THE PURITANS IN POWER

T0381896

THE PURITANS IN POWER

A STUDY IN THE HISTORY OF THE
ENGLISH CHURCH FROM 1640 TO 1660

by

G. B. TATHAM, M.A.
Fellow of Trinity College, Cambridge

Cambridge:
at the University Press
1913

CAMBRIDGE
UNIVERSITY PRESS

University Printing House, Cambridge CB2 8BS, United Kingdom

Published in the United States of America by Cambridge University Press, New York

Cambridge University Press is part of the University of Cambridge.

It furthers the University's mission by disseminating knowledge in the pursuit of education, learning and research at the highest international levels of excellence.

www.cambridge.org
Information on this title: www.cambridge.org/9781107633704

First published 1913
First paperback edition 2014

A catalogue record for this publication is available from the British Library

ISBN 978-1-107-63370-4 Paperback

PREFACE

THE object of the following sketch is to illustrate the effect of the Puritan Revolution upon the Church of England and upon the Universities as institutions closely connected with the Church. In pursuing this purpose I have had in mind the immediate and material results of the revolution rather than the influence exercised upon religious thought, upon the future history of parties within the Church, or upon the relations of the Church to Dissent. I have not attempted, except by way of the shortest possible introduction, to analyse the development of the Puritan movement or to trace the steps which brought it into conflict with the school of Archbishop Laud—a field which has provided ample material for independent investigation. My aim has been to collect evidence descriptive of the methods by means of which the revolution was accomplished and generally illustrative of the outward aspects of the Puritan regime. If in the course of the discussion I have touched upon matters of polemical interest it has not been with the object of providing weapons to the armoury of either side in the dispute.

I am very deeply indebted to Professor Firth for giving me access to some valuable notes and for his generous assistance at all times. To the Venerable Archdeacon Cunningham also I wish to express my sincere thanks for much advice and for his interest in a work with the conclusions of which he did not always agree.

G. B. T.

TRINITY COLLEGE.
September, 1913

CONTENTS

ERRATA

PAGE	LINE			
82	24.	*For*	"Robert" *read* "Roger"	
127	25.	„	"Croydon" *read* "Croyden"	
184	30.	„	"Gerald" *read* "Gerard"	
187	6.	„	"Heylin" *read* "Heylyn"	
188	30.	„	"Acts" *read* "Arts"	
247	22.	„	"Duncan" *read* "Duncon"	

CHAPTER I

THE PRELUDE

THE brief period of Puritan ascendency which succeeded the Great Civil War forms the concluding phase of what has generally been regarded as a distinct epoch in English ecclesiastical history. But though a revolution which saw the overthrow of episcopal government, the abolition of the liturgy of the English Church, and the deprivation of a third of its ordained ministers is obviously a subject which cannot be described without reference to the events which preceded it, yet the whole history of the Puritan movement is so complex that an attempt to summarise the causes and tendencies is a task of no ordinary difficulty.

One is faced at the outset by the question of terminology. The name " Puritan," by which we are accustomed to designate the forces which lay at the back of a great religious and social upheaval, is itself full of pitfalls, because it was and is used to describe tendencies of thought, superficially alike, but really distinct. In the first place, its most common use in modern language draws attention to that aspect of its meaning which is historically the least important. To modern ears the word naturally suggests the dour look and the sombre habit, familiar in fiction and in art, as typifying an austere code of morals and a harsh and narrow outlook upon life. But though this view of Puritanism as a social and moral force is a direct inheritance from the sixteenth century and is true, to a certain degree, of what then came into being, the word had another and an historically older signification which is apt to be forgotten. Primarily the Puritans stood for purity in church life rather than for purity in personal life or conduct, which was thought of as a corollary. Their demand was for a complete reformation, for the abolition, in matters of religious worship and ecclesiastical government, of all that had been superimposed upon primitive forms.

So much may be premised of the Puritans, but when one seeks to define their position more accurately, generalisation at once becomes hazardous. For Puritanism was not a creed endowed with defined dogmas and a constructive ecclesiastical policy; it was rather an attitude of mind which expressed itself not in one form only or with an equal degree of insistence. As a constructive force, Puritan thought in England was destined to follow two main lines of development, the Presbyterian and the Independent, but while it is to some extent inevitable, in speaking of the earlier phases of Puritanism, that one should employ these names for purposes of distinction, it is important to guard against the error of ascribing to movements in the embryonic stage the characteristics by which they ultimately came to be known, and of assuming the existence, from the beginning, of doctrines which were in fact only gradually formulated. The end of the sixteenth and the beginning of the seventeenth centuries was essentially a period of evolution in religious thought, and it was only by degrees that opinions began to run in well-defined channels. Presbyterianism, of course, became at an early stage a recognised model of ecclesiastical government, but it would be untrue to say that English Puritanism, under Elizabeth and James I, was represented

by a Presbyterian or an Independent party.   The body
of Puritan feeling in the country had not at that time
become identified with any party or parties : it existed
rather as an influence which directed men's minds more
or less forcibly towards a further reformation in the
Church.   For the present purpose it will be more
instructive to analyse the fundamental principles which
characterised its two main currents.

The key-note of the Puritan position was the
acceptance of the Bible as the one infallible authority
before which all institutions in the Church must stand or
fall.   To some extent this attitude was common to the
whole Reformation movement, but whereas the more
moderate reformers had been content to do away with
all that seemed contrary to Scripture, the Puritans went
further and demanded the abolition of all for which the
Bible offered no positive warrant.   In this lies the
explanation of their attitude towards the ecclesiastical
system which was being built up in the English Church.
It explains their dislike of the hierarchy, for even if some
form of Episcopacy could be traced in the New Testament,
the same could not be said of deans and canons ; it
explains also their attitude towards the festivals of the
Church and indeed towards all non-primitive institutions
which the Reformation in England had not finally
abolished.   On this, the destructive, side Puritan feeling
was tolerably unanimous and definite.   Here, however,
unanimity ended, for it is in their theories of ecclesiastical
government, of the functions of the ministry and of the
relation of the Church to the State that the differences
between the two great Puritan parties become apparent.
On the one hand, Presbyterianism, as the name implies,
rested upon a system of government by presbyters or
elders, under which the congregation is controlled by the
ministers and elders whom it has itself elected, the

collection of congregations in a district by the Presbytery
or Classis composed of ministers and elders, and the
whole country by a General Assembly. It claimed
authority from the constitution of the primitive Church,
as revealed in the books of the New Testament, and it
owed the form in which it was established after the
Reformation chiefly to the work of Calvin. The system
is essentially national; it recognises the jurisdiction of a
supreme power, and in this lies its fundamental difference
from the Independent theory.

The Independents, like the Presbyterians, sought
their model of Church government in the New Testament,
but while the attention of the Presbyterians had been
directed towards the governmental machinery, they had
been influenced by the example of the self-sufficing and
autonomous churches which sprang up in the wake
of missionary enterprise[1]. Carrying out the principle
which they perceived in the position of those churches,
they claimed that the individual congregation had full
power to elect its own officers and to manage its own
affairs and that it owed obedience to no authority save
that of its Master.

Intimately connected with these theories of government within the Church were the respective views of
the relation of the Church to the civil power. The
Presbyterians, with the theocracies of Old Testament
history before their eyes, endeavoured to build up a
polity in which the secular authority should be strictly
subordinated to the Church. In this respect their
teaching resembled that of the Romanists and stood in
marked opposition to the growing Erastianism in the
English Church. The Independents, on the other hand,
in this less faithful to scriptural tradition, while they

[1] See the Independents' Catechism published by M. C. Burrage:
The Early English Dissenters, ii, 156-7.

repudiated State control and the institution of tithes, were debarred from the assertion of ecclesiastical supremacy by the absence from their system of any supreme ecclesiastical authority. With them the ultimate triumph of right principles would be secured by entrusting the State to a "rule of the saints," that is to say, government by men directly inspired by God. The idea of inspiration was common to both views, with the difference that the one conceived the gift of the Spirit as flowing mainly through an ordained ministry while the other held that it was subject to no such limitation.

A divergence of opinion upon a subject so important is naturally seen most clearly in the conception of the ministry. If the Church were the oracle of God, then the ordained ministers of the Church must be considered to occupy a position analogous to the Jewish prophets, and therefore the Presbyterian ministry was accorded a prestige which was probably greater than that enjoyed by the ministers of the Anglican Church. It was greater because in the Presbyterian system the sacraments did not possess so full a spiritual significance, and therefore the personal influence of the ministry, as the medium through which God's purpose was revealed, was relatively enhanced. With the Independents on the other hand, the fact of ordination was in comparison unimportant, and many of the most influential preachers were laymen. The essential question was whether a man were possessed of the spiritual gift, and it was the decision of this question which chiefly engaged the attention of the Committee appointed by Cromwell in March 1653/4 for the approbation of public preachers. This belief not only in the existence of direct inspiration, but also in the possibility of discerning its presence, explains much in the actions and utterances of Independent preachers which would otherwise be unmeaning.

These points of difference in religious opinion, which were destined to become prominent during the constitutional and ecclesiastical experiments of the Interregnum, were dormant in the Puritanism of the years which preceded the Rebellion. In what relation did Puritan thought, thus diversified, stand to the system which was taking shape in the Church of England as by law established?

If it can be said that no clearly defined position can be postulated in the case of Puritanism before the Civil War, the same is to a great extent true of the Church of England, for it also was in the evolutionary stage. The Church was indeed established on the basis of episcopal government and was possessed of a liturgy and a code of doctrine, but the limits had not been defined so strictly as to exclude the Puritan altogether or so clearly as to avoid the possibility of controversy. It was this circumstance which gave the opportunity, as it provided the justification, of the Puritan attack. But the issue was from the beginning complicated by the fact that the purely religious problems in the conflict did not stand alone, but were, at all events during the critical period of the struggle, merged in questions of secular politics. In the second place, the religious problems themselves were not the outcome of an orderly development, but owed their very nature to the action of a series of opposite and mutually incompatible forces. The peculiar circumstances in which the Reformation was inaugurated under Henry VIII, the advance made under Edward VI, and the subsequent counter-Reformation under Mary were of themselves factors well calculated to render the religious question in England one of extreme difficulty, nor was the solution for the moment brought appreciably nearer by that famous venture in ecclesiastical politics which posterity has agreed to misname the Elizabethan "Settlement." Up to that point, the broad issue had been the alternative between Roman Catholicism and the Protestant systems which had taken root on the Continent. From that point begins the movement towards the re-establishment of a Church, which should avoid either alternative and be national in a sense that one owing allegiance to the teaching of either Rome or Geneva could never be. The system was imposed from above and owed its foundation to the strength of the Government: both then and later the voluntary acceptance of it by the country as a whole was hindered by the fact that, while Calvinism and Lutheranism were recognised models possessed of a definite programme, the Elizabethan *via media* appeared as something new. Accordingly, it was never accepted by the more advanced Puritans as a final settlement, but only as an intermediate stage on the road to complete reform[1], and the demands of the Puritan representatives at the Hampton Court Conference in 1604 really amounted to a claim that the English Church should be modelled on a Calvinistic basis[2].

Such a claim received no more encouragement from James I than it had from Elizabeth. Elizabeth's attitude had been dictated principally by motives of public policy; James' experience had taught him that the claims of the Presbyterians accorded ill with his theory of kingship, but he viewed the question also from the standpoint of the theologian. At the same time, the position of the English Church became more clearly defined, and its anti-Puritan tendency more pronounced, by the broadening of its field of apologetics. On the one hand,

[1] Mandell Creighton: *Laud's position in the History of the English Church* (Laud Commemoration Lectures), p. 8; H. O. Wakeman: *The Church and the Puritans*, p. 10.
[2] H. O. Wakeman: *The Church and the Puritans*, p. 72.

by appealing to the Fathers and the Schoolmen, and by developing the theory of the historical continuity of the English Church, its defenders definitely parted company with those who regarded the Reformation as a break with the past. On the other hand, the spread of the doctrine of Arminius among the more advanced divines of the Church of England set up a barrier against those who followed Calvin on the subjects of Grace and Predestination.

Throughout James' reign, nonconformity and separation were discouraged, but the general acceptance of the "orthodox" liturgy and system of Church government was due to the fact that the times still allowed a considerable measure of latitude. Scrupulous compliance was not rigidly enforced, and many even of the clergy were really Puritans at heart[1]. Under these conditions, open opposition was confined to a minority, and many who were lukewarm in their affection for Episcopacy and entirely hostile to extreme views, were prepared to accept the existing state of things, to set differences aside, and to turn their attention to a reformation of the religious life by means of a stricter discipline. But if separatism were deprecated, it is important to remember that freedom of thought within the limits of the Church was not the ideal towards which either party was striving. In spite of the popular cant about liberty for tender consciences, of which that age heard so much and understood so little, true tolerance was as foreign to the mind of the Puritan as it was to the " Anglo Catholic." The breaking-point would be reached when the extreme views of either side came into contact, and the struggle, when it arose, would be not for toleration, but for supremacy.

The accession of Charles I marked an important

---

[1] S. R. Gardiner: *Hist. of Eng.* 1603–42, iii, 241–2.

point in the development of the ecclesiastical question. The new King had inherited many of his father's views on civil and religious policy and his unwillingness to brook popular opposition in either sphere, but he was in every way a more attractive figure, and if he possessed no greater capacity to rule in a difficult age, he yet brought to the task a real wish for his country's welfare, a deeply religious mind and the power to play the part of a king with dignity. His frequent want of judgment in a crisis was due partly to the fact that he was a man with no gift for statesmanship and partly to a fatal tendency to be guided by ill-considered advice and to select his counsellors rather on grounds of sentiment than of reason. His arbitrary conduct arose from his conception of the regal power, a conception which had been common to his predecessors and had yet to be proved impracticable. At the same time, it must be conceded that the problems with which he was called upon to deal, though identical in kind, had assumed a more serious aspect than they had presented in the preceding reign, and to this, rather than to any personal inferiority, must be attributed the fact that he did not succeed in avoiding failure where his father had only missed success.

It was during the first fifteen years of Charles' reign, and especially during the eleven years during which he governed without a Parliament, that the ground was prepared for the revolution in Church and State. On the side of the Church, the policy which the King sanctioned, and indeed encouraged, will always be connected with the name of William Laud.

Laud's rise, though he obtained his highest prefer- ments late in life, was characteristic of the age in which he lived. It was founded in academic surroundings, and the presidentship of St John's College, Oxford, was the first step in his upward progress. He became Dean of Gloucester in 1616, Bishop of St David's in 1621, Dean of the Chapel Royal and Bishop of Bath and Wells in 1626, Bishop of London in 1628, Chancellor of Oxford University in 1629, and Archbishop of Canterbury, on the death of George Abbot, in 1633. Such, in brief, was his distinguished career, and, from the accession of Charles, it would not be too much to say that his was the ruling mind in ecclesiastical affairs. He was essentially an exponent of the "Anglo Catholic" school and, in point of doctrine, an Arminian, but the peculiar importance of his influence on the Church lay in his character and general attitude of mind.

At the time when he was called upon to assume a position of authority, there was much that gave cause for dissatisfaction to one who set a value on conformity and "decent dignified ceremonialism" in the services of the Church. Abbot, his predecessor in the see of Canterbury, was at heart a Puritan, and at the beginning of Charles' reign a majority certainly of the laity, and probably also of the clergy, were what may be called Puritan Episcopalians, that is to say, accepted government by bishops without sacrificing the Calvinistic opinions of the earlier post-Reformation period. Conformity, in fact, to the Church doctrine, as Laud conceived it, did not exist, and various and contradictory tenets were freely promulgated by the clergy. In external matters, the state of affairs was still more displeasing. Reports from the dioceses revealed that the churches in many places "lay nastily," the buildings dirty, and even the fabric in a ruinous condition[1]. The services were often performed without any regard to dignity or even decency, ministers were careless and "insufficient" in the discharge of their duties ; the communion table not

[1] G. G. Perry : *Hist. of the Church of England*, i, 489.

infrequently stood in the body of the church, emblematic of opinions on the sacrament in themselves eminently distasteful to Laud, and was there treated as a convenient article of furniture rather than as the centre of the Church's most solemn service. All this Laud felt to be a reproach and an offence, likely, if unreformed, to drive men to the Church of Rome.

"I found," he writes, "that with the contempt of outward worship of God the inward fell away apace, and profaneness began boldly to show itself. I could speak with no conscientious person almost that was wavering in religion, but the great motive which wrought upon them to disaffect or think meanly of the Church of England, was that the external worship of God was so lost, and the churches themselves suffered to lie in such a base and slovenly fashion in most places of the kingdom[1]."

To the reform of external worship, accordingly, Laud addressed himself and, up to a certain point, he would have received the support of all, irrespective of party, who cared for the welfare of religion. The bad state of repair in churches, and still more the want of an efficient ministry offended Puritans as well as others[2], but the line of reform which they favoured differed both in degree and in kind from that which Laud proposed to adopt. The outward adornment of churches they did not desire, and what they wished to cultivate in the clergy was first and foremost the gift of preaching. Laud's measures, on the other hand, ran, in many respects directly counter to this.

The articles in Laud's Metropolitical Visitation of

[1] Quoted by M. Creighton: *Laud's position in the History of the English Church* (Laud Commemoration Lectures), p. 18.
[2] See Richard Baxter's account of the clergy in the neighbourhood of his home in Shropshire. *Reliquiae Baxterianae* (1696), pp. 1–2.

the diocese of Winchester in 1635 do not suggest an extensive ritualistic movement, and indeed in this respect are only concerned with the ordinary ecclesiastical furniture and ornaments.   Inquiry is made as to whether there is a bible and a prayer-book "fairly and substantially bound," a font of stone, a comely pulpit, a comely large surplice, a fair communion cup, with a cover of silver, a flagon of silver, tin, or pewter, to put the wine in, with "all other things and ornaments necessary for the celebration of divine service, and administration of the sacraments."   The communion table was to be "convenient and decent...with a carpet of silk, or some other decent stuff, continually laid upon the same at time of divine service, and a fair linen cloth thereon, at the time of the receiving of the Holy Communion."   The clergy were to officiate in surplice and hood[1].   Nor do the Canons of 1640, which represent the high-water-mark in official injunctions on the subject, carry us much further.

It is expressly stated that "the standing of the communion table sideway under the east window of every chancel or chapel, is in its own nature indifferent," but in view of the Advertisements of Queen Elizabeth and the continuous custom in the royal chapels and elsewhere, which effectually cleared the practice of any "just suspicion of popish superstition," it is thought fit "that all churches and chapels do conform themselves in this particular to the example of the cathedral or mother churches, saving always the general liberty left to the bishop by law, during the time of administration of the Holy Communion."   The declaration, however, went on to declare that this situation did not imply that the communion table ought to be esteemed "a true and proper altar, wherein Christ is again really sacrificed;

---

[1] Laud's *Works*, v, 421, 453.

but it is and may be called an altar by us in that sense in which the primitive Church called it an altar and in no other." To protect the table so placed from irreverent treatment and abuse, it should be "decently severed with rails" from the body of the church.

One other direction there was which caused trouble in the future. The synod who had drawn up the Canons declared that it was "very meet and behoveful" that all persons should do "reverence and obeisance both at their coming in and going out of the said churches... according to the most ancient custom of the primitive Church in the purest times," as an act for the advancement of God's majesty, but that in the practice or omission of this the apostle's rule should be observed "which is, that they which use this rite, despise not them who use it not, and that they who use it not, condemn not those that use it[1]."

In practice, it is probable that a rather more elaborate ritual obtained in some places; the use of copes was enjoined in cathedrals and episcopal chapels in accordance with the 24th Canon of 1603, and stained-glass windows were repaired or newly introduced, but the points already mentioned were sufficient to supply the grounds on which the Puritan party based their contention that Laud and his followers were bringing in "Popish Innovations."

In view of the ritualistic developments of modern times, it comes at first as a surprise that such comparatively modest measures of reform should raise such serious opposition. The explanation lies in the circumstances of the age. On the one hand, hardly two generations had passed since England had been under a Roman Catholic Government, and to those who were unable to take a more than superficial view of the

[1] Laud's *Works*, v, 624-6.

tendency of events, it may well have seemed that the same fate still threatened the country. On the other hand, the position taken up by the predominant school of English churchmen was still too novel to be familiar. A great part of the new policy the Puritans did not understand, and what they understood they did not like. For there is no doubt that the divergence of view between the two parties went much deeper than a mere question of forms, and that the order prescribed by Laud represented doctrines which were opposed to those held by his opponents. To the Puritan who regarded the Holy Communion merely as a commemorative act, there was nothing indecent in the old state of affairs, and the table standing as an ordinary piece of furniture in the body of the church effectively typified his views. When the table was removed to the east end of the chancel, furnished with hangings and ornaments, and separated from the people by rails, when kneeling at the reception of the Elements was enjoined, and the act of bowing encouraged, it was obvious that the inward meaning had not remained unaffected. Laud might honestly dissociate himself from the eucharistic opinions of the Roman Church: the doctrinal distinction, though in reality broad enough, was too subtle to convince Puritan suspicion, while the outward resemblance to Roman forms was an argument which struck the eye and was readily accepted.

The charge that Laud inclined towards Roman Catholicism is effectually refuted by his controversy with Fisher the Jesuit, but his view of the position and historical continuity of the Church of England made him appear to be in closer agreement with Rome than he actually was, and an age which had been astonished to hear Sheldon deny that the Pope was Anti-Christ was not likely to regard favourably one who allowed the Roman Church to be a true Church. Nor were Laud's measures in a real sense "innovations"—"an unlucky word," as Clarendon remarks, which "cozened very many honest men into apprehensions very prejudicial to the King and to the Church[1]." That his opponents had any justification for so regarding them was due to the fact that the general practice in the matter of Church services during the two preceding reigns had been much more Puritan in tone than the precept of authority had warranted, but hardly any of Laud's directions were strictly "new[2]." The position of the communion table "in the place where the altar stood" could be referred to Queen Elizabeth's Injunctions of 1559, the use of surplice and cope to the Advertisements of 1566, the practice of bowing towards the east could be said to have been "usual" in the same reign[3], while images, either in stone or glass, had been allowed even by Calvin, so that they were used not for idolatrous purpose but "in docendo et admonendo[4]." The Puritans might indeed cite the twenty-third Injunction of 1559 against paintings and monuments and argue that the spirit of the law was being contravened ; Laud's appeal was to the letter and to practice, and on the mere point of novelty his position was unassailable. Assuming that the Elizabethan statutes had left the law indefinite, it became a question of interpretation, and of which of two possible lines of development should be pursued. The crux of the matter was that Laud had chosen the anti-Puritan interpretation.

But it was not only in forms and external matters that Laud's policy conflicted with Puritan sentiment. We have seen that the attribution of a semi-prophetic character to the ministry was common among the Puritans in general, and especially among the Presbyterians, and

[1] Clarendon : *Hist. of the Rebellion* (ed. Macray), i, 128.
[2] Cf. W. Bright : *Waymarks in Church History*, p. 338.
[3] Laud's *Works*, iv, 201.   [4] *Ibid.* iv, 199.

this naturally led them to regard the exercise of preaching as the primary duty of the minister and the most important part of their religious service. The pulpit rather than the press was the mouthpiece of controversial as well as of pastoral theology, and they demanded a large liberty in the matter of discussion. With such a demand Laud had little sympathy. Though by no means undervaluing the gift of tongues, his own religious temperament led him to distrust the unbridled language of somewhat ill-instructed men[1].

In a letter to Vossius, written in July 1629, Laud had said that he had always laboured to prevent the public discussion of difficult and intricate subjects lest piety and charity should be dishonoured under the pretext of truth, and that he had ever counselled moderation lest everything should be thrown into confusion by fiery minds to which religion was not the highest care[2], and imperfectly as he may seem to have fulfilled the part of an apostle of moderation, this description of his life's purpose would not be an untrue or an unsuitable epitaph. Charles' declaration of November 1628, which was almost certainly inspired by Laud, breathed the same spirit in expressing the desire that in those "unhappy differences, which have for so many hundred years, in different times and places, exercised the Church of Christ...all further curious search be laid aside, and these disputes shut up

---

[1] A somewhat similar attitude was adopted by the Bishop of Winchester in a speech on the case of a minister named Vicars who was brought before the High Commission Court. "I will not speake against preaching," he said, "nor against those that preach twise upon every Sunday...but I would he would preach lesse and consider what he saith." S. R. Gardiner: *Cases in the Star Chamber and High Commission Court* (Camden Soc.), p. 234.

[2] "Omnem ego semper movi lapidem, ne publice scopulosae illae et perplexae quaestiones coram populo tractarentur; ne pietatem et charitatem sub specie veri violaremus. Moderata semper suasi, ne fervida ingenia, et quibus religio non est summae curae, turbarent omnia." Laud's *Works*, vi, 265.

in God's promises as they be generally set forth to us in the Holy Scriptures and the general meaning of the Articles of the Church of England according to them[1]." He did not aim at doctrinal conformity, but his conception of the function of the Church caused him to dislike all preaching which did not take place under its supervision and authority, especially at a time when much of the eloquence was certain to be directed against his own government. His object was comprehension, but a comprehension which was to be achieved by a reverent reserve on controversial points and without the sacrifice of outward conformity. It was this double characteristic which rendered his purpose impracticable. Though not consciously desiring to restrain liberty of thought within the Church he was compelled to restrain liberty of speech, while his insistence upon outward conformity to an unpopular form prevented that mutual consent without which comprehension is impossible.

But there was another reason for Laud's attitude towards preaching. The pulpit had also a very considerable political importance, and though Elizabeth had contrived to keep its influence chiefly in her own interest, under James and Charles it had become an instrument of attack. The danger had lately been increased by the appearance of a class of irregular preachers who occupied a position to some extent independent of the ordinary parochial system. These "lecturers" as they were called, owed their rise to the eagerness of Puritan congregations to supplement the official ministrations of the Church, and were generally appointed by some private person or corporation which had raised a subscription for their maintenance. Early in the reign of Charles I, a body of twelve London Puritans had formed themselves into a society known as the Feoffees for Impropriations, and

[1] Quoted by W. H. Hutton : *William Laud*, p. 59.

T. P.   2

had raised a fund for buying up tithes which had fallen into the hands of laymen, and by means of this were enabled to support a considerable number of lecturers of their own persuasion. So appointed, the lecturers avoided the necessity of subscription and were not bound to perform the service in accordance with the orders of the Church. They regarded themselves, in fact, as more or less exempt from the jurisdiction of their ecclesiastical superiors, and in districts like Northamptonshire, where there was much Nonconformity, they were a constant source of trouble[1]. They were looked upon with profound distrust by the King and the Church party as likely to fill the minds of the people with discontent against the established order both ecclesiastical and secular.

The general attitude towards liberty of preaching, therefore, adopted by the Government had been one of restriction. As early as 1622 a series of " Directions concerning Preachers " had been issued at the instance of the King. In a letter to the Archbishop, James recalled that in former times preaching had been kept under strict control, and remarked upon the fact that "at this present divers young students by reading of late writers, and ungrounded divines, do broach many times unprofitable, unsound, seditious, and dangerous doctrines, to the scandall of the Church, and disquiet of the State and present Government." The directions therefore proceeded strictly to define the limits which the preacher was to observe and to prohibit entirely any discussion of "matters of state, and the differences between Princes and the People[2]." Some similar directions, belonging to the same date, a copy of which is preserved in the Baker Collection, also allude to the chief defects of the Puritan

[1] J. E. Bailey : *Life of Fuller*, pp. 42–3.
[2] Rushworth : *Historical Collections*, i, 64–5.

sermons. Mention is made of "a sowing up in points of Divinity too deep for the capacity of the people...or an ignorant meddling with civil matters...or a venting of their own distast or a smoothing up of these idle fancies which in this blessed time of so long a peace doe boyle in the braines of an unadvised people[1]."

On Laud's accession to a position of influence in Charles' councils, the same policy had been continued. In a paper containing "considerations for the better settling of Church government," presented by him to the King in 1629, the substance of which was afterwards embodied in a series of official instructions, he recommended "that a special care be had over the lecturers in every diocess, which by reason of their pay are the people's creatures, and blow the bellows of their sedition[2]." As Bishop of London he had come into contact with the Feoffees for Impropriations, with the result that the society was suppressed by an order of the Court of Exchequer in February 1633[3], and as Archbishop he continued his attack on the system as a whole. In the account of his province, drawn up in the first year of his archiepiscopate, he desires the King "that no layman whatsoever, and least of all companies or corporations, may, under any pretence of giving to the Church or otherwise, have power to put in or put out any lecturer or other minister."

Charles supported him wholeheartedly. "Certainlie," he wrote in the margin of the above account, "I cannot hould fitt that anie Lay Person or Corporation whatsoever, should have the Power thease Men would take to themselves[4]." Accordingly the lecturers were placed under supervision, and it was ordered that they should

---

[1] Baker Collection, vol. xxvii, Fol. 139.   [2] Rushworth, ii, 7.
[3] S. R. Gardiner: *Hist. of Eng.* 1603-42, vii, 258-9.
[4] Laud's *Works*, v, 321.

read the service according to the liturgy in surplice and hood, and should be obliged to take upon them livings with cure of souls[1]. This enabled the bishops to use their authority and to suspend offenders for sedition or unsound doctrine, a power which they saw cause to exercise with considerable frequency.

These restrictions and orders dictated the lines on which the Church service was to be conducted, and assumed a right to control the religious worship of the people : the publication of what was known as the " Declaration of Sports " in 1618 raised the whole question of Sunday observance. The issue of this declaration, by which official approbation was accorded to the time-honoured practice of indulging in dances and other forms of recreation after the attendance at divine worship on Sundays, was caused by the state of affairs observed by King James during his progress from Scotland. Puritan influence had been sufficiently strong in some parts of the country, notably in Lancashire, to suppress what were generally regarded as " lawful recreations," and from this were argued two distinct dangers. On the one hand, the Roman Catholics, who were numerous in Lancashire, would be deterred from coming over to the Church of England ; on the other, the " common and meaner sort of people " would be prevented " from using such exercises as may make their bodies more able for war." A further danger would be found in the fact that the place of these healthy recreations would be taken by "tipling and filthy drunkenness " and " idle and discontented speeches in their ale-houses[2]." In October 1633, the Declaration was reissued under Laud's sanction and ordered to be read in the churches. The Puritans attacked it on the grounds that such a use of the Lord's Day was not only unsanctioned, but even directly prohibited in the Bible,

[1] Laud's *Works*, v, 312.   [2] Rushworth, ii, 194.

and that it tended to encourage immorality and vice. A considerable number of the clergy declined to read it, and some suffered suspension for their persistent refusal. In the history of his trial, Laud maintained that he "ever laboured" that Sunday should be kept holy, "but yet free from a superstitious holiness[1]," and his action may be taken as a protest against the general attitude of mind represented in the opposition[2].

The cleavage of opinion between Puritans and "Anglo Catholics" on the subjects alluded to was not a new factor in the political situation at the time of Laud's ascendency. The period of his rule, however, brought the antagonism to the critical point, and therefore a discussion of the means by which he, in conjunction with the King, strove to impose his system upon the country forms a natural corollary to an account of the main points in dispute. The two measures for enforcing conformity, which afterwards became the principal objects of the Puritans' attack, were the High Commission Court and the "Etcetera Oath."

The High Commission Court, in the form in which it existed under Charles I, dated from the time of Whitgift's campaign against Nonconformity. Its constitution, and still more its procedure, was open to grave objections on legal grounds, and on this head its jurisdiction had always been resented. Under Abbot's influence, however, its action had been tempered by a certain moderation[3], and it was left for Laud to bring out its full power as an engine of repression.

It was disliked, though not for the same reasons nor with equal justification, by several widely different classes.

---

[1] Laud's *Works*, iv, 252.

[2] Ranke thinks that Laud's object in attacking the religious strictness of the Puritans, especially in the matter of Sunday observance, was to "attract the people to his side." *Hist. of England*, ii, 49.

[3] S. R. Gardiner: *Hist. of Eng.* 1603-42, vii, 254.

It was hated by the Puritans because it imposed upon them a system of worship of which they disapproved ; it was hated by a certain section of the nobility and gentry because it was a stern censor of morals : it was hated by the lawyers because of its rivalry with the civil courts and because, though an ecclesiastical tribunal, it inflicted civil penalties[1].   Clarendon himself condemns it in strong terms.   " It had much overflowed the banks which should have contained it," he says, " not only in meddling with things that in truth were not properly within their [*i.e.* the bishops'] connusance : but extending their sentences and judgments in matters triable before them, beyond that degree that was justifiable," while by over-riding the common law they had alienated the lawyers and made " almost a whole profession, if not their enemy, yet very undevoted to them[2]."

As to its relations to Nonconformity, it is probable that the court has been on the whole unjustly condemned[3], but it is difficult to speak with certainty on this point on account of the paucity of first-hand evidence.   Those records of its proceedings which have been published[4] extend only from October 1631 to June 1632, a period, it is important to remember, anterior to Laud's appointment to the archbishopric and therefore to the time of his greatest influence.   But the evidence of these records shows that, at that time at any rate, though the ecclesiastical business occupied a considerable proportion of the commissioners' attention, their activities were by no means exercised exclusively in that direction.

[1] W. H. Frere : *Hist. of the Eng. Church in the reigns of Elizabeth and James I*, p. 354.

[2] Clarendon: *Hist. of the Rebellion* (ed. Macray), i, 372.

[3] W. H. Hutton : *Hist. of the English Church from the accession of Charles I to the death of Anne*, p. 69.

[4] S. R. Gardiner: *Cases in the Star Chamber and High Commission Court* (Camden Soc.).

The general impression gained by a perusal of the cases connected with Nonconformity is that the sentences for false doctrine or for holding conventicles were severe, and that the behaviour of the bishops and the lay members of the court towards prisoners was usually harsh. The prisoners themselves in many cases could not be brought to take the oath to give true answers, maintaining that they dared not or that they knew not what they should swear to[1], but the most striking feature of the examinations is the light thrown on the kind of opposition that Laud was endeavouring to overcome. "The Lord hath wrought that in me that I need not to use it," replied one to the question whether he used the Lord's Prayer[2]. "I am a minister of the Gospel of Christ, and the Lord hath qualified me," was the answer of another, a conventicle preacher named Latropp, when asked to produce his orders[3]. These, and similar replies, though undoubtedly representing extreme cases, reveal the gulf that separated Laud from the attainment of his ideal, and the practical impossibility of reconciling views so hopelessly at variance.

The "Etcetera Oath" was the popular name given to the oath, prescribed by the sixth Canon of 1640, against "all innovations in doctrine and government," and was derived from the fact that the oath required an undertaking not "to alter the government of this Church by archbishops, bishops, deans, and archdeacons, etc., as it stands now established[4]." The insertion of the "etcetera" in place of a long list of offices and officers was, of course, dictated by a desire for greater brevity, but never was disregard of legal accuracy visited with more sudden

[1] S. R. Gardiner: *Cases in the Star Chamber and High Commission Court* (Camden Soc.), p. 285.
[2] *Ibid.* p. 188. [3] *Ibid.* p. 281.
[4] Laud's *Works*, v, 623.

judgment. To some extent, it is true that the technical objection to the wording was a quibble and that the real opposition was directed against the whole tenor of the oath[1].

"Those that were against it," writes Baxter, "said, 1. that Episcopacy was either contra jus divinum, or at best not jure divino, and therefore mutable when the King and Parliament pleased. 2. Or at least that it was undeniable, that Archbishops, and Deans, and Chapters, and Archdeacons etc., were not all Jure Divino: nay, that the English frame of Diocesans having many hundred Parish Churches under one Bishop in fini gradus, was not only against the word of God, but destructive of all the Episcopacy which was known in the Church at least for 200 years[2]."

But, incredible as it may seem, there was a genuine distrust of the "blind Et Cœtera" and what it might involve. Nothing, in fact, could have better brought out the real point at issue as illustrating the Puritan suspicion, and it is not altogether surprising if, as Baxter states, an oath, which was or seemed to be imposed "for the unalterable subjecting" of men to diocesans, should become a chief means to alienate them from episcopal government[3].

In the actual carrying out of his scheme of government, it is probable that Laud suffered at the hands of those subordinate officials of the Church to whom the work of producing conformity was necessarily entrusted, just as his cause was prejudiced by the indiscretion of men like Sibthorpe and Mainwaring. It is certain that the interests of the Church were affected by the close connection which had sprung up between civil and

[1] S. R. Gardiner: *Hist. of Eng.* 1603-42, ix, 146.
[2] *Reliquiae Baxterianae* (1696), p. 15.
[3] *Ibid.* p. 16.

ecclesiastical affairs. Not only had the interests of the Laudian and Court parties become identical, but Laud himself and others of the bishops as well occupied an important place in Court politics and the King's favour, while Juxon, as Bishop of London, became Lord High Treasurer. The result was that they incurred the additional odium of being connected with an unpopular policy in affairs of State. This aspect of the alliance was from every point of view a mistake, and is responsible for much of the bitter hostility with which the bishops were viewed. Even amongst the courtiers considerable resentment was felt at the undue power conferred upon them, and the animosity extended to the clergy as well. Men looked upon the Church, says Clarendon, "as the gulph ready to swallow up all the great offices[1]."

During the eleven years of Charles' personal government, then, the opposition to secular and ecclesiastical policy alike was kept in check, and Puritans were obliged to contemplate the consolidation of Laud's influence without the means of active resistance. The observance of the order and ceremonies of the Church were strictly enforced and open revolt was crushed with a heavy hand. The cases of Leighton, Prynne, Bastwick and Burton revealed at once the strength of the authority and the bitterness of the opposition, and postponement merely had the effect of increasing the violence of the inevitable storm. On April 13, 1640, the Short Parliament met and, among the long list of grievances to which it immediately turned its attention, the question of religion obtained a prominent place. But even then, though the tendency of the Commons was to regard the Laudian party as the "enemies of the Church and Country," the remarkable point was the comparative moderation of tone

---

[1] *History of the Rebellion* (ed. Macray), i, 132. See also C. H. Simpkinson: *Life and Times of William Laud*, p. 148.

which was still preserved. The distinguishing note of Pym's speech, delivered on April 17, was a plea for liberty and a comprehensive treatment of the questions at issue[1], and for the moment nothing was said of the more radical changes which were fast approaching. The fatal decision which led Charles to dissolve the Parliament after it had sat for three weeks, ruined whatever slight prospects there remained of a peaceful adjustment of differences, for in the Long Parliament, which met on the 3rd of the following November, the active opposition of the country was gathered together in a more powerful and a more ominous shape.

The actual strength of the several ecclesiastical parties between the date of the meeting of the Long Parliament and the outbreak of the war is not easy to gauge, and the latter event, though it divided the nation into two distinct camps, did not give any clear indication of the feeling of the country on the religious difficulty. Many sacrificed their views on Church questions for their loyalty to the King, and others sacrificed their loyalty to the King for their views on Church questions. The great mass of the people were probably not profoundly convinced either for or against Episcopacy, and amid much misrepresentation and misunderstanding "both sides found such reception generally with the people as they were inclined to the persons[2]." It needed, in fact, outside influence of policy or affection to determine which party they should support.

The Laudian party, though in some respects the most powerful force in the State, was not strong numerically. Even of the clergy not more than half could be regarded as whole-hearted supporters of his system, and amongst the laity it was decidedly weak.

---

[1] Gardiner: *Hist. of Eng.* 1603-42, ix, 103-4.
[2] Clarendon: *Hist. of the Rebellion* (ed. Macray), i, 124.

A section of the Court party and a few of the better class families adhered to it, but in Parliament, in the House of Lords, as well as in the Commons, and amongst the middle and lower classes it had found very little acceptance.

But though the extreme Anglicans were without a large following, Episcopacy was supported, on less ambitious grounds, by a considerable proportion of the nation. This section of what may be called the episcopal party included many different types, some friendly to Laud and others openly hostile. It included, for example, such broad-minded churchmen as Prideaux and Ussher, who would have favoured some scheme of comprehension on the basis of a modified Episcopacy: it included, again, such men as Williams, some time Archbishop of York, whose churchmanship was tempered by motives of policy and expediency, one who regarded the Calvinists as a force in the State to which concessions must be made[1]. The real strength of the party lay in the affection which inspired men's minds[2] for the traditional form of worship, and the rooted aversion to the extravagances of the Puritan teaching. The majority of the supporters of Episcopacy cared little for the high pretensions expressed in the views of Laud, Hall[3] and others.

---

[1] Dr Gardiner, indeed, thought that "if Williams had been trusted by Charles instead of Laud, there would have been no civil war" (vi, 340), and that, but for certain defects in character, he might even have become the "Burke of the ecclesiastical politics of the seventeenth century" (vii, 18), but he was before all things an opportunist and his conduct in affairs was to a great extent dictated by his personal antagonism to Laud.

[2] Ranke : *Hist. of England*, ii, 291-2.

[3] Gardiner and Ranke differ as to the nature of Charles' episcopal appointments in the autumn of 1641. Ranke states that Hall's moderation had brought him under suspicion of being inclined to Presbyterianism, but he was the author of *Episcopacy by Divine Right*, and was one of the "impeached Bishops." See Ranke, ii, 304, and Gardiner, x, 41.

The balance of power really lay with the moderate men on the other side, not necessarily militant Puritans, but men who were opposed to Laud and felt that some change was needed without knowing what form they wished it to take. There was a good deal of latent Presbyterianism amongst the lower and middle classes, but in the Commons of the Long Parliament it was not at first a very definite force. How far a distinct purpose to overthrow Episcopacy is to be traced in the actions of the popular leaders from the beginning is a question which has never been conclusively answered, but, in any case, it must have been confined to a very few. During the early debates on religion Lords Saye and Brooke in the Upper House, and Nathaniel Fiennes and Sir Harry Vane, the younger, in the Lower, were, says Clarendon, the only men who were believed to be "for root and branch[1]." With the majority of the reforming party, and even with Pym himself, the development of an ecclesiastical policy was a matter of time. But the very vagueness of their attitude and their want of a constructive policy in the end constituted the chief element of danger to the Church. At the critical moment in the course of the war, the Commons, so constituted, were able to accept a ready-made ecclesiastical system as the price of the much-needed military assistance of the Scots. Had they at that time been intent on the establishment of a definite system of their own, the negotiations with the Scots would probably have fallen through, for the Scots army would not have taken the field on any other terms.

In the Long Parliament, representatives of nearly all shades of opinion confronted one another, but, as the inevitable result of the circumstances in which the elections had taken place, the Puritan element was

[1] Clarendon : *Hist. of the Rebellion* (ed. Macray), i, 309.

relatively stronger there than in the nation as a whole. But even so, there was no general agreement, even amongst the avowed opponents of the existing system, as to the measure of change which was needed, whether, in fact, it should be a reform or a revolution. Schemes embodying each of these alternatives were possible and were actually formulated, but the only one which assumed any practical importance was one which aimed at the total overthrow of episcopal government. The fact that such a line of action was adopted by a Parliament in which its whole-hearted supporters were at first a minority was due in the first place to motives of political expediency, and in the second place to the influence of external events reacting on the position of the Parliamentary party. The line of development, therefore, which it will be necessary to follow here is the one which shows the steps by which the "Root and Branch" policy, as it was called, gained acceptance and led finally to the utter overthrow of Episcopacy.

As soon as the Long Parliament had assembled, the antagonism to the bishops made itself heard in the cry for their abolition. As early as November 18, Baillie could write that "all here are weary of bishops[1]," and it was apparent to all that the question was being hurried to the front. But the event by which the controversy in all its aspects was first raised, was the presentation on December 11, 1640, of a petition against Episcopacy signed by 15,000 Londoners[2]. The petition went over the whole ground in dispute between the supporters of episcopal government and the extreme Puritans, and advocated the abolition of bishops as "members of the Beast" and the entire destruction of that whole system of ecclesiastical government. The conservative feeling both

---

[1] Baillie: *Letters* (1841), i, 274.
[2] Printed in Rushworth, iv, 93-6.

in Parliament and in the country was still too strong to
allow the popular leaders to adopt a policy so revolutionary
in character, but their position was complicated by their
dependence upon Puritan support and especially the
support of Puritan London.   Parliament, as Ranke has
remarked[1], "was connected with the disaffection of the
city through religious ideas," and in order to carry through
their policy of reform in civil affairs, Pym and his followers
saw clearly the necessity of fostering the discontent in
religious matters.   Hence, though for the moment
nothing was done, the petitioners were favourably
received.

But the example set by London proved infectious,
and in the course of January 1641, many numerously
signed petitions breathing a similar spirit were sent up
from various counties.   The country, in fact, appeared
more ready to deal with the subject than did the Parliament, and it was only the unwillingness of the House
which delayed the petitions so long[2].   At the end of the
same month, a petition of rather a different character
was presented in the names of some eight hundred
ministers, which purported to represent the wishes of the
more moderate party among the clergy.   Its contents, as
far as it is possible to judge them from the rough notes
taken during its discussion in committee[3], embodied a
sufficiently large scheme of reform, but it provided,
probably intentionally, a contrast to the more revolutionary
proposals contained in the "Root and Branch" petitions.

Contemporary royalist writers allege that these
petitions were "manufactured" and that they provide no
indication of the state of public opinion.   Dr John Walker,
for example, speaking of the hostile petitions as a whole,

[1] Ranke: *Hist. of England*, ii, 393.
[2] W. A. Shaw: *Hist. of the Eng. Ch.* 1640–60, i, p. 19.
[3] *Ibid.* i, p. 24.

says[1] that they were "generally framed by Dr Burgess
and his Junto in London, and from thence transmitted to
their correspondents ; who, by persuasions, and threaten-
ings, and all the methods imaginable, procur'd hands to
them," while "great numbers of the subscribers were
poor ignorant fellows, and persons of the meanest
capacities, as well as quality." According to Clarendon[2]
a petition, "very modest and dutiful," was prepared to
communicate to those who were desired to sign it. Very
few signatures sufficed to fill the paper on which the
petition itself was written, and when this was done, other
sheets were annexed and duly signed. Lastly, the
original petition was cut off, and a new one, "suitable to
the design in hand," substituted, so that "men found
their names subscribed to petitions of which they before
had never heard." A similar method, according to
Walker, was followed in the matter of the Ministers'
petition, which for this reason he describes as a "plain
forgery[3]."

What actually seems to have been done in the case
of the last-mentioned petition, and probably in other
petitions also, was sufficient to give colour to these
reports. The various petitions with their appended
signatures from each district were forwarded to a committee in London, who drafted a fresh petition which
professedly embodied the sense of all, and affixed the
whole mass of signatures to it. Obviously, if this final
draft contained clauses to which any signatory had not
subscribed, the proceeding justifies Clarendon's condemnation, but, in the case of the Ministers' petition at
least, this does not appear to have been done.

---

[1] John Walker : *Sufferings of the Clergy*, Pt. i, p. 8. His book was
written early in the eighteenth century and was published in 1714.
[2] Clarendon : *Hist. of the Rebellion* (ed. Macray), i, 271.
[3] Walker : *Sufferings of the Clergy*, Pt. i, p. 15.

A more convincing argument against the contention that these petitions represented the sense of the nation might be found in the existence of an almost equal number of petitions from the other side, which, while favouring the reform of abuses, express the desire that the form of government should be preserved and sectarianism suppressed. Thus a petition from Cornwall prayed the Parliament " to continue the reverenc'd office, and punish the offending persons of Bishops, to have in high account and eternize...the divine and excellent forms of Common-Prayer, to correct brain-forg'd doctrine[1] " etc., and a similar petition from Chester, while recognising the value of reforms already made, alludes to the organised attack on the existing system carried on through the medium of the press and the pulpit, which led the petitioners to fear that the desire was " to introduce an absolute innovation of Presbyterall Government." They conceive that " of all the distempers that at present threaten the welfare of this State, there is none more worthy the mature and grave consideration of this Honourable Assembly, than to stop the Torrent of such spirits before they swell beyond the bounds of Government[2]."

The latter petition was said to be signed by four noblemen, fourscore and odd knights and esquires, seventy divines, three hundred and odd gentlemen and above 6000 freeholders and other inhabitants of the county, so that the evidence of petitions as illustrating the weight of public opinion is contradictory and of very little value.

On February 8, 1641, the actual discussion of the " Root and Branch " proposals was first broached over the question of whether the London petition and the Ministers' petition should be referred to a committee[3].

---

[1] Brit. Mus. 669, f. 4, 64.   [2] *Ibid.* f. 4, 16.
[3] S. R. Gardiner : *Hist. of Eng.* 1603-42, ix, 276.

The debate which took place on this occasion is extremely interesting as illustrating the point of cleavage between the two great parties on this, the question of the hour. It is noticeable that though the division of opinion on the question of the abolition of Episcopacy and all that it involved was perfectly clear and well-defined, the hostility to the bishops was equally marked in almost all the speeches which were delivered. Finally, the debate ended in a compromise[1]. Both petitions were to be committed, but the discussion of the main point at issue, the maintenance of Episcopacy, was reserved for a future occasion. Still, the question was only postponed. During the spring, both Houses were more or less constantly engaged on the question of religion. A committee of the Commons had been appointed to consider the "Ministers' Remonstrance," and the fruits of their labours appeared in a report submitting questions for discussion. As a result of these recommendations bills were formed early in March, recommending the prevention of pluralities, the removal of the bishops from the peerage and the Privy Council, and the exclusion of clergymen generally from the commission of the peace[2]. On March 1, the House of Lords also appointed a committee of thirty lay peers and ten bishops "to take into consideration all innovations in the Church concerning religion," and directed that the committee should " have power to send for what learned divines their lordships shall please, for their better information." In accordance with these directions a sub-committee of divines was formed which met in the Deanery of Westminster under the presidency of the Dean, Williams, Bishop of Lincoln[3]. Laud himself viewed the appointment of this body with disfavour

[1] S. R. Gardiner: *Hist. of Eng.* 1603-42, ix, 287.
[2] Stoughton: *The Church of the Civil Wars*, p. 126.
[3] *Ibid.* p. 119 and *Lords' Journals*, iv, 174, 180.

as likely to tamper with doctrines as well as ceremonies, and their proposals certainly represented a considerable measure of reform, and showed, in some points, a distinctly Puritan tone. Nothing, however, was destined to come of the committee's work. By the middle of May, when its sessions came to an end, more violent counsels were being adopted.

In the first place, the ground had been cleared by two acts, which, though constitutional in form, were really of an equally revolutionary character. On May 10, 1641, the Parliament secured its own permanence by the passing of the act to provide against dissolution without its consent, and two days latter, Strafford, its most formidable enemy, was executed on Tower Hill.

On the very day of the latter event, the Commons were sitting to hear Dr John Hacket argue the case for the cathedral establishments. Rumour of impending reform had created considerable alarm in the ranks of the episcopalian clergy, and, as the assistance of counsel was not admitted, Hacket had been deputed to urge their claims before the House. He was opposed by Cornelius Burgess, but, after hearing both speakers, the Parliament determined to put the matter temporarily aside[1]. The attack on the bishops next came under consideration. A bill for the exclusion of the clergy from secular offices, and for the removal of the bishops from the House of Lords had already passed the Commons and had been sent up to the Lords on May 1. Here it had not unnaturally encountered opposition, and the Upper House had finally agreed to the exclusion of the clergy from secular offices, but had decided that the bishops should retain their seats[2]. This rejection of a measure upon which they had set their hearts would not have been

---

[1] Stoughton: *Church of the Civil Wars*, pp. 142–4.
[2] *Ibid.* p. 145, and Gardiner: *Hist. of Eng.* 1603–42, ix, 347.

endured by the Commons, and a dead-lock would probably have been the result had not the issue involved been unexpectedly raised in another and a more direct form. On May 27, while the Commons were discussing a petition from Lincolnshire praying for the abolition of episcopal government, Sir Edward Dering suddenly and without previous notice brought forward a bill for the "utter abolishing and taking away of all Archbishops, Bishops," and the whole body of the episcopal and capitular establishment. The motion emanated from the extreme party of reformers, but Dering's motives in proposing it are shrouded in some mystery, for he was at that time regarded as one of the more moderate among the Puritans. In the short speech in which he introduced the bill, he announced that if his former hopes of a "full reformation" could be revived, he would reconsider his opinion on the present proposal, and his action seems to have been dictated either by a desire to raise the question in a definite form or to induce the Lords to accept the bishops' exclusion[1]. After some demur, the bill was proceeded with, and passed its first reading by a majority of 135 to 108. On June 11, it had reached the committee stage[2]. On June 21, the younger Vane brought forward a proposal to replace the authority of the bishops by a commission, half lay, half clerical, in each diocese[3] and on July 17 the substance of his scheme was accepted with the difference that the clerical element was to be excluded entirely[4]. On June 15, the Commons had passed a resolution to the effect that Deans and Chapters should be abolished, and that their lands should be devoted to the advancement of learning and piety.

---

[1] Stoughton: *Church of the Civil Wars*, pp. 146–7, and Gardiner: *Hist. of Eng.* 1603–42, ix, 382.

[2] Gardiner: *Hist. of Eng.* 1603–42, ix, 387.

[3] *Ibid.* ix, 390.

[4] *Ibid.* ix, 408.

They also resolved that the forfeited lands should be entrusted to feoffees and that the bishops' lands should be given to the King[1].

It appeared as if the final abolition of episcopal government was about to become an accomplished fact, but at this point the progress was checked. Early in August, the King set out for Scotland, and the Parliamentary leaders, unwilling for the moment to arouse unnecessary hostility, allowed the "Root and Branch" bill to drop[2]. On the reassembling of Parliament in the following October, it was abandoned, and the question was for the moment shelved. One solid result of the debates on Episcopacy was, however, soon to be consummated. On October 21, a second Bishops' Exclusion Bill was introduced in the Commons. There was still a strong feeling of opposition in the Lords, but on February 5 it was allowed to pass, and obtained the King's sanction on February 13, 1641/2[3]. For the present this represented the limits in the progress of the attack upon the hierarchy.

The outbreak of the Civil War at once placed the matter upon a different footing, and rendered possible that which had been found impracticable while peace was outwardly maintained. In the first place, the negotiations with the Scots obliged the Parliament to declare itself more unequivocally on the subject of Church government, for it was clear that the abolition of Episcopacy would be a necessary preliminary to an understanding. Accordingly a bill for that purpose was introduced in the Commons on December 30, 1642, and passed both houses on January 26, following[4]. An additional motive, which may have influenced the initial step, as it certainly served

[1] Stoughton : *Church of the Civil Wars*, p. 156 ; Rushworth, iv, 285.
[2] Gardiner : *Hist. of Eng.* 1603–42, x, 1.
[3] *Ibid.* x, 37, 163, 165.
[4] *Commons' Journals*, ii, 906 ; *Lords' Journals*, v, 572.

ultimately to make it irrevocable, was the necessity of providing for the expenses of the war out of the property of the Church.

The idea of sequestrating ecclesiastical property for one purpose or another did not originate with the outbreak of the war; from 1641 onwards several schemes with this object had been put forward and discussed. But during the early years of the war, bishops and the members of cathedral bodies were treated on the same footing as other "delinquents," that is to say, their estates were seized and the revenues were applied "to the use, and for the maintaining of the army and forces raised by the Parliament, and such other uses as shall be directed by both Houses of Parliament[1]." In the course of time, however, the march of political events, and particularly the financial obligations to the Scots, necessitated the adoption of some more radical methods with respect to ecclesiastical property. In these circumstances, a proposal was brought forward in September 1645, that both episcopal and capitular lands should be sold, and the proceeds devoted to State purposes[2]. Nothing came of this measure, but a similar proposal touching episcopal lands only was brought forward in the following year, and on October 9, 1646, passed both Houses. Two years and a half later, on April 30, 1649, the lands of the Deans and Chapters met with the same fate.

In alienating the church property, the Parliamentary leaders do not appear to have had the purpose of sealing the overthrow of Episcopacy more effectively than they had hitherto done, but such nevertheless was the practical result of their action. It is necessary to draw a clear

---

[1] *Acts and Ordinances of the Interregnum* (Ed. C. H. Firth and R. S. Rait), i, 106, 109.
[2] W. A. Shaw: *Hist. of the Eng. Ch.* 1640–60, ii, 210.

distinction between this ordinance, which decreed that the lands should be sold outright, and the earlier ordinances which had merely sequestrated the revenues. As long as the revenues only were touched, the bishops were in the position of other "delinquents," capable of rehabilitation, but the sale of their lands, by depriving them of their position and means of subsistence, struck a blow at the constitution of their order. The King's assent to the abolition bill of January 26, 1642/3, had been demanded in the Parliament's propositions at Oxford in February of the same year, and again at the treaty of Uxbridge in January 1644/5; it had also formed part of the Newcastle propositions in July 1646. It is rather remarkable that in the Heads of the Proposals, put forward in August 1647, after the sale of episcopal lands had been decreed and partially carried out, the demand should, for the first time, assume a more moderate form and require only that an act should be passed "to take away all coercive power, authority, and jurisdiction of Bishops," thus tacitly conceding the continuance of the office. The explanation, of course, lies in the fact that the last mentioned propositions emanated from the Army leaders who did not consider themselves bound by the former policy of the Parliament any more than they shared their views on Church government, but in reality the ordinance which authorised the sales had considerably complicated the whole question. It had created, in the persons of the buyers, a vested interest opposed to any settlement which did not confirm the abolition of Episcopacy, and to such terms Charles would never agree. The difficulty was to prove one of the rocks on which the final negotiations broke down.

The abolition of the liturgy accompanied the overthrow of episcopal government. The Book of Common

Prayer had not at first been assailed when the Long Parliament met; it was at that time, says Clarendon, "much reverenced throughout the Kingdom[1]," and the attack upon it was gradual and was directed, in the first instance, against certain forms contained in the book rather than against the book as a whole. The Lords' Committee on innovations, appointed on March 1, 1640/1, had discussed revision, but their proposals on this and other subjects came to nothing. The Commons' resolutions on innovations, passed in September 1641, while directing that communion-tables should be moved, rails taken away, chancels levelled, and all ritualistic accessories abolished, contained no mention of the Prayer Book, and at one point in the debate Culpeper was able to carry a resolution that it should remain without alteration and be observed with all reverence[2]. Nor did the subject appear in the Grand Remonstrance, though a rather more hostile spirit had been evinced in the preliminary debates. The "declarations on Church Reform" of April 8, and the "Nineteen Propositions" of June 1, 1642, refer vaguely to a reform of the liturgy[3], but no radical change seems to have been contemplated until the adoption of the Presbyterian model necessitated the disuse of traditional forms and the substitution of the Directory for Public Worship.

The ordinance for taking away the Book of Common Prayer was passed on January 4, 1644/5[4]. On the same day the Lords passed the Act of Attainder against Laud. He had been impeached of high treason on December 18, 1640, and from that date, although his trial did not actually begin until 1644, he had

[1] Clarendon : *Hist. of the Rebellion* (ed. Macray), i, 383.
[2] *Ibid.* i, 384, note
[3] S. R. Gardiner, *Constitutional Documents*, pp. 247, 252.
[4] *Acts and Ordinances of the Interregnum* (Ed. C. H. Firth and R. S. Rait), i, 582.

been in imprisonment, and had thus been withdrawn from the conflict during the years which witnessed the overthrow of the English Church. His execution took place on January 10, 1644/5, and by this act of injustice, the Long Parliament crowned their work of destruction.

CHAPTER II

THE PAROCHIAL CLERGY

ANY one who sets out to estimate the general standard of piety and learning among the clergy of the seventeenth century, is confronted with the existence of two apparently quite distinct classes, the one eminent for the virtues and attainments which the other as conspicuously lacked. In the high offices of the Church were men of great parts and holy life, not unfit to be compared with the English ecclesiastics of any preceding or succeeding age, men whose characters, as well as their positions, claimed general respect. In an age when academic distinction was the surest road to preferment, the Universities were well-provided with eminent divines, and many of the London parishes and a certain number of country cures were no less fortunate. The encomium, bestowed upon such by Clarendon, is hardly overdrawn when he speaks of "the Church flourishing with learned and extraordinary men," and states that "there was not one Churchman in any degree of favour or acceptance... of a scandalous insufficiency in learning, or of a more scandalous condition of life; but, on the contrary, most of them of confessed eminent parts in knowledge, and of virtuous or unblemished lives[1]." On the other hand, the ordinary country clergyman and, indeed, the inferior clergy taken as a whole, appear as belonging to another

[1] Clarendon: *Hist. of the Rebellion* (ed. Macray), i, 95, 97.

class, lower in social status, in education, and in general qualifications.

The traditional explanation of this disparity has been the poverty of benefices, the ranks from which the great majority of the clergy were drawn and the low estimation in which the clerical profession was held by the genteel classes. To some extent this is a correct explanation, but Macaulay's estimate of the clergy in the latter part of the seventeenth century[1], which has been largely responsible for it, was elaborately answered by Churchill Babington in 1849 and in some points disproved[2]. The controversy between these two writers turned on the use of authorities, and on how far the country parson of contemporary satire might be considered as a true picture.

The evidence of seventeenth century writers is not wanting, but it is somewhat contradictory, and the popularity of the less favourable view is probably due to the dramatists whose works are naturally more widely known than those of preachers or pamphleteers. One or two of the latter kind may, however, be noticed as giving a less fanciful sketch.

In an interesting book, published early in the century, the writer, himself a clergyman, expostulates with the gentry of his day for contributing towards the contempt in which the lower ranks of the clergy were held, by refusing to allow their sons to take orders, and speaks of the office being entrusted to "the basest of the people and lowest sort...because the wise men of the world, men of might, and the noble, hold it derogatorie to their dignities[3]." A not dissimilar line was taken in 1670 by

---

[1] Macaulay : *Hist. of Eng.* (popular ed. 1895), i, 158–163.
[2] Churchill Babington : *Mr Macaulay's Character of the Clergy...* *considered.*
[3] Richard Bernard : *The Faithfull Shepheard,* p. 5.

John Eachard, the Master of St Catharine's Hall, Cambridge, in a tract entitled *The Grounds and Occasions of the Contempt of the Clergy.*

This work is written in a light and satirical vein and was probably intended to exaggerate the case, but the main purpose of the author was to draw attention to an evil and was serious enough. A large part of his tract is devoted to the inadequate education which the clergy received and to the consequent absurdities of the common manner of preaching, but he goes on to describe the private lives of the country clergy and their extreme poverty by which "their sacred profession is much disparaged, and their doctrine undervalued[1]."

" I am almost confident," he writes, "that since the Reformation, nothing has more hindred people from a just estimation of a form of prayer, and our holy Liturgy, than employing a company of boyes or old illiterate mumblers, to read the service[2]."

The chief causes of the evil state of affairs he thought were the facts that the ministry was overstocked and underpaid and that the gentry designed "not onely the weak, the lame, and usually the most ill-favour'd of their children for the office of the ministry, but also such as they intend to settle nothing upon for their subsistance; leaving them wholly to the bare hopes of Church preferment[3]."

The publication of the tract aroused a considerable amount of indignation and led to a series of "answers" and "replies." It is noticeable, however, that Eachard's critics did not deny that the clergy were poor or that there were cases of gross ignorance : they quarrel rather with his method of dealing with the subject and with the reasons

[1] *Grounds and Occasions of the Contempt of the Clergy* (1670), p. 82.
[2] *Ibid.* p. 106.
[3] *Ibid.* pp. 111, 115, 118.

which he had assigned for the existence of the evil. "It is a grave subject you enquire into," one of his opponents told him, "and such as in sober sadness deserves to be enquired into, but the manner of your enquiry is too facetious and jocular." His work, in fact, was calculated to make the clergy "more obnoxious and contemptible than yet we are[1]."

" I freely grant," says the same writer, "among the many 1000 clergymen that are in England, divers may be dull and heavy, but why should this reflect more upon the whole body of the clergy to their dishonour, than the learning of some does to their honour[2]." This ignorance, however, was due to "want of books, want of time to make the best use of those few we have, and want of converse with learned men[3]," and the contempt in which they were held was due to the hostility of the Roman Catholics, the Nonconformists and the young "blades," who sought to foster it, rather than to the circumstances of their own condition. As to that part of Eachard's tract that dealt with their poverty, he wishes that he could confute it, "but (though you hyperbolize grievously in that part of your discourse) there is too much truth in it to be contradicted[4]." Another writer, while contending that Eachard's account had made the poverty of the clergy appear " far more extreme and desperate than in truth it is," also admits the truth of the general statement[5].

So also Barnabas Oley, in his preface to the edition of George Herbert's *Priest to the Temple*, published in 1671, alludes to their poverty as a well-known fact, "so far from being a Ground of Contempt, that it is a Cause

[1] *An answer to a letter of Enquiry into the Grounds, etc.* (1671), p. 78 and preface.

[2] *Ibid.* p. 24.   [3] *Ibid.* p. 45.   [4] *Ibid.* p. 82.

[5] *A vindication of the Clergy from the contempt imposed upon them, etc.* (1672), p. 28. Quoted by Churchill Babington, p. 60.

of Commiseration and Honour." The low social standing of the clergy, on the other hand, he seeks to refute by instancing several cases in which members of noble families had entered the profession. " Though the vulgar," he says, "ordinarily do not, yet the Nobility and Gentry do distinguish and abstract the Errors of the man, from the Holy Calling, and not think their dear relation degraded by Receiving Holy Orders[1]."

There is a general consensus of agreement, then, that the clergy of the seventeenth century were poor—poorer probably than in the periods which preceded and succeeded. The Reformation had impoverished · the revenues of the Church and, at the same time, the substitution of married clergy, in a system designed for the support of celibates, had added to the difficulties of the situation, and rendered the servants of the Church relatively worse off than they had been in pre-Reformation days. Again, the increased value of land in the eighteenth century brought with it a corresponding rise in the value of country livings and may have contributed to the improvement in the social condition of the clerical profession in the age which succeeded, but George Herbert's " Country Parson " is essentially the picture of a poor man. " The furniture of his house," is described as " very plain, but clean, whole, and sweet, as sweet as his garden can make ; for he hath no mony for such things, charity being his only perfume, which deserves

---

[1] See also *Hieragonisticon or Corah's Doom* (1672). Eachard published answers to the three tracts cited above, under the titles *Some Observations upon the Answers to an Enquiry, etc.*, *A letter to T. D. the author of Hieragonisticon*, *A letter to B. O. the publisher of Mr Herbert's Country Parson*, and *A letter to the author of a Vindication of the Clergy*. His answers maintain the same spirit of raillery that had characterised his original work, but he takes some pains to show that his object had not been to bring the clergy into contempt. For a short *résumé* of some of these authorities see Bruce Blaxland : *The Struggle with Puritanism*, pp. 151-3.

cost when he can spare it[1]," and this may probably be taken as a typical description.

But, in spite of this, it may be doubted whether the material prosperity of the clergy in the seventeenth century was on a much lower level than it is at the present day. The average income of a country clergyman was undoubtedly very low, but livings which would even now be considered substantial were not as uncommon as is generally supposed[2]. In the second place, incomes of thirty or forty pounds a year, on which some clergymen had to subsist, do not represent an equal sum at the present day, because the standard of living in the middle and lower classes was on a much more modest scale, and expenses, especially in the isolation of a country village, would be fewer and smaller. The economic conditions, in fact, were entirely different, and the lack of what would now be regarded as the ordinary accessories of a respectable household cannot be taken as a necessary indication of extreme poverty. Even Eachard's picture of a country clergyman's ill-supplied house and library of a dozen books and "a boudget of old stitch'd sermons[3]" is not so far from the truth as it appears, and this is shown by an interesting inventory of a contemporary parsonage— that of Prestwich in Lancashire, the contents of which were sequestrated from the rector, Isaac Allen, in 1645[4]. This was a good living, worth, according to Walker, £400 a year[5], but the total furniture and household stuff

[1] G. Herbert: *A Priest to the Temple* (1671), p. 36.

[2] The articles of accusation presented against the clergy of Cambridgeshire before the local Parliamentary Committee, generally give the value of the living and show that the average income of twenty-four parishes was roughly £87 per ann. (Brit. Mus. Add. MSS. 15,672), but in Walker's list, in the second part of the *Sufferings of the Clergy*, livings of £300 and £400, and even more, are not uncommon.

[3] *Grounds and Occasions of the Contempt, etc.* p. 87.

[4] See Appendix I.

[5] John Walker: *Sufferings of the Clergy*, Pt. ii. 183.

of what seems to have been a large house, was only valued at a little over sixty-one pounds, and the rector's modest library ("not prized") contained no more than a hundred and fifty books. In fact, even though the very poorest vicarages have now been improved by schemes for augmentation, so that the average value of livings has been raised, it must be conceded that the modern clergyman has a much more difficult position to support. For there can be very little question but that one of the principal differences, which distinguish the modern country clergyman from his predecessor of the seventeenth century, is that of social status.

The strata of society in the seventeenth century were set on broader and less complex lines than those of to-day. On the one hand, a wider gap separated the nobility and landed gentry from what would now be called the middle classes, but, on the other, below this main division there were fewer of those subtle grades which characterise the modern social arrangement. It was not, therefore, that the clergy were recruited from a different class, but rather that they were drawn from a greater number of classes. The nobility and upper classes did not favour orders as a profession for their sons. Members of good families were of course, to be found not infrequently among the clergy, but Barnabas Oley's instances prove that it was the exception rather than the rule. The Church no longer offered positions of such pomp and circumstance as it had in the days of the great statesmen prelates of pre-Reformation times, although its high places were still the seats of power and influence, and the way was left open for men of humbler extraction who had the ability to attain to it. Laud himself started with no "family interest" or any advantages beyond what his own worth gave him, and the famous Jeremy Taylor was the son of a Cambridge barber. But though the gulf fixed between the classes was not so formidable but that merit could overcome it, it was yet wide enough to make a very real difference between the people on the opposite sides. The system probably had the advantage of bringing the most able men to the front, but it did nothing for those whose lot fell in humbler stations. The ordinary parish priest had little prospect of ever becoming anything more, and, as the office was ill-paid and somewhat despised, it required a considerable measure of self-sacrifice in a man of social position, like George Herbert, who deliberately chose to serve the Church in this humble capacity[1]. There was no dearth of candidates for orders—indeed Eachard complains that they were too numerous in his day— but the conditions of life naturally affected their standard.

The mere fact that the clergy were ill-paid and were largely drawn from the humbler ranks of society only touches the question of their efficiency indirectly and in so far as it deprived them of opportunities and education, and the fact that a certain number were ill-fitted for the profession must be attributed partly to the general laxity of Church discipline which Laud had set himself to reform. The evil undoubtedly existed, and the ecclesiastical visitations of the reign of Charles I revealed many facts which called for redress among the clergy as well as among the churches. When, for example, in 1625, John Cosin carried out his visitation as archdeacon of the East Riding of Yorkshire he found a generally unsatisfactory state of affairs. If the queries contained in his visitation articles may be accepted as evidence of the kind of irregularities which he expected to encounter, it would seem that lack of episcopal ordination and simony

---

[1] George Herbert's "Country Parson" is supposed to be likely to bring up his eldest son to his own profession. His younger children he will probably bind apprentices to trades. *A Priest to the Temple* (1671), p. 33.

were not unknown, while there are indications of considerable laxity in the performance of the Church services[1]. "Well may your Worship terme these tymes of neglect," writes one of his correspondents at this time, "for even in the clergy I fynd great defect in the performance of reall duties[2]."

The visitations of 1638 again show the inner workings of Laud's system, and give a very fair idea of the condition of the ordinary parish of the time. As in 1625, cases of irregularity and neglect are common. At Histon in Cambridgeshire, for example, it was reported that Mr Slegg, the vicar, " never served the cure himself, but takes all the profitts and getts young Scholars to read prayers and preach, but whether laymen or no will not be known, because the Churchwardens dare not displease Mr Slegg[3]." At S. Mary's in Wisbech, it was stated that Mr Edward Furnis, the vicar, "receiveth the profits but doth not serve the cure well, sometimes wee have prayers on Sundays and sometimes not," various instances of neglect being cited. More commonly the cause of complaint was breach of the Canons. At S. Peter's in Wisbech, a number of witnesses testified to various irregularities. "We are informed that the Communion hath been received sitting. Our curate doth not preach in his hood. Our vicar doth serve 2 cures, the one 2 miles from the other. No catechising but in Lent. No sermons in the afternoon...the Sacrament is not performed according to the 24th article of the 4th Cap. The 26th article altogether neglected," and so forth. In Streatham it was reported that "the minister turneth his face towards the west when he kneeleth," and at Elm the vicar was presented "for not wearing a hood contrary to

---

[1] *Cosin's Correspondence* (Surtees Soc.), i, pp. xviii, 106.
[2] *Ibid.* p. 82, Letter from Robert Claphamson, notary-public at York.
[3] Baker Collection (B.M.), vol. vi, fol. 322.

the 24th article," for not catechising except in Lent, and
for not observing the orders mentioned in the sixth
article. At Emneth the minister did not catechise and
did not use the form of prayer provided in the book
of articles : at Leverington it was complained that
Mr Bayley, the incumbent, did not preach in a surplice
and did not read the second service, and that he allowed
his son, who was not in orders, to read prayers.

In many cases, there were, of course, extenuating
circumstances which appear to have been taken as an
excuse. Bayley, for example, explained that his son had
been obliged to read prayers because he himself was ill,
and on account of the "scarcitie of ministers to officiate."
Similarly Edward Furnis of Wisbech was excused on
the ground of sickness.

Of the presentment of parishioners, also, there are
several instances. At Coveney it was reported that
" Many of the hamlet of Maney who ought to bring their
children to this Church to be baptized have carried them
to Doddington." " Roger Beaumont and Thomasine his
wife " were presented " for not repairing to their parish
church att the time of divine service." At Streatham,
Thomas Low was presented for not paying his rate to
the church, and Robert Turner for not receiving the
Communion at Easter, while at Leverington many
parishioners were said to be absent from prayers. There
are also some quaint instances of disagreement between
the clergyman and his parishioners. In the report from
Leverington it was alleged that : " Mr Bayley did strike
one Thomas Laryware in the Church upon a Sunday and
putteth Cattell in the Churchyard." To this Bayley, the
vicar, appears to have replied that " the said Laryware
misbehaveing himselfe by laughing he being neere him
gave the said Laryware with his hand a little stroake
on his head." With regard to the second charge

" Mr Bayley saith that he hath not putt any cattell into the Churchyard this 20 years...and further alleageth that he letteth the Churchyard to the parishioners there, and the cattell which are putt in are by them[1]."

From other parts the reports were more serious. In the diocese of Lincoln, Laud was informed that "in divers parts of that diocese many both of clergy and laity are excessively given to drunkenness," and in Gloucester Bishop Goodman reported that though "to his knowledge he never gave holy orders to an unworthy person," yet he was "forced to ordain some very mean ministers[2]," while in the diocese of Rochester a clergyman was sentenced " for drunkenness, profaning of marriages, and making men live in perpetual adultery, that he is a briber, a beggar, a drunkard, a Bedlam[3]." Nor was this all. " It is certain," says Mr Hutton, "that in many cases the grossest irreverence prevailed in the use of parish churches[4]."

This was the state of affairs reported to the bishops in 1638. Some two years later, a somewhat similar picture is revealed in the various petitions, hostile to Episcopacy and the clergy of the Church of England, which were presented to the Long Parliament. The Kent petition against Episcopacy, for example, which was introduced into the House of Commons by Sir Edward Dering in January 1641, speaks of "the great increase of idle, lewd, dissolute, ignorant and erronious men in the ministry, which swarme like locusts of Egypt over the whole kingdome[5]," and an equally unfavourable

[1] These cases are taken from the Ely Diocese Visitation Book (Ely Episcopal Register, B. 3).
[2] W. H. Hutton : *Hist. of the English Church from the accession of Charles I to the death of Anne*, p. 60.
[3] *Ibid.* p. 71.
[4] *Ibid.* p. 50 ; see also Stoughton : *Church of the Civil Wars*, p. 30.
[5] *Proceedings in Kent*, ed. by L. B. Larking (Camden Soc. 1861), pp. 31–2.

spirit permeates other documents of a like nature. A certain margin must, of course, be allowed for the exaggeration of avowed enemies to the prevailing system, while the evidence supplied by the petitions of individual parishes must, for reasons to be given later, in many cases be discounted altogether ; but, taken in conjunction with the bishops' reports, the natural assumption is that the complaints were not without foundation. Even amongst the parochial petitions, a few stray facts, gleaned from the mass of less reliable material, occasionally throw additional light upon the character of the clergy, and not always to their credit[1].

Still, Walker himself, who denies the credibility of the charges brought against the clergy, reasonably admits that it would be "false, as well as ridiculous, to affirm, that there were not in those (or indeed any other times) among the whole body of the clergy, any men of wicked lives, and such as were even a reproach and scandal to their function[2]." A certain number of such cases were inevitable at any period, but the available evidence suggests that the general state of affairs could not be regarded as either healthy or satisfactory.

The strength of the Laudians and Puritans respectively among the clergy was on a very different scale to that in the lay population. According to the *Valor Beneficiorum*, published in 1695, there appear to have then been, roughly speaking, about eight thousand six hundred benefices in England and Wales. A rather later authority[3] states that there were over nine thousand, but the former is probably the more reliable figure. Walker's list of parochial sequestrations contained just

---

[1] See, for example, a letter to Sir Edward Dering from a minister named Nicols, practically admitting faults. *Proceedings in Kent*, pp. 110–111.

[2] Walker : *Sufferings of the Clergy*, Pt. i, 72.

[3] J. Withers : *Remarks on Dr Walker's late Preface to the Attempt*, 1717.

over two thousand names, from which some reduction must be made for those cases where the same man is mentioned more than once. But this list, as we shall see later on, was incomplete, and the probability is that the number of ejections was considerably larger than that. John Withers, one of Walker's critics, seemed prepared to admit, from the evidence supplied by the printed list of clergy ejected by the Parliament in Hampshire, that a third of the total number, that is to say about three thousand, were ejected[1]. He shows indeed that the proportion in Norfolk, Cambridge, and Suffolk, according to Walker, only worked out at a little under a sixth, but these counties were essentially Puritan in tone and therefore not a fair test, especially as the proportion varies enormously. Practically all those who were sequestered would be royalists, and nearly all " High " Churchmen, and yet we must suppose that a certain number escaped ejection either by conforming or some other means. Altogether, counting those who were ejected and those who escaped, it does not seem unreasonable to place the number of Laudian clergy at about four thousand. The genuine Puritans, on the other hand, were in a very distinct minority, and probably did not number a thousand in all. The balance was with those who had not identified themselves with the extremists on either side. This last fact, as has already been seen, holds good for the lay population also, but here the similarity ends, for the Laudians had little or no following amongst the mass of the people.

But though the lower classes were undoubtedly hostile to the system in Church as well as in State, the real influence of mobs is apt to be overestimated, and to appear proportionate to the disturbance which they

[1] J. Withers : *Remarks on Dr Walker's late Preface to the Attempt*, 6th remark.

create. As a matter of fact, the hostility of this class to the Established Church cannot have been the result of enlightened speculation on the respective claims of Episcopacy and Presbytery to be considered *jure divino*, but was rather due to a vague sense of oppression, coupled with an innate propensity for faction.

In any case, it will be seen that the weight of the clergy was distributed in precisely opposite proportion to that of the laity, and that the reforms most popular with the one were the most disliked by the other. Having arrived at this point, it is more or less of a platitude to point out that the clergy were, very often, out of sympathy with the views which recommended themselves to their parishioners. We should, indeed, be led to expect that the popularity or the reverse of any individual parish priest was very much a personal matter, and that, in country districts especially, this would have counted for more than differences on questions of ritual and Church government. On the whole this impression is borne out by the general attitude of the parishes during the course of the sequestrations. It is difficult to imagine that the underlying Puritanism of the rustic population would, if left to itself, have taken any very concrete form, had not external events reacted upon it. One thing, however, all classes seem to have had very clearly in their minds, namely, an intense dread of anything that savoured of popery. The orders enforced by the Laudian bishops were misinterpreted by the Puritans to bear this construction, and therefore, in parishes where the Laudian system was in vogue, in spite of the opposition of the general wishes of the parish, strained relations were often created.

The latent discontent which undoubtedly existed in many parishes under Laud's *régime* was soon to receive an impetus from the course which events were taking. With the meeting of the Long Parliament in November

1640, a new complexion was put upon religious affairs. The supremacy of the Laudian party, which had been all powerful while Charles' personal rule had lasted, and had escaped attack by the dissolution of the Short Parliament, was at once successfully assailed. In a very short space of time, Laud was in prison, and the Puritan spirit throughout the country was let loose.

At first the hostility to the Established Church, both in and out of Parliament, was cautiously displayed. The most noticeable feature of the growing assertion of the prevalent discontent was evinced in the petitions and complaints which, side by side with the larger motions directed against Episcopacy as a whole, now began to be presented by various parishes throughout the kingdom. The *Commons' Journals* from 1640 onwards are full of such petitions, illustrative of the effect produced in the parishes throughout certain districts by the trend of events. At first they take the form of complaints or informations against the clergyman of the parish, usually on the ground that he was disaffected to the Parliament, but not infrequently containing more serious charges.

The general tenor of these petitions accorded well with the spirit which was then animating Parliament, where antagonism to Laud was rife. One of their earliest actions had been to appoint a Grand Committee of Religion to deal with ecclesiastical affairs generally, but the work occasioned by the petitions increased so fast that further arrangements had to be made. On November 23, 1640, a sub-committee of the Grand Committee was formed with Sir Edward Dering as chairman[1]; on December 12, the "Committee for Scandalous Ministers" was first nominated[2].

So ready did the Commons appear to receive these

---

[1] *Proceedings in Kent*, p. 80.
[2] W. A. Shaw: *Hist. of the Eng. Ch.* 1640-60, ii, 177.

indications of feeling that Clarendon and other royalist writers have accused them of deliberately exploiting the popular discontent. In support of this contention, for example, Walker quotes a printed leaflet which, he says, was unofficially circulated by the leaders of the Puritan party in the Parliament[1]. In this the earnest desire and expectation of the Parliament was expressed that "all ingenuous persons in every county of the kingdom, will be very active to improve the present opportunity, by giving a true information of all the parishes in their several counties," with the further assurance that the Committee desired "informations from all parties."

With regard to the petitions themselves which were presented in response to this appeal, Walker states that they were generally the work of a body of ignorant sectaries, often "the meanest and most vicious" in the parish, and expresses his disgust that "a few of the rabble, much the least and worst part of their parish (and sometimes a single person, though a profligate drunken blasphemer, though a profest enemy to his minister, and made so either by reproof for his vices, or by prosecution for his inconformity) should be heard in Parliament against a clergyman[2]."

There can be little doubt that, as in the case of the county petitions against Episcopacy, a good deal was done by way of private instigation, to procure signatures to the petitions, and that they hardly ever represent the spontaneous action of the parish. It is certain that these parochial movements were attended with a considerable amount of corrupt practice.

The somewhat precarious position of the Long Parliament, during the initial stages of their existence, rendered them peculiarly suspicious of hostility, and quick to stamp out what might be regarded as a covert

[1] Walker: *Sufferings of the Clergy*, Pt. i, 64.   [2] *Ibid.* p. 71.

attack. Although, therefore, the parochial petitions dealt with a variety of subjects, it was chiefly the charges of "disaffection" which attracted their attention, and it is evident from cases in the *Commons' Journals* that to be guilty of this offence was of itself sufficient to condemn to imprisonment[1]. At the same time, it is improbable, at that date at all events, that the Parliament, though ready to receive petitions, took any official steps to promote them.

In connection with the second point, brought forward by Walker, that is to say the character of the petitioners, the evidence supplied by the proceedings of Sir Edward Dering's Committee is extremely instructive[2]. This was one of the offshoots of the original Committee for Religion (already described), and, in the course of its existence, it dealt with numerous petitions from the county of Kent. It may be that these were not quite characteristic of the petitions throughout the country, but the impression derived from them is not such as to warrant Walker's violent generalisations. Perhaps the most common complaints are those of non-residence or neglect of duties, "innovations in doctrine," and disputes about tithes. There are very few charges of drunkenness and hardly any of vice. On the other hand, several of the petitions dealt with the questions of the insufficient number of clergy to serve the churches in the county, and the insufficient stipends of those who did so, subjects which might well engage the attention of a committee bent only upon improving the service of the Church. There are also a number of petitions in favour of the clergyman,

---

[1] Thus, there is an order of January 22, 1640/1, that "Geo. Preston, Vicar of Rothersthorpe, for very scandolous speeches, spoken by him against this House, (the which words are contained in a Petition delivered into this House, and were all clearly proved...) be forthwith committed to the prison at the Gatehouse." *Commons' Journals*, ii, 71.

[2] Given in the *Proceedings in Kent*.

though not so much with a view to rebutting charges, as with the purpose of obtaining for him some augmentation of income.

But, at the same time, there is no lack of cases in which bad feeling and discontent are revealed. These are usually numerously signed, but one or two instances which occur in the course of the proceedings show how little a wealth of signatures may mean. In the case of Dr Meric Casaubon, vicar of Minster and Monkton, we have both the petitions of his two parishes and his reply to the articles of complaint[1]. He was charged with observing the innovations, with exorbitant demands in the matter of tithes, and with neglect of his cure, and although his replies appear satisfactory, he seems to have suffered ejection. The next evidence on the subject is contained in a letter written to Casaubon by six of his former parishioners in 1647. The letter has an interest beyond the mere point at issue as showing into what hands the sequestered livings sometimes fell, and it is worth reproducing at length.

"We cannot but let you know," the parishioners write, "of our great sufferings under Mr Culmer which you cannot but be sensible of. These 3 last sabbaths we have had tumults in our church between the poor people and Mr Culmer, the poor people being resolved he shall not continue there: And we whose names are under subscribed, doe fere that the difference if not suddainely prevented will be the cause of bloodshed. We desire your worship to be pleased to doe as some other of your own coate doth at this present, that is to desire your living againe, and that your parishioners may keepe in there hands there tithes and to be accountable to your worship for them, and if you think not fit to come there your selfe that you would endeavour to get order to send

<hr>
[1] *Proceedings in Kent*, pp. 104-110.

a curate that he may officiate for you, and we shall ever remain your humble parishioners[1]."

This must be read in the light of the fact that six years previously Casaubon had been ejected on a petition signed by thirty-three from Minster and four from Monkton. This in itself throws light on the capricious feeling of the inhabitants, but the remarkable fact is that of the six parishioners who signed this letter, asking Casaubon to return, all but one had also signed the petition urging that he should be supplanted.

It might, of course, be possible to explain this by merely assuming that the parishioners in question had learnt wisdom by experience, and had found that Puritanism in the person of Mr Culmer was even less to be desired than the ceremonial innovations and other short-comings of Casaubon, but the case of another Kent minister named Richard Tray suggests the possibility of another explanation.

On February 8, 1640/1, a petition against this minister was presented to the House of Commons[2]. It was attested by eight members of his parish of Lidsing and Bredhurst, and dealt with several charges, neglect of his cure, being "very contentious" and "a stirrer up of suits" and "given to fighting," while he was further accused of betraying the confidences of a sick man. The materials for his defence, which Tray sent to an influential friend in London, contained, besides a refutation of the charges, signed by various witnesses, a testimonial

---

[1] A copy of this letter was sent to Walker by John Lewis, Casaubon's successor in the living of Minster (MSS. J. Walker, c. 7. fol. 111). Concerning Culmer, Lewis says, "no man was ever more hated than he, and to this day spoken of by those that remember him with all the dislike imaginable. He went by the name of 'blew dick' and has left behind him the character of a very turbulent, unquiet and debauched man." Walker makes no use of this information, so perhaps it reached him too late for incorporation in his book. The letter is dated Sept. 23, 1710.

[2] *Proceedings in Kent*, pp. 160–173.

in his favour signed by twenty-three parishioners. They also included signed confessions from five out of his eight accusers, admitting that they had been prevailed upon to give their signatures to the petition by the malpractices of one Edward Alchorne, whose name had headed the list. Three of these had signed when " overtaken with drink," one had been bribed, and another had been deceived by a misrepresentation of the facts. The proceedings do not show what reception was given to this mass of evidence, but Walker states that about this time Tray was ejected from the living of S. Mary's in Hoo by the Committee for Plundered Ministers[1].

The peculiar circumstances of Tray's case stand alone as far as the extant records of the proceedings in Kent are concerned, but, having regard to the times, there is at all events a presumption that what happened in one place may have also happened elsewhere. Of the actual merits of his case it should not be difficult to judge if signatures to documents mean anything. Certainly, it would be hazardous to build too much upon the testimony of men whose signatures could, on their own showing, be so easily obtained, but the contrast between the certificate in Tray's favour with its twenty-three names and the petition against him with its dubious eight, leaves little room for doubt that in this case his accusation was due to private animosity.

The conditions under which the petitions were made rendered it possible for anyone who entertained a private grudge against his minister to use this most effective means of satisfying his vengeance, nor would it generally be difficult to persuade the unthinking rustic that he too had a grievance. The persistent mention of disputes concerning tithes, which occur again and again in the petitions, may go a certain way towards accounting for

[1] Walker : *Sufferings of the Clergy*, Pt. ii, 379.

some at least of the signatures. Considerations of this sort, coupled with the more direct evidence of a few ascertained cases, make it impossible to regard these petitions as a reliable criterion of the country's feeling. They reveal the local effect of political events at times of violent change. A very similar tendency is observable amid the reaction of the Restoration. For example, we find the inhabitants of the town of Yeldon presenting a petition to the Lords in June 1660, in which they pray that their rector, Mr William Dell, may be deprived of the living for disloyal speeches in reference to the King and for general neglect of his cure[1].

As time went on, the petitions changed somewhat in character and took the form of requests that "lecturers" might be appointed to preach at stated times in the parish church. Accordingly towards the end of 1642 and the beginning of 1643, orders became common appointing lecturers to preach, and requiring the regular minister to allow him the use of his pulpit and threatening punishment in case of refusal[2].

The regular parish clergy, upon whom these unwelcome visitors were imposed, very naturally objected strongly, and consequently often suffered punishment for

[1] *Hist. MSS. Com. 7th Rep.* Appendix, H. of Lords, pp. 101-2.

[2] The following are examples :

"Nov. 26, 1642. 'The humble petition of divers of the Inhabitants of St Ives was this Day read

Ordered, that the Order formerly made, for Mr Tookey to be Lecturer of S. Ives in the county of Huntingdon, shall be revived, and confirmed.

Resolved, that Mr Downehall, vicar of S. Ives, and Mr Reynolds the curate there, be forthwith sent for, as delinquents, for their contempt in refusing to obey the orders of this House, for admitting M. Tookey to be lecturer there.'" *Commons' Journals*, ii, 864.

"Dec. 31, 1642. 'Ordered, that Mr George Green, Master of Arts, and in Orders, be recommended unto the Parish of Sutton, in the Isle of Ely, in the County of Cambridge, to be their lecturer, to preach there every Thursday in the week : And the Vicar is hereby required to permit him the free Use of the Pulpit, to exercise his Function, upon the days aforesaid, accordingly.'" *Commons' Journals*, ii, 909.

their behaviour. Dr Shaw, indeed, contends that "to such action of the Commons there cannot be the slightest objection from one point of view," inasmuch as the lecturer did not interfere with the incumbent's stipend or the regular services[1]; but it must be admitted that it was an action well calculated to arouse animosity. Leaving out of the question the mere personal annoyance of having his own ministrations supplemented in this high-handed manner, there was a further very legitimate grievance. At such a period of active controversy in matters secular and religious, the sermons of the Puritan lecturers would necessarily be filled with much hostile criticism of the opposite party, and if the legitimate incumbent were a royalist and a "High" Churchman, as he was tolerably certain to be, he would very properly resent what he regarded as false and dangerous doctrines being discharged from his own pulpit into the ears of his own congregation.

Instances of resistance on the part of the incumbents are common among the entries in the *Commons' Journals.* The vicar of "Andevor," for example, "gave a command to lock the Church doors," saying that "Rather than Mr Symonds should preach there, by Order of Parliament, he would lose his life," and that "the Church was as much his own, as his own house[2]." Occasionally other, and possibly more effective, methods were pursued to thwart the intention of the Parliament. The inhabitants of Pinner set forth that "whereas this House did formerly recommend Mr Philip Goodwyn to be lecturer there, to preach every Sunday in the afternoon,...the Curate, to elude this order, does expound every Afternoon, till six of clock[3]." The curate in question no doubt felt that the

[1] W. A. Shaw : *Hist. of the Eng. Ch.* 1640–60, ii, 183.
[2] *Commons' Journals*, ii, 735, Aug. 24, 1642.
[3] *Ibid.* ii, 723, Aug. 17, 1642.

end justified the means, but in this case, one is almost led to sympathise with his congregation.

Very few cases are recorded in which the clergyman of the parish gave his consent, but at Beales in Suffolk, a certificate was signed by the parson, John Shardelow, "declaring his consent, that the parishioners should make choice of Mr Jo. Clerke to be lecturer to the said parishioners[1]."

The institution of these lectures appealed, as a rule, to the religious requirements of the people who still favoured preaching, but, even amongst the people, the lecturer was not always popular.

A very interesting instance is provided by the case of S. James at Dover, where the churchwardens and parishioners complained "of a great disturbance and interruption in the Church, in the time of Divine Service; occasioned by some, who in opposition to an order of the House, would hinder Mr Vincent, recommended by this House to be their lecturer[2]." This instance, taken in conjunction with somewhat similar demonstrations elsewhere, seems to show that, in some cases at all events, the lecturers were appointed in opposition to the wishes of a section of the parish.

But the *raison d'être* of the lecturers was not only religious: they had a political importance as well, and the influence exercised by them upon public opinion was undoubtedly very great. Of course, as soon as the war broke out, self-preservation became the first law, and questions of public morality could not be too closely considered; but even while peace was outwardly maintained, the Parliament had imprisoned royalist clergy for no other offence than "disaffection." The lecturers provided the Parliament's antidote to the royalist doctrines

---

[1] *Commons' Journals*, iii, 17, Mar. 24, 1642/3.
[2] *Ibid.* ii, 673, July 14, 1642.

of the episcopal clergy, and there can be little doubt that their utility from the Parliamentary point of view was as much political as religious. On August 11, 1643, an order was read in the Commons "for sending divers godly Ministers into divers Counties,...to possess the people with the truth and justice of the Parliament's cause in taking up of defensive arms[1]." In this respect, the lecturers acted as Parliamentary agents in the parishes where they gained a foothold[2], just as the royalist clergy supported the cause of the King. To lose sight of the interaction of secular and religious affairs, is to miss the true interpretation of events throughout the whole struggle.

Another factor, of an entirely different kind, should also be borne in mind. Although the interest in the questions at issue permeated practically every corner of the land, and caused a revolution in nearly every village, there were nevertheless some few favoured spots where the course of the war, as well as the reasons which promoted it, made little impression. Waterbeach in Cambridgeshire seems to have been a case in point, for the seventeenth century "passed over this village very lightly[3]." Where the personal affection between the clergyman and his parishioners counted for more than the political relations between the King and his Parliament, or where the position or insignificance of a village lent it a degree of immunity, it is possible that the even tenor of the village life would not be very greatly disturbed. Such cases, however, were not very numerous.

---

[1] *Commons' Journals*, iii, 202.
[2] Clarendon : *Hist. of the Rebellion*, ii, 319.
[3] W. K. Clay : *History of Waterbeach*, p. 16.

CHAPTER III

THE SEQUESTRATION COMMITTEES

It has already been seen that the number of petitions directed against the parochial clergy had, even in the first few months of the sitting of the Long Parliament, necessitated the creation of additional bodies to deal with the business. At first, the various committees sat in London, and it is probable that the great majority of cases with which they dealt came from districts within more or less easy access of the metropolis. But with the outbreak of the war, and with the consequent increased importance of widening the sphere of the Parliamentary influence, a further delegation of powers was found expedient.

At an early stage of the war the Parliament had adopted the policy of appointing special committees for the defence or the administration of counties or districts, and amongst others a whole series of committees had been called into being by the ordinance, of March 27, 1643, "for sequestring notorious delinquents' estates[1]." The purpose of the committees created by this ordinance was purely political and was concerned solely with the sequestration of the property of those who had been in arms against the Parliament or who had voluntarily assisted or contributed towards the maintenance of the royalist forces. It was not till later that the Parliament began to entrust the local authorities with a special power in the case of ecclesiastical offenders, and then it was only as a part of a more general jurisdiction. One of the earliest instances of this extension of authority was the

---

[1] *Acts and Ordinances of the Interregnum* (Ed. C. H. Firth and R. S. Rait), i, 106.

ordinance of January 22, 1643/4 "for regulating the
University of Cambridge, and for removing of Scandalous
Ministers in the seven Associated Counties" of Essex,
Norfolk, Suffolk, Hertford, Cambridge, Huntingdon and
Lincoln. This ordinance began by stating that many complaints had been received from the well-affected inhabitants
of the counties that the service of the Parliament was
retarded, the enemy strengthened, and the people's souls
starved by their "idle, ill-affected, and scandalous clergy,"
and that many that would give evidence against such
scandalous ministers were not able to travel to London.
The ordinance therefore directed the Earl of Manchester,
who had been appointed to the command of the army of
the Association on August 10, 1643, to establish one or
more committees in every county to assist him in carrying
out the instructions of the Parliament. The committees
were empowered to call before them "all Provosts,
Masters, and Fellowes of Colledges, all Students, and
Members of the University, and all Ministers in any
County of the Association, and all Schoole-Masters that
are scandalous in their lives, or ill-affected to the
Parliament, or Fomenters of this unnaturall Warre, or
that shall wilfully refuse obedience to the Ordinances of
Parliament, or that have deserted their ordinary places
of residence, not being imployed in the service of the
King and Parliament[1]." They were further authorised
to summon witnesses and examine evidence for the
purpose of a report to the Earl of Manchester, who was
to eject such as he should judge unfit for their places.
A similar formula was adopted in later ordinances giving
a like power to the committees in other counties and
districts. It will at once be seen that a great deal of
emphasis was laid upon what may be called the "political"

---

[1] *Acts and Ordinances of the Interregnum* (Ed. C. H. Firth and
R. S. Rait), i, 371.

misdemeanours, quite apart from considerations of immorality or vicious life[1].

When the committees in the Eastern Association were appointed, the Earl of Manchester sent them a copy of directions which were to guide their actions in carrying out their orders.

The object of the Parliament in appointing these local bodies was sufficiently well indicated in the ordinance already quoted, but if any doubt remained on this head, the directions now issued must have set it at rest. Everything was to be done to encourage the people to bring forward their complaints, if they had any to bring. The committees were to sit in such places that "all parties, by the easiness of access, may be encouraged to address themselves" to them, and the clerk of the committee was to be salaried so that he should not be led to discourage the people by demanding fees. Most important of all was the sixth clause, which ran as follows:

" Because it is found by sad experience, that parishioners are not forward to complain of their ministers, although they be very scandalous, but having this price and power in their hands, yet want hearts to make use thereof, too many being enemies to that blessed reformation so much by the Parliament desired, and loth to come under a powerfull ministry; and some sparing their ministers because such ministers to gain the good opinions of their people do spare them in their tythes & therefore are esteemed quiet men or the like, you are therefore required to call unto you some well-affected men within every hundred, who, having no private engagements, but intending to further the publique reformation

---

[1] Fuller records that many moderate men of the Parliamentary party were much grieved at the severity by which "some clergymen, blameless for life, and orthodox for doctrine, were only ejected on the account of their faithfulness to the King's cause." *Church Hist.* xi, p. 207, quoted in J. E. Bailey's *Life of Fuller*, p. 237.

may be required and encouraged by you to inquire after the doctrines, lives, and conversations of all ministers and schoolmasters, and to give you information both what can be deposed, and who can depose the same[1]."

The existence of these "informers," as they have with some justice been styled, presents a problem in many respects analogous to that involved in the consideration of whether or no the signatures to the earlier petitions were obtained fraudulently. The question here is whether the agents or informers appointed by the sequestrators acted merely in the character of "inspectors" in the various parishes or as intermediaries between the discontented parishioners and the committee, or whether, as Walker[2] and others have alleged, they deliberately "got up" the cases against the clergy.

In the first place, it must be considered that the Eastern counties generally were Puritan in tone, and at the outbreak of the war had sided with the Parliament. Also, there are indications that, in some places at any rate, there was a certain amount of ill-feeling between the clergy and their parishioners. The ground, therefore, was not altogether ill-prepared for the work of the sequestrators.

But against this must be set the gratuitous admission on the part of the Earl of Manchester himself, that "parishioners were not forward to complain," and that some were "enemies to the intended reformation." Coming on the top of these two statements, the appointment of agents to seek the information which the parishioners themselves had failed to bring, and to produce the witnesses who had refused to come forward of their own free will, tends to prove that artificial

[1] A transcript of these directions, addressed to the Lincolnshire committee, is in the Walker Collection ; MS. J. Walker, c. 6, fol. 17.

[2] Walker : *Sufferings of the Clergy*, Pt. i, 118.

assistance was needed before the "many complaints of the well-affected" could be brought to the birth.

Cole, the antiquarian, in a short preface to his MS. copy of the articles preferred against the clergy before the Essex committee, reflects upon the probable result of the directions given by the Earl of Manchester to the sequestrators. "Of how wicked a tendency," he says, "such a proceeding must be at that time, when people's spirits were heated by religious disputes, may easily be discerned when we reflect what the consequence of such encouragement would be for informers even at this time. Everyone," he goes on, "who has had it in his power to make observations on the nature of country people must be convinced how easily they are to be influenced, particularly against their superiors, and more especially when their interest coincides with encouragement[1]."

It is, as Cole points out, not a question of party but of human nature. Some ten years before the time of the sequestrations of the loyal Episcopalians, an advocate in the High Commission Court had occasion to indicate the fallacy of accepting the evidence brought against Puritan clergy by a section of their parishioners. In the case of a minister named Vicars who had been summoned before this court on charges of heretical doctrine, testimony had been brought to the fact that some of the witnesses for the prosecution were "capital enemies of Mr Viccars and...backbiters of their neighbours[2]" and Gwyn, his advocate, in addressing the court, pointed out that "it was an easy matter for a company joyning themselves (as his accusers did) to pick holes in any man's sermons for three years' space[3]."

The cases of Casaubon and Tray[4] are instances to

---

[1] Brit. Mus. Add. MSS. 5829, fol. 2.
[2] *Cases in the Star Chamber and High Commission Court*, p. 211.
[3] *Ibid.* p. 220.   [4] See *ante*, pp. 58–60.

some extent of the unrepresentative character of many accusations, and various cases of a later date afford additional evidence of a similar kind.

In 1644, for example, eleven gentlemen of Norwich presented a petition to the Earl of Manchester on behalf of two ejected clergymen named Williams and Locke[1]. The petitioners admitted that the two ministers in question had been "observant of ceremonies imposed by coercive power," that there had been some difference with their neighbours on a question of Church rights, and that they had "opposed sectaries in their preachinge," but although this had been the cause of "the late harsh and uncharitable persecution against them," the committee appointed by Manchester had been "too readie and forward to promote and countenance" it.

The ejected clergymen were said to be "learned and orthodox divines, sedulous and industrious in their sacred functions...of honest life and exemplary conversation," while it was further asserted that no one denied this favourable character to them save "some few sectaries savouringe Independencie."

Again, in 1646, a somewhat similar petition from the inhabitants of Monk Soham in Suffolk was addressed to the Committee for Plundered Ministers on behalf of their minister, Thomas Rogerson[2]. The petitioners certified that they had "knowne Thomas Rogerson clarke Mr in Arts, for many years past, never haueinge given any just scandall in his life, but orthodox in doctrine, and of an honest godly conversacon, he haueinge never done any thinge, to any of our knowledge in opposicon to any the pliaments ordinances. Wee conceive him," they proceed, "a very fitt object, for the due consideracon of the noble committee in restoreinge him to his liveinge

---

[1] *Manchester Papers* (Record Office), 552.
[2] MS. J. Walker, c. 4, fol. 398.

of Muncke Soham; he being a man of learninge and abilityes and fittinge to discharge the duty of that place." The petition, which is dated July 9, 1646, is signed by twenty-two inhabitants of the parish, by eight clergymen and five others. Even the minister, to whom the rectory had been sequestrated, offered, on receiving preferment elsewhere, to vacate the living of Monk Soham, if the committee would restore it to Rogerson. "I confesse," he wrote, "that I have beene the willinger to make this certificate because I have heard some who were the chief meanes of putting him out to say that he was prosecuted out of Malice and I doe believe it[1]."

From the fact that one of the clergymen who signs the petition, John Brinsley of Yarmouth, was a Puritan and was himself ejected at the Restoration[2], it would seem possible that Thomas Rogerson was either a Puritan or had leanings in that direction. But if this were the case, by whom and for what offence was Rogerson ejected, for it is evident that his sequestration was regretted by some at least in the parish? It is impossible to avoid the conclusion, elsewhere seen to be probable, that in this case, as in others, the sequestration was largely due to the agency of a hostile cabal[3].

---

[1] MS. J. Walker, fol. 397.

[2] Calamy: *Abridgment of Mr Baxter's History of his Life and Times* (1713), ii, 477.

[3] Another case, taken from the period of the Protectorate, may be cited in this connection. In November 1657, Thomas Fitch petitioned the Government for permission to preach. He stated that, eighteen months previously, he had been ejected from his living of Sutton Courtney by the committee for Berkshire, but he had the testimony of "divers eminent ministers" for his "fitness for the service." Commissioners were appointed to examine his case and confirmed his statement that "the information (against him) was unduly prosecuted and indirect means used with the witnesses." They declared that the witnesses were "not of credit," and an order was subsequently issued allowing him to preach. *Cal. of S. P. Dom.* 1657-8, p. 150. See also the account of the plots against Martin Blake of Barnstaple, given in J. F. Chanter's *Life of Martin Blake.*

Sometimes the feeling in favour of the ejected clergyman took a less orderly course and manifested itself in open violence. An example of this is found in a riot which took place at Soham in Cambridgeshire, as a result of the appointment of a Parliamentary nominee in place of the regular incumbent. Exeter, the vicar, had been deprived of the living in 1644, principally for drunkenness, innovations, and disaffection to the Parliament, the charges being attested by nine witnesses[1]. A certain John Fenton had then been appointed to the cure, but at what date it does not appear. On July 9, 1647, the Committee for Plundered Ministers found it necessary to issue an order requiring the parishioners to pay tithes to Fenton[2], but more serious troubles seem to have followed, and apparently some of the inhabitants were ordered into the custody of the sergeant-at-arms. At all events, on August 14, " Mr Dalton, Mr Story, and Mr Clarke, Justices of Peace in the Countie of Cambridge," certified to the committee that, in view of the "threats, boldness and insolent carriage of divers malignants in the said countie questioning the said justices authoritie to their face, they durst not at presente...assist the serjeant at Armes of the house of Comons his deputie in execution of the order of the 29th of July last for bringing Samuel Thornton and Thomas Eaton before this Committee in safe custody ; one of them having assaulted and beaten the serjeant's deputie and threatned his death[3]." Upon the receipt of this intelligence, the committee repeated the order, and further required the Sheriff of the county and all deputy Lieutenants and Justices of the Peace to assist in its execution, and to see that Fenton was securely settled in

---

[1] Brit. Mus. Add. MSS. 15,672, fol. 21.
[2] Brit. Mus. Add. MSS. 15,671, fol. 110 b.
[3] *Ibid.* fol. 173 b.

the possession of his living[1]. The only result of this seems to have been an increased disturbance, headed by Exeter and others, which assumed such serious proportions that on October 12 the committee decided to write to Sir Thomas Fairfax to ask for military assistance[2].

It would, of course, be possible to regard this riot as occasioned solely by Exeter and a few confederates, and not in any sense as a manifestation of the feeling of the parish, nor is it possible to say what were in reality its characteristics[3]. In view of the fact that military assistance had to be called in, the presumption is that a considerable number of men were implicated, and that the demonstration was at all events tolerably well supported. The chief importance of the instance, however, lies in the fact that Exeter had been sequestrated as a result of charges brought by nine of his parishioners and that if the rising in his favour represented the feeling of the parish, then obviously the attack upon him did not.

Numerous examples, to prove the corrupt practices of accusers and the injustice of the Parliamentary committees, may be found in Walker's *Sufferings of the Clergy*. They were largely taken from original papers, many of which are still preserved in his MS. Collection, and in view of evidence from other sources, they acquire an even greater degree of credibility.

Before the question of the justice of the sequestrators' proceedings can be satisfactorily answered, it is necessary to consider what motives were really actuating them and what was the purpose which they had in view. In their defence it must be said that their object was always clearly avowed, nor, under the circumstances, was it

---

[1] Brit. Mus. Add. MSS. 15,671, fol. 208. [2] *Ibid.* fol. 241.

[3] See an ordinance of Aug. 23, 1647, for "Keeping in Godly Ministers, placed in livings by authority of Parliament." *Acts and Ordinances of the Interregnum* (Ed. C. H. Firth and R. S. Rait), i, 999. This shows that it was found necessary to legislate against attempts to dislodge intruders.

unnatural. The pulpit exercised a powerful influence, not only in religious matters, but also in the realm of party politics. To capture these outpost positions, left by the enemy, was a matter of political necessity which neither party overlooked[1]. In considering, therefore, the work of the sequestrators, it must be remembered that the removal of "scandal" in the lives, and even in the doctrines, of the clergy was only a part of their avowed object, and that the eradication of political "disaffection" always held a prominent place in their minds. That this was so, is well borne out by the extant records of their proceedings in Cambridgeshire and Leicestershire[2]. In the articles of accusation preferred against the clergy in the former county we find that the charges of refusing the Covenant, speaking against the Covenant, refusing to read the Parliamentary proclamations and the like are those most commonly brought forward. In twenty-nine recorded cases, there are twenty-seven charges of dis- affection or disobedience to the Parliament; twenty-two of neglect of cure; twenty-one of "innovations in religion"; eleven of drunkenness or "frequenting of ale houses"; six of immorality and six of swearing and quarrelling. Besides these, there are twelve cases in which disputes between the clergyman and his parishioners, on the subject of tithe and the like, take the form of a charge against the incumbent[3]. In one recorded case in

[1] Cf. a letter from the King to Goring (Nalson Papers, i, 17). "Being informed that there are yet within our quarters divers ministers, who either by their doctrine teach or by their behaviour countenance Rebellion, we command you to make strict enquiry for all such Clergymen within your quarters, and to apprehend them immediately, and send them to Oxford, if possible, or otherwise to keep them in custody till further orders." *Hist. MSS. Com.* 13th Rep., Duke of Portland's MSS. App., Pt. i, p. 212.

[2] Brit. Mus. Add. MSS. 15,672 and MS. J. Walker, c. 11.

[3] It even seems as if the removal of scandal, as part of the work of the Committee for Plundered Ministers, had been an afterthought. See *Commons' Journals*, iii, 183, July 27, 1643. "Ordered, That the Committee for

Devonshire an ejected clergyman obtained a certificate
from the committee stating that he had been deprived
for " disaffection " only[1].

It has been affirmed that disaffection and "innovation"
were the genuine causes of ejection, and that the charges
of immorality were only included to strengthen the case
and endow it with an appearance of justification. But
though the former proposition is probably true in the
great majority of cases, the latter contains a fallacy.
The comparatively small number of the charges of
ill-life, if it can be used as an argument at all, would be
in favour of the truth of those particular accusations,
because, if they were false, and included merely for the
sake of appearance, there is no obvious reason why they
should not have been included for a similar purpose
against the rest of the accused clergy. It is rarely
possible now to decide the merits of any individual case.
Walker himself does not deny that there may have been
cases where charges of vice were justified, but the
conditions under which the accusations were brought
make it necessary to require further corroboration for the
facts with which they deal.

One of the genuine evils which the Puritans endeavoured to abolish was pluralism, and, in certain parts
of the country, cases in which a clergyman was deprived
on that ground are not uncommon. It appears, however, that where no other charge was produced, the
clergyman was allowed to choose which of his benefices
he would retain.

With regard to the actual proceedings of the sequestrators' court there unfortunately only remain incomplete

Plundered Ministers shall have power to consider of the Informations against
scandalous Ministers, though there be no Malignancy proved against him."
[1] George Pierce or Pearse of Tiverton, see *Sufferings of the Clergy*,
Pt. ii, 327. The certificate itself is in the Walker Collection. MS.
J. Walker, c. 4, fol. 207.

and partial accounts. The directions to the sequestrators had instructed them to allow the accused a copy of the depositions against him, and fourteen days " or there-abouts " in which to make his defence. It is further evident, from some brief orders prefixed to the articles exhibited before the sequestrators in Leicestershire[1], that these directions were obeyed, and that opportunities were given for a defence to be made. So far this was fair enough, although the time allowed to the accused seems rather short. The directions next ordain that "the party accused should not be present at the taking the depositions." This, Neal states[2], was on account of the "insolent and unmannerly behaviour of some of the clergy before the commissioners " when the witnesses were examined in their presence, but he does not cite his authority for this statement. Failing this, therefore, the accused party seems to have been obliged to hand in a list of "interrogatories" which were to be put to the witnesses, as well as his more explicit answer to the charges.

The number of witnesses for the prosecution in individual cases varied, in Cambridgeshire, between three and twenty, and averaged about ten. Of their character it is not possible to discover much. In one case the two churchwardens gave evidence against the vicar, but in several instances the witness was unable to sign his name. For the most part, where their callings are mentioned, they appear to have been local tradesmen. Thus in the case of Thomas Lee, rector of Newton, the witnesses were Richard Rose, saddler, John Johnson, baker, William Nicholas, weaver, Edmund Scotten, "gent.," and so on[3]. Jeremy Stephens' papers, quoted by

---

[1] MS. J. Walker, c. 11, fol. 4.
[2] *History of the Puritans* (ed. 1822), iii, 108, note.
[3] Brit. Mus. Add. MSS. 15,672, fol. 14.

Walker[1], give a highly-coloured account of the witnesses who appeared before the Northampton committee, but Jeremy Stephens' evidence, as coming from one who had himself suffered deprivation, must be received with caution. It would, however, be tolerably safe to assume that they were almost invariably recruited from the lower classes[2]. In the absence, however, of any further information, the mere numbers of the witnesses prove very little. On the other hand, it is possible to form a clearer opinion of the evidence which they gave.

As it appears in the records of the Cambridgeshire sequestrations, it takes the form of depositions with the names of the deponents annexed. The character of these attestations thus presented is necessarily varied, but they included much that was absurd, and a good deal which could not, properly speaking, have been accepted as evidence at all. Thus, Nicholas Felton[3] of Streatham was charged, amongst other offences, with refusing to repair his hedges, and the vicar of Foulmire[4] with "profaning the Sabbath day by bowling"; while in the case of a charge of swearing brought against Robert Grimer, vicar of Wicken, three witnesses solemnly deposed "that they living remote from him, and haueing little converse with him, haue not heard him sweare as they remember, but they haue heard divers of the parish affirme that he doth often use to sweare," a form of evidence which merited the well-known comment of Mr Justice Stareleigh. Other witnesses in the case, brought forward to attest the fact that certain words hostile to the Parliamentary cause had been used in a sermon, affirmed that they were,

[1] Walker: *Sufferings of the Clergy*, Pt. i, p. 92.
[2] In the case of Dr Cheney Rowe, rector of Orwell, and Fellow of Trinity, Cambridge, although a brother Fellow gave evidence against him, the other witnesses appear to have been of the lower class, for example, a "yeoman," and a grocer. (Brit. Mus. Add. MSS. 15,672, fol. 48.)
[3] Brit. Mus. Add. MSS. 15,672, fol. 1.   [4] *Ibid.* fol. 44.

indeed, present on the occasion in question, but "perceiving his (the preacher's) straine to run wholly that way," that is to say, unfavourably to the Parliament, "they left the Church before the conclusion of his sermon, wherein it is affirmed those words were uttered[1]." These instances are, of course, more or less exceptional, and we have no means of knowing whether the type of evidence offered in the last two examples was accepted by the court as satisfactory.

The Cambridgeshire committee's book gives no account of any answers given by the accused clergy, and only mentions that in the one case " Mr Peacock, Vicar of Swaffham-Prior having time given him to put in his answer to the articles exhib:ted against him to this Comittee until the present Saturday by ten of the clock in the forenoon hath fayled to appear or return his answers accordingly[2]." The Leicestershire book, on the other hand, contains several answers and interrogatories, though they are not found by any means in every case. On the whole, it would seem probable that the accused clergy for the most part neglected to avail themselves of such opportunity of defence as was granted to them, either because they had already fled, or because they would not recognise the jurisdiction of the court.

In the case of the committees in the Associated Counties, at any rate, it appears that the witnesses were heard on oath, but as neither the Cambridgeshire nor the Leicestershire records give any account of the actual hearing of the case or the examination of the witnesses, it is practically impossible to form an opinion of the justice of the system or the fairness of the judges. The convictions appear to have been wholesale, for of the thirty accused clergymen, whose names appear in the Cambridgeshire book, not one escaped sequestration.

[1] Brit. Mus. Add. MSS. 15,672, fol. 40.   [2] *Ibid.* fol. 5.

A rather fuller record of the proceedings before these county committees is found in the case of Isaac Allen, the rector of Prestwich in Lancashire, tried at Manchester on November 10, 1643, before the local committee consisting of Colonel Ralph Asheton, John Bradshaw, Robert Hyde, Rowland Hunt and Thomas Birche, Esquires. He was indicted on nine charges, the chief of which were that he had not publicly instructed his congregation as to which side they ought to take in the struggle between King and Parliament, that he had refused at first to read the Covenant in Church, on the ground that it was contrary to the oath of allegiance and supremacy, and that when at last he had done so, he had said that, for his own part, he could not take it, and had otherwise encouraged his congregation to follow his example, and that he had been in company with Lord Strange in Manchester and had assisted him in the siege with money. There were fifteen witnesses against him, and all the charges were concerned with political offences.

His defence reveals him in the pathetic position of a man who was driven by force of circumstances out of the attitude of neutrality which he had endeavoured to adopt. Probably with the view of protecting himself from possible violence from the royalist soldiers he had sought and obtained in the previous June a paper under the hand of the Earl of Derby, the royalist commander in Lancashire, certifying that he had suffered much from the enemy and was faithful and loyal to the King[1]. The course of the war, however, had not favoured the royalist cause, and he now found himself obliged to explain his former caution. He admitted that he had not been satisfied as to the lawfulness of taking up arms, but he

[1] MS. J. Walker, c. 5, fol. 292. This is apparently the original certificate, dated from Lathom.

denied that he had ever encouraged anyone to oppose the Parliament, but, on the contrary, had publicly desired that his example, in not taking the Covenant, "might not be a president to any." Most of his parish, including his own servants, had taken it. He denied also that he had assisted Lord Strange with money, and affirmed that he had only accompanied him to Manchester in the hope that a settlement of differences might result from the visit. For a testimony to his own good life and service in the parish, he referred to those who had been constant members of his congregation, and he excepted against the characters of those who appeared against him. They had "much perverted and depraved" his words and actions, and had, as he was informed, formed a malicious plot to oust him from his living. Some of them were men of "meane capacity" and others could not even write their names. He stated that he had been present at the examination of only one of the witnesses, and finding that he was not on oath, he had desired the commissioners to put some questions which "would have discovered the untruth of his testimonie." This the commissioners had refused to do, and Allen had then left the court voluntarily[1]. A second hearing of the case took place on April 2, 1645[2], and Allen eventually suffered sequestration, but his subsequent history is not of immediate interest.

Another full account of a somewhat similar trial is contained in the narrative written by a clergyman named Bushnell, describing the process of his cause before one of Oliver Cromwell's commissions for ejecting scandalous

---

[1] The examination of the witnesses against Allen and his answer, together with several other papers relating to the case, are to be found in the Walker Collection, MS. J. Walker, c. 5, fol. 275–297.

[2] The proceedings at the second trial have been printed in the *Royalist Composition Papers*, edited by J. H. Stanning (Lancashire and Cheshire Rec. Soc.), p. 18.

ministers. The times were, of course, different, but the conditions and the composition of the two tribunals were not unlike, and the case is instructive up to a certain point.

Bushnell's charges against his judges and accusers are varied. He asserts that the signatures to the petition against him were forged, and complains that hearsay evidence was accepted by the court, that his witnesses were turned out during the hearing of the case, but that the witnesses for the prosecution were allowed to remain and no evidence reflecting on their characters was admitted. He further charges the commissioners with being open to bribery[1]. An answer to some of his charges was afterwards published by Humphrey Chambers, who had been one of the commissioners in question, but as is usual in such cases, it is not easy, between their conflicting statements, to strike the mean of truth.

Of the character of those who sat on the county sequestration committees it is difficult to speak with certainty, for the few accounts of them which have survived come almost entirely from a hostile point of view. Walker's description[2], for example, of the Northamptonshire committee was taken from the manuscript papers of Jeremy Stephens, who was deprived of his living of Wootton in that county, and it is impossible to accept the evidence of such a prejudiced witness without further corroboration. The composition of the committees varied no doubt locally, but it does not seem that the leading Puritan families were numerously represented, and the work, which could hardly have been congenial to a refined temperament, was left to the rougher members of the party. The powers of the committees extended to

---

[1] See *A narrative of the proceedings of the Commissioners* etc. by Walter Bushnell (London 1660).

[2] Walker : *Sufferings of the Clergy*, Pt. i, pp. 90-2.

lay as well as clerical delinquents, and that their characters as well as their methods of procedure were the objects of general attack is suggested by a document known as the "Declaration of the County of Dorset," printed in June 1648. The Declaration asks that the county should no longer be subjugated "to the boundless lusts and unlimited power of beggarly and broken Committees, consisting generally of the tail of the gentry, men of ruinous fortunes and despicable estates, whose insatiate desires prompt them to continual projects of pilling and stripping," and to their "Emissaries—generally the most shirking and cunning beggars that can be picked out of a County[1]."

Their procedure in court has been illustrated already, and there is evidence that their method of dealing with confiscated property was equally open to exception. The Hereford committee not only occupied the sequestrated houses belonging to the Chapter and formerly inhabited by the Canons and Prebendaries, but in one or two cases defrayed the cost of repairs, to the amount of ten pounds, out of the ecclesiastical revenues[2]. The committees appear also in some cases to have made use of the witnesses for the prosecution as their agents in enforcing the sentence. Thus, in the case of Robert Exeter, the vicar of Soham in Cambridgeshire, one of the witnesses delivered the summons, while in the case of Crosland, the vicar of Bottisham, two of the witnesses, Robert Brand and Thomas Jolly, were appointed to receive the profits of the living during the sequestration[3]. An entry in the accounts of the same committee shows that an even more unblushing method of rewarding

---

[1] Quoted in A. R. Bayley's *Civil War in Dorset*, p. 352.

[2] See Walker's *Sufferings of the Clergy*, Pt. i, p. 90. This is taken from an abstract of the original proceedings of the committee, supplied to Walker by a Herefordshire clergyman. See G. B. Tatham, *Dr John Walker*, p. 97.

[3] Brit. Mus. Add. MSS. 15,672, fol. 22, 4.

informers was sometimes adopted[1]. In view of previous evidence in the same direction, this further indication of co-operation between judges and witnesses, slight as it is, has a considerable significance.

The sequestration committees were after all only subordinate institutions: they were subject to various higher powers. The Cambridgeshire committee, for example, was answerable in the first place to the Earl of Manchester, and, to some extent, to the Committee for Plundered Ministers in London. This last-mentioned body, again, was itself answerable to the Parliament.

The Committee for Plundered Ministers, which sat in the Exchequer Court at Westminster, had been appointed on December 31, 1642[2], and in point of time, therefore, comes before the county committees, but as the particular aspect of its work with which we are now chiefly concerned was subsequent to the actual sequestrations, it has been convenient to postpone the discussion of it. It was by far the most permanent of the committees appointed by the Parliament to deal with ecclesiastical affairs, and in course of time it gradually absorbed a great part of the duties of other bodies. It continued in existence until the dissolution of the Rump in 1653.

Its original purpose, as its name vaguely implies, was to deal with the cases of those Puritan ministers who had lost their benefices through adherence to the Parliamentary cause, but before very long the business of depriving unfit and "insufficient" clergymen, which had formerly belonged to the Committee for Scandalous Ministers, was handed over to it[3], an enlargement of powers

---

[1] " Paid to Thomas Soper for discovering John Stagg to be a delinquent ...7. 0" is an item in "A note of the charges" incurred in connection with the sequestrations in Cambridge. *State Papers Domestic*, vol. DXL.

[2] *Commons' Journals*, ii, 909.

[3] W. A. Shaw: *Hist. of the Eng. Ch.* 1640–60, ii, 189.

which led to the royalist taunt that it was a committee, not for plundered, but for plundering ministers. "The real design of the faction," says Walker, "in appointing this Committee, was to erect a standing tribunal for the ruin of the regular clergy[1]."

Besides dealing with a certain number of cases for sequestration which had not come before the county committees, and occasionally appointing incumbents to vacant cures, it fell to the lot of this committee to act as a court of appeal, to decide cases where there were two claimants for a living, or where the ejected minister endeavoured to regain what he considered to be his rights. A series of resolutions and orders entered in their minute book under date August 1645, show some of the rules which regulated their actions. It was resolved that, where a minister was put out of one living for scandal, he ought also to lose any other preferment of which he might happen to be possessed. It was ordered that no man's living should be sequestrated from him until his cause had been considered, and that, where a cause was depending, no order should be made until both parties had been heard[2]. There are several instances in which the committee granted to an accused minister facilities for making his defence[3], and in the hearing of the case both sides were not infrequently represented by counsel. Their procedure, in fact, stands in marked contrast to that of the local committees, and though they were regarded by the royalists as the instruments of tyranny, the count against them is much less strong.

Their task was by no means an easy one amid the petitions and counter-petitions and general hard swearing

---

[1] Walker : *Sufferings of the Clergy*, Pt. i, p. 73.

[2] Brit. Mus. Add. MSS. 15,669, fol. 239.

[3] See for instance the case of Richard Locksmith (Add. MSS. 15,670, fol. 103), and that of Dr Holliday (Add. MSS. 15,671, fol. 257).

which characterised the numerous cases which came under their view, but they seem to have considered grievances, heard what was to be said on each side, and to have been ready to correct injustice whenever it did not clash with public policy. Two or three instances may be cited from the minutes of their proceedings.

John Baker, the vicar of Bartlow in Cambridgeshire, had been sequestrated from his living in 1644[1], and appears to have died not very long afterwards, for on July 10, 1645[2], we find an order from the committee that "the sequestration is ended and determined by the death of the said Mr Baker," and that therefore the patron was justified in presenting Mr Richard Weller to the living. After this decision had been made, however, the attention of the committee was drawn to the fact that, since Baker's ejection, the cure had been served by one William Hinton, and that, if Weller were appointed, Hinton would be "deprived of satisfaccon after much pains by him taken in the cure of the said Church." It was further suggested that several "exceptions" were "alleged" against Richard Weller. The proceedings were therefore stayed "till the said cause be heard and this Committee's pleasure be further knowne[3]." On September 27, the case was referred to the Committee of Parliament for the County of Cambridge[4], who appear to have delayed the matter, for they are requested, in a subsequent order, to make greater "speede and dispatch[5]." On November 25, Hinton having several times failed to appear, the committee decided that Weller was regularly presented to the living and all concerned

---

[1] Brit. Mus. Add. MSS. 15,672, fol. 12.
[2] Brit. Mus. Add. MSS. 15,669, fol. 110.
[3] *Ibid.* fol. 120 *b*.
[4] *Ibid.* fol. 177.
[5] *Ibid.* fol. 204.

were required to yield obedience to this decision[1]. Hinton then appears to have petitioned for some "satisfaction" on account of his past services in Bartlow, for a request of this nature is referred in turn to the Cambridge committee who are directed to "examine and determine the same as to justice shall appertaine[2]."

In the case of Orwell, in the same county, Dr Cheney Rowe, the rector, a Fellow of Trinity, had been ejected in 1644 for drunkenness and non-residence[3]. On July 12, 1647, an entry in the book of the Committee for Plundered Ministers mentions a complaint received from Rowe to the effect that the rectory of Orwell was a sinecure, and that therefore he was sequestrated for non-residence unjustly. In view of this complaint, the sequestrators are required to show cause why he should not be reinstated[4]. Delay seems to have been the rule in all these cases, and two months elapsed before the case was heard. The sequestrators did not appear, but the intruding minister, Brooks by name, came forward to vindicate his right to the living, pointing out that "scandall" had also formed a part of the charge against Rowe. This explanation appears to have been accepted by the committee, for they found in favour of Brooks, and gave it as their opinion that it was "not proper for them to intermeddle in the said cause," and they therefore dismissed it, leaving Dr Rowe "to seeke his reliefe where else he shall see cause[5]."

---

[1] Brit. Mus. Add. MSS. 15,669, fol. 212.

[2] *Ibid.* fol. 235. In considering the justice of the committee in this case, it is important to notice that Weller was almost certainly a Puritan, or at all events conformed to the new order. See the note on Bartlow in the Augmentation Books (Lambeth), "Mr Weller is or very lately was minister here a very able man."

[3] Brit. Mus. Add. MSS. 15,672, fol. 48 *b*.

[4] Brit. Mus. Add. MSS. 15,671, fol. 138 *b*.

[5] *Ibid.* fol. 204 *b*, 215.

A third case was that of George Beardhall or Beardsall, the vicar of Arkesden, whose name appears in the Cambridgeshire Sequestration Book as being brought before that committee on October 23, 1644, for disaffection to the Parliament and neglect of his cure[1]. On October 23, 1645, he complained to the Committee for Plundered Ministers "that he was ejected out of the said vicarage after he had given a satisfactorie answere and been acquitted," and therefore desired that "he may be heard by his witnesses." The Cambridgeshire committee were, upon this, required to give an account of their proceedings in the case, and to examine Beardhall's witnesses, if that had not already been done[2]. By the following March, however, the case still remained unheard, for an order, dated March 7, directs the Cambridgeshire committee to examine the witnesses against Beardhall, and to give him notice of the examination "to ye end that hee may be present (if hee will) at ye sayd heareing[3]." The case ultimately appears to have gone against him, and on April 25, it was ordered that the vicarage should stand sequestrated to Samuel Ball, "minister of the word[4]."

In this case, the committee, by referring the case to the original tribunal, seem to have failed in their function as a court of appeal, and it is, indeed, unusual to find instances in which a former verdict was reversed. That this was sometimes done, however, is proved by the case of Martin Blake of Barnstaple, who was ultimately reinstated in his living by the Committee for Plundered

---

[1] Brit. Mus. Add. MSS. 15,672, fol. 42.
[2] Brit. Mus. Add. MSS. 15,669, fol. 199.
[3] Brit. Mus. Add. MSS. 15,670, fol. 34 b.
[4] Ibid. fol. 72. Failing to regain his living by these means, Beardhall appears to have resorted to violence. In the course of 1647, he forced his way into the vicarage and refused to surrender it, so that he came again under the view of the committee. BM. Add. MSS. 15,671, fol. 129 b, 154 b, 168.

Ministers in spite of the machinations of a hostile party[1].

The question of the number of Episcopalian clergy who were deprived of their livings by the Parliamentary committees during the period of the Civil War and Commonwealth is a subject which has often engaged the attention of historians, but it is one which is likely to remain an unsolved problem. The wild calculations which have sometimes been made vary between two extremes, in accordance with the political bias of the calculator, and provide no indication of reliable figures. Walker himself, who attempted a work which few people would have the patience to emulate, was obliged to confess failure, and his numbers are manifestly incomplete. His actual list, compiled at the cost of infinite labour, contains the names of about 2300 parochial clergy, but his own estimate of the total was 7000 or even more[2]. Tories of his day, in fact, regarded the ejections as practically universal, and it was even suggested that all had been turned out except 450—the exact number, it was observed, of Baal's priests[3]. On the other hand, supporters of the Puritan party, both then and afterwards, were no less assiduous in throwing discredit on the evidence and reducing the numbers to comparative insignificance. In modern times, a serious attempt has been made to arrive at a probable figure in Mr Stoughton's *Church of the Commonwealth.*

Mr Stoughton remarks upon the fact that the question of numbers has always been treated as a party question, and says with justice that "the proper subject of investigation would be found, not in numerical statistics,

[1] A full account of this interesting case will be found in J. F. Chanter's *Life of Martin Blake.*
[2] *Sufferings of the Clergy,* p. xviii.
[3] See a letter in the Walker Collection, G. B. Tatham, *Dr John Walker,* App. i, p. 227.

but in the rules laid down to regulate the sequestrations[1]."
At the same time, it is an unsound argument of his to say
that the desire of the Episcopalians so to exalt the
numbers is shortsighted, because "the more sequestrations there might be, the more open to censure must have
been the conduct of the clergy," for, as we have seen, it
is not altogether "incredible that the enormous number
imagined by some" were "expelled on political or ecclesiastical grounds alone." He rightly rejects Walker's
extreme figures and points out that if such a vast number
had been ejected, one would expect that at the Restoration a comparatively large number would have returned
to their livings. On the other hand, he rejects the
wholly untenable view of the Nonconformists that, although 2000 were ejected, half of these were allowed to
return during the Commonwealth and Protectorate.

In the attempt to arrive at an approximate figure,
however, he makes a curious slip. He gives the number
contained in Walker's list as 1339, nearly a thousand
below the actual figures, and this error probably threw
out his calculation. He refers to Baillie's letters, to a tract
in the Harleian Miscellany, to British Museum Add. MSS.
15,669, which he calls "a list of sequestrations in Essex[2],"
and to the computation given by John Withers[3], and
concludes by giving 2000 or 2500 as the outside limit.

It is, of course, impossible to arrive at anything more
than an approximate figure. The sources from which an
accurate list might have been compiled are no longer
forthcoming, for the minutes of the Committee for
Plundered Ministers are incomplete, and those of the
local sequestration committees have, except in a very few

---

[1] Stoughton : *The Church of the Commonwealth*, p. 540.
[2] It is in reality the first of three volumes of proceedings of the Committee
for Plundered Ministers.
[3] John Withers : *Remarks on Dr Walker's late Preface to the Attempt.*

cases, disappeared altogether. Without these valuable records the field of investigation becomes so vast that the collection of such details as have survived must be left to the patient research of local historians.

The documents of which Walker made use can, of course, be supplemented considerably. For example, besides the proceedings of the Committee for Plundered Ministers, there are the records of the Committee for Compounding, calendared among the State Papers, a MS. Register giving the names of incumbents of livings in 1650[1], and the House of Lords' Papers, among which are found numerous petitions for restitution presented by deprived clergymen in 1660. It happens also that for the three counties of Cambridge, Dorset and Leicester, some original record remains of the proceedings of the local committees. For these three counties, therefore, it is possible to draw up a list of sequestrations, not indeed exhaustive, but as complete as we can now hope to obtain. Any argument as to the total number in the country at large must be based on the evidence which these three cases provide.

The proceedings of the Dorset committee have been carefully edited by Mr C. H. Mayo. They extend from September 1646 to May 1650 and consist chiefly of orders relating to sequestration from and appointment to livings within the county. They give the fullest and, in some respects, the most instructive view of the local machinery in working. There were at that time about 250 livings in the county, and these proceedings, taken in conjunction with other available sources of information, give satisfactory evidence of some 74 cases of sequestration or just under 30 per cent.

The Cambridge committee's book[2], from which several extracts have been given in the earlier part of this

---

[1] Brit. Mus. Lans. MSS. 459.   [2] Brit. Mus. Add. MSS. 15,672.

chapter, has not been published, but it has been used by Mr Alfred Kingston in the thorough examination which he appends to his history of East Anglia during the Civil War. The entries take the form of depositions made by witnesses for the prosecution against various clergymen between September 1643 and the end of 1644, followed by a few orders of a later date. Mr Kingston's researches into this and other records, published and unpublished, show that from 68, out of a total of 155 livings, the incumbents were ejected, giving a percentage of about 44.

The Leicester committee's book[1] is similar in form to the last, except that the answers and "interrogatories" handed in by the accused clergy are in some cases included. The available evidence in this county gives a list of 86 sequestrations for the two hundred livings in the county, or a percentage of 43.

The geographical position of these counties, representing respectively the south-west, the east and the midlands of England, is fortunate, because, had the evidence come from one quarter of the country only, it would have been more hazardous to have argued from the part to the whole. If, then, we may take them as being typical of the counties generally—and there is no reason to suppose that they are not—we find that they show an average percentage of 39 sequestrations to the total number of livings. Now there were at that time roughly 8,600 livings in England[2], which means between 3,000 and 3,500 sequestrations. If an approximate number be required, therefore, these are the figures which the evidence supports and at that we must leave it[3].

[1] The MS. is in the Walker Collection in the Bodleian Library. MS. J. Walker, c. 11, fol. 4–81. It has not been published.
[2] This number is taken from *Valor Beneficiorum* published in 1695.
[3] For a fuller discussion of the subject see G. B. Tatham: *Dr John Walker and the Sufferings of the Clergy*, pp. 124–32.

From a historical point of view, however, the actual numbers have little importance, for the reasons for which the clergy were deprived were so frequently other than religious that they merely serve to indicate the extent of the upheaval engendered by the Civil War.

CHAPTER IV

THE REGULATION OF CAMBRIDGE UNIVERSITY

As it was the University which educated and trained men for the ministry of the Church, and set its stamp upon their religious views and opinions, the regulation of Oxford and Cambridge was a necessary part of the ecclesiastical reform which the Puritans set out to accomplish. "Whilst the Universities continued unreform'd," says Walker, "their work was but half done[1]." Both had come under the influence of Laud's *régime*, though not in an equal measure, for Oxford, as the natural home of his teaching, and later as the headquarters of the King's cause, had been more thoroughly permeated with the spirit of his churchmanship and royalist principles.

On the other hand, it is customary to regard Cambridge as more under the influence of Puritanism. The past history of the University lends support to the view, and it is probable that of the Cambridge men who played prominent parts in the events of the Civil War and Interregnum, the greater number were ranged on the side of the Parliament. But in 1640, though there was a decided Puritan undercurrent, the new school of thought had been firmly planted. As early as 1629, Laud, then Bishop of London, was giving his attention to the matter, for in a paper containing "considerations for the better

[1] *Sufferings of the Clergy*, p. 108.

settling of the Church Government," presented to the
King in that year, he recommends "that Emanuel and
Sydney Colleges in Cambridge, which are the nurseries of
Puritanism, may from time to time be provided of grave
and orthodox men for their governors[1]."

It has already been remarked that one of the leading
motives of Laud's insistence on a strict observance of
forms and ceremonies was to reclaim the worship of the
Church from the neglect and the slovenly practices into
which it had fallen. In this direction, much remained to
be done at Cambridge. A report drawn up either by
Richard Sterne or John Cosin in 1636, dealing with
"certain disorders" which called for the Archbishop's
notice, reveals the fact that a great measure of neglect
and irregularity prevailed throughout the University.
The report dealt with two classes of disorder, the neglect
of discipline, and the neglect of religion.

It was not the first time in Charles' reign that the
neglect of discipline in the University had engaged the
attention of the authorities. In the very first year after
his accession, he had had occasion to direct the then
Chancellor of the University, Thomas, Earl of Suffolk,
to write to the Vice-Chancellor and Heads of Houses in
order that they might consider "what are, or have been,
the true occasions of this general offence taken at the
government, and what are fit to be remedies thereof."
In the letter which the Chancellor addressed to the
University authorities, in accordance with this direction,
he conjured them to "be all of· one minde, as one intire
man, to bring home that long banisht pilgrim, discipline,
by whose absence the famous nursery of literature and
good manners is in the eye of the state much declined[2]."

[1] Rushworth : *Historical Collections*, ii, p. 7.
[2] Heywood and Wright : *Cambridge Transactions during the Puritan Period*, ii, 335-7.

The report of 1636 showed that this reformation had been only imperfectly carried out. Some of the complaints were concerned with mere external forms. Notice was taken of the disuse of academic dress and the aesthetic tendencies observable in the apparel of the students, the "light and gay" garments, "with stockings of diverse colours reversed one upon another." Another subject of complaint was the neglect of fast days, upon which, Laud was informed, "are generally the best suppers of ye whole week[1]." D'Ewes, we are told, who spent a short time at St John's, was glad to get away from "the swearing, drinking, rioting, and hatred of all piety and virtue abounding generally in Cambridge[2]."

In matters connected with religion, the disorders were of a sufficiently serious kind. In Great St Mary's the fabric had been very much neglected and the service was very negligently performed and was "commonly posted over and cut short at ye pleasure of him that is sent thither to read it." It was the same in the college chapels. Trinity had "been long noted to be very negligent of their chappell and of their prayers in it." In King's "some of the Quiremen" could not sing, and were "diverse of them very negligent": in Caius unordained persons conducted the services, and so on. A noticeable allusion is made to certain Puritan tendencies. The "bidding prayers" before the sermons were "not only neglected but by most men also mainly opposed and misliked," and had given place to "such private fancies and several prayers of every man's own making (and sometimes sudden conceiving too)." In "Bennett college" they "use to sing long psalms of their own appointing," and the same custom was followed in Emmanuel[3]. In Laud's report on his

[1] C. H. Cooper: *Annals of Cambridge*, iii, 280.
[2] Life of D'Ewes, quoted in Bailey's *Life of Fuller*, p. 114.
[3] C. H. Cooper: *Annals of Cambridge*, iii, 280-3.

province for the year 1639, he still found "by my Lord the Bishop's account, that there are divers particulars of moment, and very fit for redress, presented to him in his late...visitation, and most of them in the University and town of Cambridge[1]." But he exerted himself to effect a change in the existing state of affairs, and the traces of his influence are apparent in many directions.

Those who now succeeded to positions of authority in the University were, in many cases, members of the new Church party, men who would carry out reforms on the lines laid down by Laud, and it is significant of the tendency of the time that of the nine heads of houses appointed between 1630 and 1640, six were of this stamp[2]. Under their auspices, the religious life, in point of doctrine and of ritual, assumed a form and an appearance more in accordance with the new school of thought. "The greatest alteration," says Fuller, "was in their chapels, most of them being graced with the accession of organs. ...Some," he records, "took great distaste thereat, as attendancy to superstition[3]."

Dr John Cosin, who was appointed to the mastership of Peterhouse on February 8, 1635, is a good example of the new school. A bill for plate furnished to him for the college chapel is still extant[4], and provides additional evidence on the subject of one of the charges afterwards brought forward at Laud's trial. On that occasion, one witness deposed that "in Peterhouse Chapel there was a glorious new altar set up, and mounted on steps, to

[1] C. H. Cooper: *Annals of Cambridge*, iii, 294.

[2] Lany of Pembroke (appointed 1630), Martin of Queens' (1631), Comber of Trinity (1631), Sterne of Jesus (1633), Beale of St John's (1633), and Cosin of Peterhouse (1635). The remaining three were Love of Corpus (1632), Brownrig of St Catharine's (1635) and Holdsworth of Emmanuel (1637).

[3] *Hist. of Cambridge* (1840 ed.), p. 233.

[4] Printed in *Cosin's Correspondence* (Surtees Soc.), i, 223.

which the Master, Fellowes, Schollers bowed, and were enjoyned to bow by Doctor Cosens the Master who set it up, that there were basons, candlestickes, tapers standing on it, and a great crucifix hanging over it," while another testified that there was "on the altar a pot which they usually called the incense pot[1]."

In Trinity College extensive alterations were carried out in the chapel, in accordance with the new ideas[2], and in July 1637, the organ was painted and gilded at a cost of fifty pounds[3]. Similar alterations and additions were made in other colleges[4].

Nor was the trend of opinion evinced only in externals. In June 1632, Nathaniel Barnard had been prosecuted in the Consistory Court on account of a sermon preached by him in Great St Mary's on May 6. The principal exceptions taken to his sermon were that he had contravened the royal declaration against discussing controversial subjects in the pulpit, that he had inveighed against those who read sermons, instead of preaching, and those who followed ritualistic innovations. He had further affirmed that treason against the State was a worse crime than treason against the King, and he had

---

[1] Prynne : *Canterburies Doome*, p. 73. "For the Sencor 36 ozs. 4 cwts. at 8*s*. the ounce, is £14. 9*s*. 6*d*." is an item in the bill mentioned above, and this has been adduced as evidence of the use of incense in the chapel, but the passage from *Canterburies Doome*, does not suggest that the censer was used except for ornament. It is hardly likely that the burning of incense, had it actually been practised, would have escaped special mention. Cf. *Cosin's Correspondence* (Surtees Soc.), i, 223.

[2] June 15, 1636. "Agreed by ye Mr and ye Seniors to set our Communion table in our chappell as it is in Cathedrall churches and chappels at ye upper end and ye ground to be raysed and that ye chappell be adorned accordingly." Jan. 14, 1636/7. "It was concluded for ye beautifying of ye chappel and ye decent adorning of ye Communion table doe authorise and constitute Fra. Kinaston Sen. Bursar of ye Coll. for ye performance of ye same and doe committ ye contrivance of ye whole worke forthwith to bee performed by him." Trinity Seniors' *Conclusion Book*.

[3] *Ibid.*

[4] See *College Hist. Series*, Jesus, p. 105 and St John's, p. 113.

T. P.   7

given additional offence by praying that God would honour the Gospel with the Queen's conversion. Barnard denied some points contained in the objections and justified others, and, though he consented to submit, he refused to accept the form of recantation drawn up by Dr Comber, the Vice-Chancellor, and the Heads. He was deprived of his post as lecturer at S. Sepulchre's and was summoned to appear before the High Commission Court[1].

In 1637 the attention of the Heads was engaged by three sermons, which, from the matter contained in them, as well as from the controversy to which they gave rise, are of considerable interest. The first two emanated from the opposite extremes. In July, Anthony Sparrow of Queens' was questioned by the Vice-Chancellor on the subject of a sermon in which he was alleged to have justified the doctrine of auricular confession[2], and on August 14, Mr Riley of Trinity was charged by Dr Martin, President of Queens', for that "in his ordinary course att Saint Maryes, he did state the cheife and principall of the controversyes of predestination in theise words,

---

[1] Pending this, the Consistory committed him, on October 15, to the safe custody of Thomas Buck, one of the Esquire Bedells, in default of sufficient sureties for his appearance. Almost immediately afterwards he escaped, but was recaptured and committed to prison in Cambridge.

See a letter from Dr Comber to Mr Lucas, the secretary to the Chancellor, the Earl of Holland, dated October 21, 1632. He acquaints him "with the unfortunate escape of Mr Bernard, who this Sunday, whilst Mr Buck our senior beadle attended upon me to S. Mary's sermon, hath made a secret escape from the servant that had the charge of him. We have sent many horsemen after him with hue and cry." *Hist. MSS. Com.* 12*th Rep.*, Earl Cowper's MSS., App. I, Vol. i, p. 479. He refused to recant when brought before the High Commission on Nov. 8, and is said to have died in prison.

Papers relating to Barnard's case are to be found in the Cambridge University Library MSS. Mm. vi, 54, ff. 1–24. See also Heywood and Wright, *Transactions in the Puritan Period*, ii, 392.

[2] *Acta Curiae* preserved in the University Registry, and Cooper's *Annals of Cambridge*, iii, 288.

or to this effecte, non ideo eliguntur quia iusti, sed ideo iusti quia eliguntur, contrary to His Majesty's declaration, and did then and there likewyse interprett a publique Article of the Church of England in his private sense and opinion concerning concupiscence in ye regenerate, expressely likewise against his sacred Majesty's declaration[1]." Both preachers were compelled to produce copies of their sermons, but no definite action was taken, and on August 14 Sparrow's case was dismissed[2].

Greater interest, however, was attached to the case of Sylvester Adams of Peterhouse, who on June 25, had preached a public sermon on the text : " Whose sins ye remit, they are remitted, and whose sins ye retain, they are retained[3]."

On July 17, the Heads ordered him to appear in a month's time and to bring in a copy of his sermon, but the copy produced does not seem to have been satisfactory and the case dragged on into the winter, Adams being forbidden , on November 20, to leave the town without the Vice-Chancellor's permission. On December 4, Adams was admonished, and ordered to deliver a true copy of his sermon " as he preached it (without quotation)."

" Being demanded whether he doth hould that the Confession of all knowne sinns unto a Priest, is ye only ordinary revealed meanes for salvacon, he saith that he doth not hould it. Secondly whether he doth hould that God doth not ordinarily pardon such knowne sinnes beforementioned, without such confession as is before mentioned."

No answer is recorded to the second part of the interrogation, but on December 16, the Vice-Chancellor was entreated " to conceave a forme of acknowledgment,

---

[1] *Acta Curiae.* [2] *Ibid.*
[3] S. John xx, 23.

which should be propounded to Mr Adams to see if he would voluntarily undertake it."

Two days later, Adams appeared again, and was charged by the Vice-Chancellor with delivering the doctrine, "That a speciall confession unto a Priest actually when time or opportunity presents itselfe or otherwise in explicite intention and resolution of all our Sinnes Committed after Baptisme so farre forth as wee doe remember is necessary unto saluation, not only necessitate precepti, but also necessitate medii, so that according to the ordinary and revealed means appoynted by Christ there can be noe saluation without the aforesaid Confession." To this Adams replied that he had said nothing in his sermon which he believed to be contrary to the doctrine of the Church of England. A form of recantation was then read over and the question was put to the Heads whether it was "a fitt recantation to be made by Mr Adams in regard of the matter delivered in his sermon."

The voting of the thirteen Heads who were present discovered a considerable divergence of opinion. Only four gave an unqualified assent, Ward of Sidney, Bainbrigg of Christ's, Love of Corpus Christi, and Batchcroft of Gonville and Caius. Five voted against the form of the recantation, Cosin of Peterhouse, Lany of Pembroke, Martin of Queens', Sterne of Jesus and Eden of Trinity Hall. The remaining four, namely Collins of King's, Smith of Magdalene, Comber of Trinity and Holdsworth of Emmanuel, were in favour of postponement and their vote carried the day. On March 2, 1638, the question was brought up again and the Heads decided, by a majority of seven to five, counting Brownrig the Vice-Chancellor's vote as one, that Adams should either submit to the recantation or be dealt with in accordance with the University Statute "de concionibus." Adams refused to give way, and it may be assumed that the sentence was duly enforced.

The four Heads who had previously voted for the recantation, again supported the Vice-Chancellor's ruling, and they were joined on this occasion by Holdsworth, who had previously favoured a postponement, and Paske of Clare, who had not been present at the earlier vote. The "non-placets" were weakened by the absence of Martin and Eden. Collins, however, voted with them and so did Beale of St John's, another whose vote had not been recorded on the first division. Comber seems to have been absent.

It will be observed that the opposition to the Vice-Chancellor's sentence came chiefly from those whose election to the masterships of their colleges has already been mentioned as a sign of the increasing influence of Laud's school, and their objections were generally based on the ground that such a condemnation of the practice of confession was not in accordance with the doctrine of the Church. The one exception was Eden, the only layman present. Eden was a Puritan and sat in the Long Parliament, so that his objection must have been founded on different reasons.

The importance of the case must not be pressed too far, but it is interesting as illustrating the existence of two distinct parties amongst the Heads, and the views which they put forward on what was, to some extent, a test question. Then as now, there seems to have been considerable difference of opinion as to what was the teaching of the Church of England on the question of Confession, and though it may be doubted whether the minority were correct in thinking that the wording of the censure and recantation ran counter to orthodox doctrine, it was on the Articles and the Liturgy, as they understood them, that they took their stand. In this, as in other

points round which controversy was then raging, the
latitude and want of strict definition which characterised
the written doctrine of the Church of England, enabled
each side to pose as the champions of orthodoxy with
a fair show of consistency[1].

With the summoning of the Short Parliament, the
balance of power began to undergo a change, and the
party which had been slowly making its way towards
supremacy in the University, found itself thrown back by
the advancing tide of Puritan feeling. One of the first
acts of the Short Parliament was to make an inquiry
into a sermon preached by Dr Beale, the Master of
St John's, in 1635, in which he was said to have
attacked the authority of Parliament[2], and proceedings
against Dr Cosin were initiated by the Long Parliament
in November 1640. They were instigated by one Peter
Smart, who had been an antagonist of Cosin's at Durham[3]
and resulted in the passing of a series of resolutions on
January 22, 1641, in which the Commons declared that
the Doctor was "unfit and unworthy to be a governor
in either of the Universities, or to continue any longer
head or Governor of any college, or to hold and enjoy
any ecclesiastical promotions[4]." On December 7, the
Commons appointed a committee, under Sir Henry
Mildmay, to examine what had been done in violation of
the statutes of Emmanuel[5], and on the 22nd of the same
month, a committee was appointed to consider the abuses
in matters of religion and civil government, either done
or suffered by the Universities[6].

On June 4, 1641, the last-mentioned committee was
revived, and was instructed to prepare a bill for regulating

[1] See Appendix for a fuller account of the voting.
[2] C. H. Cooper: *Annals*, iii, p. 300.   [3] See *Dict. Nat. Biog.*, Cosin, John.
[4] C. H. Cooper: *Annals*, iii, 306, 309–10.
[5] *Ibid.* 306, see also Walker: *Sufferings of the Clergy*, p. 108.
[6] C. H. Cooper: *Annals*, iii, 307.

the Universities. Such a bill was accordingly drawn up, and was read for the first time in the Commons on August 3[1]. For the moment, however, it did not proceed any further. Three days later articles were exhibited in Parliament against Dr Beale. They were concerned, firstly with his political views and his hostility to the Puritans, and secondly with the part he had taken in the recent ecclesiastical changes. He was said to have been "the sole encourager of Dr Cozins in his vice-chancellourship to tyranize in that jesuiticall, popish, and canterburian religion" and to have insisted on conformity to "papistical innovations[2]." The undoing of Laud's work was, in fact, for the moment the chief concern of the Parliament. On June 28, 1641, the Commons declared that the "injunction of doing reverence to the Communion-table" was no longer to be enforced in either University, and by an order of September 9 following, the University authorities were directed to remove the communion table from the east end of all chapels, to take away the rails and to level the chancels[3].

In the following year, Cambridge was drawn more directly into the current of political events. On June 29, the King, moved, as he said, by the warlike preparations against him, invited the University to furnish him with money at 8 per cent. interest[4]. The University of Oxford sent £10,000 and Cambridge "a fair proportion" in answer to this appeal[5]. Peterhouse sent £200, £100 from the Master and £100 from the college[6]; St John's sent £250[7]; Emmanuel and Sidney £100 each[8] and from

[1] C. H. Cooper: *Annals*, iii, 313.

[2] Heywood and Wright, *Cambridge Transactions*, ii, 442-4.

[3] C. H. Cooper: *Annals*, iii, 314, 316.   [4] *Ibid.* iii, 325.

[5] Secretary Nicholas to Sir Thos. Roe, July 20, 1642, *Cal. of S. P. Dom.* 1641-3, p. 359. See also Gardiner: *Hist. of Eng.* 1603-42, x, 212.

[6] *College Hist. Series*, Peterhouse, p. 108.   [7] *Ibid.* St John's, p. 115.

[8] *Ibid.* Emmanuel, p. 92 ; Sidney, p. 106.

Queens', the President, Dr Martin, sent £100 and Sparrow £85[1]. In some cases no doubt the record of the loan has been lost, but the above sums, if they may be taken as proportional, do not represent a very imposing total, and it is probable that a considerable part of the money subscribed came from private hands.

Within a month, the King was forced to make a further claim on the college liberality. Being informed[2], he wrote on July 24, "that all or most of the colleges in Cambridge were ready to deposit their plate in his hands for the better security and safety thereof," he offered to receive it, and to grant a dispensation from those statutes which might prevent the temporary alienation of college property[3]. The college authorities can have been under no misapprehension as to the intention of this proposal, and must have realised that the surrender of their plate was much more in the nature of a free gift, or at best a loan, than that of a deposit for purposes of safety, and in some colleges there was a noticeable reluctance to accede to the royal request. St John's, however, sent 2065½ ozs. weight[4]; Jesus 1201 ozs.[5], Queens' 1514 ozs.[6], and nearly all the colleges contributed in some measure. Christ's is said to have sent neither money nor plate[7]. The first consignment of this valuable contribution was entrusted to the care of Barnabas Oley of Clare, and was successfully convoyed by by-paths past Cromwell's watch to the King at Nottingham. A certain amount, however, was afterwards seized by

[1] *College Hist. Series*, Queens', pp. 161–2.
[2] According to Clarendon, the idea of borrowing college plate emanated from Gilbert Sheldon : *Hist. of Rebell.* ii, 330, note.
[3] C. H. Cooper: *Annals*, iii, 327.
[4] Heywood and Wright, *Cambridge Transactions*, ii, 452.
[5] *College Hist. Series*, Jesus, p. 107.
[6] *Ibid.* Queens', pp. 161–2.
[7] *Ibid.* Christ's, p. 160.

Cromwell in Cambridge, that belonging to Magdalene and Trinity Hall amongst the rest[1].

The action of the University in this matter led to the first act of violence from the Parliament. Several persons were sent up to London as prisoners for their complicity in the affair, and amongst them Drs Beale, Martin and Sterne, the Masters respectively of St John's, Queens' and Jesus[2].

During the summer and autumn of 1642, the town and neighbourhood of Cambridge were disturbed by the alarms and excursions that necessarily attended the outbreak of the war. The strategic importance of the place was fully realised by the Parliamentary leaders, and early steps were taken to foster the sympathy evinced by the townsmen. At the instigation of Cromwell, arms were sent down, and measures taken to train and exercise the inhabitants for the defence of the district[3]. On the whole, the " Town and Gown " stood for the two opposite parties and collisions between the two must have been frequent[4]. An attempt, however, on the part of the colleges to provide themselves with arms was frustrated by the vigilance of Cromwell, and a chest of muskets and ammunition purchased by Trinity Hall was seized. "The scholars of Trinity College" got possession of five chests before the Mayor could safeguard them[5], but the Parliamentary party was too strong to allow any Royalist demonstration to succeed. This may partially explain the fact that early in 1643 the college societies began to thin as the result of a general exodus. On February 23, 1642/3 the fellows of Jesus agreed to grant leave of

---

[1] *Commons' Journals*, ii, 731. See Appendix.
[2] C. H. Cooper: *Annals*, iii, 328.   [3] *Ibid.* iii, 326.
[4] The *Querela Cantabrigiensis* states that the townsmen were in the habit of firing their muskets at the college windows.
[5] C. H. Cooper: *Annals*, iii, 326-7.

absence to any of their number till Michaelmas, which
was subsequently extended to Michaelmas 1644, and most
of them availed themselves of the opportunity[1]. In April,
thirteen fellows of Trinity obtained leave of absence
varying in length from six weeks to twelve months[2], and
the King's College " Liber Communarum " shows that a
very considerable number of fellows and scholars were
absent from the years 1643 to 1646.

Cambridge in fact had ceased to be a congenial atmo-
sphere for men of royalist proclivities, for in February
a strong garrison under Cromwell had been thrown into
the town to resist a threatened attack from the forces
under Lord Capel[3].

The presence of a large number of troops was likely
to lead to the violent treatment of person and property,
and accordingly on March 4, the House of Lords issued
an order to protect the University members from
molestation and their buildings from being plundered or
spoiled.   Three days later, the Earl of Essex issued
a similar order to the officers under his command, en-
joining them to forbear to "offer any damage to the
University of Cambridge " or to any property belonging
to it[4].   But, according to a contemporary royalist account,
on February 23, preceding Essex's order, Lord Grey of
Wark had already procured a warrant for his officers "to
enter into the houses of all papists, malignants, and other
persons whatsoever that have or shall refuse to appear
at musters," or to contribute to the Parliament, "and to
seize upon all such arms, horses and ammunition, as shall
be found in their custodies, and to apprehend their said
persons."   In virtue of this order, the students were

[1] *College Hist. Series*, Jesus, pp. 109-10.
[2] Trinity Seniors' *Conclusion Book*, 1607-75, pp. 171-2.
[3] C. H. Cooper: *Annals*, iii, 337.
[4] *Ibid.* iii, 339-40.

examined and the colleges were ransacked and plundered[1].

It is difficult to say how much of substantial truth there is in contemporary accounts, but it is tolerably clear that the damage attributed to the wilful violence of the troops has been very much exaggerated. "Multitudes of soldiers," says the *Querela*, "were quartered in the colleges, and the buildings" which our devout and royal founders designed for sanctuaries of learning and piety... were made by them mere spittles, and bawdy-houses for sick and debauched souldiers, being filled with queans, drabs, fiddlers, and revels, night and day[2]." The members of St John's were driven out of the college "for above sixteen months together," and eighty soldiers "were turned loose" into Pembroke, and "charged by their officers to shift for themselves." In addition to this they "tore and defac'd the buildings, pull'd down, and burn'd, the wainscote of the chambers, the bedsteds, chairs, stools, tables and shelves for books[3]."

If what is here described had actually taken place, it might naturally be expected that some record of the damage could be traced in the contemporary college account-books, and the comparative silence of these witnesses tends to discredit the account. The Bursar's cash-book at Peterhouse shows that a not inconsiderable sum was spent in the entertainment of soldiers[4], and the "Mundum Books" of King's College prove that a certain number were billeted there, but the expenses for repairs do not "indicate anything more than reasonable wear and tear," nor was any serious damage done to the fabric[5].

---

[1] *Querela Cantabrigiensis*, Preface. Cf. an order of Parliament of the same date, granting power of martial law to Sir William Waller, *Commons' Journal*, ii, p. 975.
[2] *Querela Cantabrigiensis*, p. 15.   [3] *Sufferings of the Clergy*, p. 110.
[4] *College Hist. Series*, Peterhouse, p. 110.
[5] Willis and Clark : *Architectural Hist. of Cambridge*, i, 511-13.

The account-books of Jesus College show that the college suffered a similar imposition, but here again the traces of damage are inconsiderable. Seven shillings and a penny were paid for the "soldiers that came to be billeted. October 20, 1643," and seventeen shillings were paid "for mending windows, locks, bedsteads, etc., broken by the souldiers billetted in the College[1]." The burials of soldiers, frequently recorded in the registers of several churches in the town, afford an additional indication of the military occupation[2]. The first court of St John's was converted into a prison, and a considerable amount of damage was done, but in spite of this the admissions during the period were not entirely interrupted[3].

On the other hand, there are some indications that the relations between the colleges and the soldiers whom they were forced to entertain, were not always unfriendly, and we find that five shillings was paid at Trinity "to diuerse souldiers at seuerall times that behaved themselves very deuoutly in the chappell," and another five shillings to "some of Major Scot's souldiers who defended the chappell from the rudenesse of the rest[4]."

Damage and destruction of course there was, but the most serious at the moment was that carried out for military purposes. The material intended for the re-building of Clare College was seized for the purpose of fortifying the Castle, in the neighbourhood of which about fifteen houses had been demolished[5], and some of the timber in the St John's orchard was felled[6]. Cooper,

[1] *College Hist. Series*, Jesus, p. 110.
[2] A. Kingston, *East Anglia in the Great Civil War*, p. 148.
[3] Baker's *Hist. of St John's* (ed. Mayor), p. 633; J. E. B. Mayor: *Admissions to St John's College*; Walker: *Sufferings of the Clergy*, p. 110.
[4] Trinity Steward's accounts, 1644, quoted in Willis and Clark, *Architectural History*, ii, 576.
[5] C. H. Cooper: *Annals*, iii, 340–1.
[6] *College Hist. Series*, St John's, p. 126.

on the authority of the *Querela Cantabrigiensis*, also states that the Garret Hostel bridge, and the bridges belonging to St John's, Trinity, King's and Queens' were pulled down, but Walker is probably more accurate in saying that they were "defac'd" of stone and timber[1].

Throughout the year, in fact, there was some danger that Cambridge might become the scene of serious fighting, and the occasional proximity of the royalist forces without, combined with a constant hostile element within the town, gave the Parliamentary party some cause for anxiety[2].

It was natural that in the midst of these unacademic scenes, the course of the University life should be practically suspended. In a petition presented to the Parliament on June 5, 1643, the University drew attention to their "sad dejected estate…how our schools daily grow desolate, mourning the absence of their professours and their wonted auditories; how, in our Colleges, our numbers grow thin, and our revenues short; and what subsistence we have abroad, is for the most part involved in the common miseries: how, frighted by the neighbour noise of war, our students either quit their gowns, or abandon their studies; how our degrees lie disesteemed, and all

---

[1] C. H. Cooper: *Annals*, iii, 341; Walker: *Sufferings of the Clergy*, p. 110. The St John's bridge was a wooden structure and may have been completely destroyed, and the Trinity bridge had to undergo repair in 1651, but the King's bridge, which had been built in 1627, remained until the beginning of the last century. See Willis and Clark, *Architectural History*, i, 572, ii, 275, 638.

[2] A letter written by one of the Castle garrison on October 7, 1643, just at the time that detachments of the King's army were making demonstrations towards the Eastern counties, describes the weakness of the defence and the lack of arms and ammunition. The writer, one Robert Jordan, anticipated an attack from the "Oxford forces," being "persuaded they know as well as ourselves what a condition we are in, we having so many malignant scholars and others." *Hist. MSS. Com. 13th Rep.*, Duke of Portland's MSS., App., Pt. i, p. 135.

hopes of our Public Commencements are blasted in the bud[1]."

Term was ended in the middle of May[2], and on June 12, a Grace was passed to forego the solemnities of Public Commencement on account of the state of affairs[3]. Another ceremony to be abandoned was the Latin sermon, for at the beginning of the Easter Term, the Lady Margaret Preacher had been "furiously pursued over the market place by a confused number of soldiers, who in a barbarous uncivil manner cryed out, a Pope, a Pope, and vowed high revenge if he offered to go into the Pulpit." This is the version in the *Querela Cantabrigiensis*, and its substantial truth is attested by the fact that in the following term the sermon was suspended by Grace of the Senate, "for the avoydinge of the like tumult which threatened some danger to the Preacher in the beginning of the last term[4]." In the following year several Graces were passed to allow men to take their degrees by proxy, "ob varia in itinerando pericula," and the like[5].

The threatened siege of Cambridge never took place, and as events turned out, the University buildings were destined to suffer less from the violence of war than from the work of an authorised agent of destruction. On August 28, 1643, an ordinance of Parliament had been issued directing that all the recent ritualistic additions

---

[1] Printed in Cooper's *Annals*, iii, 347.

[2] May 15, 1643. There were granted "(there being at that tyme a cessation of tearme) dayes for all fellowes and scholars untill Michas. next following." Trinity Seniors' *Conclusion Book*. Later in the summer, a periodic outbreak of the plague took place, and we find in the *Conclusion Book* strict orders to prevent the carrying of infection "during this time of the Visitation."

[3] C. H. Cooper: *Annals*, iii, 349.

[4] *Grace Book*, Z (University Registry), ff. 455-6. Quoted by Cooper (*Annals*, iii, 358) from the Baker MS.

[5] *Grace Book*, Z.

to the appearance of churches and chapels should be demolished, and Heads of Houses were required to see that the directions were carried out in their own colleges[1]. As the colleges showed no readiness to obey the ordinance more rigorous measures were employed, and in December, William Dowsing, whose doings among the churches of the Eastern counties will be described later, arrived at Cambridge armed with a special commission from the Earl of Manchester. Some colleges took the precaution of beginning the required alterations without his assistance, and the fellows of Jesus had taken down and concealed their organ[2], but Dowsing's journal[3] shows that, in most chapels, he had ample scope. Robert Masters speaks of " the enraged rabble " who accompanied and assisted him in the execution of his work[4], and images, pictures, and inscriptions were cleared away and the raised chancels levelled in the same ruthless fashion which characterised the discharge of his commission elsewhere. According to the *Querela*, he battered and beat down " all our painted glasse, not only in the chappels ; but...in the publique schools, colledges, halls, libraries and chambers[5]," but this again is an exaggeration. Dowsing's journal mentions the destruction of glass in only three colleges, Peterhouse, St Catharine's and Clare, and there is no record of repairs on a scale so extensive as such wholesale destruction would have necessitated[6]. On the other hand, there can be no doubt of the thoroughness of the work.

[1] Quoted in Cooper's *Annals*, iii, 364.
[2] *College Hist. Series*, Jesus, p. 110.
[3] Printed from the Baker MS. in Cooper's *Annals*, iii, 364-7.
[4] *History of Corpus*, p. 149.
[5] *Querela Cantabrigiensis*, p. 17.
[6] Evelyn, who visited Cambridge in 1654, says nothing about any indications of Dowsing's handiwork, though he was in the habit of mentioning traces of the war when he observed them elsewhere.

"We had 4 Cheribims and Steps levelled" is
Dowsing's note for Trinity, and in the Bursar's accounts
the work is set out more at large :—

> To Mr Knuckles for whiting over the figures and for
> his paines and his servants   ...   .   1*s*.
> To Georg Woodruffe for taking downe the organs and
> hangings   ...   .   xv*s*.
> To Mr Jennings for taking downe the organ pipes   xlv*s*.
> Given to free Masons, bricklaiers, carpenters, up-
> holsterers for removing the hangings and railes
> in the chappell   ...   .   xxviii*s*.

The outbreak of hostilities naturally affected seriously
the material well-being of the University in another
direction.   On March 27, 1643, an ordinance had been
issued to sequester the estates of all who had taken up
arms against the Parliament or who had voluntarily contributed to the enemy's forces[1], and in virtue of this order,
the local sequestrators, always eager to deal a blow at
the University, had begun to seize college property by
way of reprisal for their contributions to the King.
On October 7, 1643, the University authorities addressed
a petition to Parliament begging protection from a course
which promised to ruin them.   They admitted that they
had sent a quantity of plate and money to the King for
the supply of his "present necessities," but disclaimed
the intention "to foment any war, which was not at that
time begun."   They prayed the Parliament to grant
them "freedom from this sequestration," and not to allow
the dutiful action of a few men towards their sovereign
to deprive "the members of the several colleges of all
possibility to continue in this University[2]."   A similar
petition was presented on December 5 by the fellows
and scholars of Trinity who complained that the sequestrators had seized their lands, distrained their tenants

[1] *Acts and Ordinances of the Interregnum* (Ed. C. H. Firth and
R. S. Rait), i, 106.
[2] C. H. Cooper: *Annals*, iii, 359.

for the rents due to the college, and driven away their cattle[1]. The action of the sequestrators, indeed, was likely to have such serious results that the Earl of Manchester, who both then and afterwards, did much to protect the interests of the University, addressed a letter on the subject to the Speaker of the House of Lords, pointing out the danger of the existing state of things and delicately suggesting that "your Lordships in your wisdoms will think it better to endeavour the reforming of the University, rather than to hazard the dissolving of it[2]."

The result of this united agitation was the issue on January 6, 1643/4 of a declaration by Parliament to the effect that the University and college property was "in no wise sequestrable, or to be seized on, or otherwise disposed of by vertue or colour" of any of the ordinances for the sequestration of delinquents' estates. The declaration, however, went on to decree that the University and college treasurers, to whom the revenues were paid, must be approved by the Earl of Manchester, and that "the said receivers, and treasurers respectively, shall pay all and every part, portion, and dividend, which they have, or shall have respectively, of all and every of the said rents or revenues, which part, portion, or dividend, shall be found to be, or to have been due or payable to any Head, Fellow, Schollar, or Officer of the said University, or of any of the said colledges or halls, being, or which shall be a delinquent, within any of the said ordinances for sequestration, either to the Committee for Sequestrations sitting at Cambridge, or otherwise as it shall be ordered by the said Earle of Manchester[3]."

The involved wording of this last clause renders the

---

[1] C. H. Cooper : *Annals*, iii, 362. [2] *Ibid.* iii, 363.

[3] *Ibid.* iii, 367. It appears from the Senior Bursar's accounts 1644, that Trinity paid £21. 10s. 0d. for "expenses for the Ordinance of Parliament to take off the Sequestration for College rents."

meaning at first sight somewhat obscure, but the sum
of the matter is that the incomes of delinquent members
of the University were to be paid to the sequestration
committee[1].

Shortly after the issue of this declaration, the Parliament proceeded to the execution of the work which they
had in view from the beginning of their sessions—the
regulation of the University.   A bill for that purpose had
been read the first time in the Commons on August 3, 1641,
but, in the midst of more urgent business, the matter had
been allowed to drop.   On June 10, 1643, the subject
had been revived in a debate on the petition from the
University praying for freedom from rates and impositions[2].
As a result of the debate a committee had been appointed
to consider some means of extending relief to the
University, and "to consider of some effectual means of
reforming it, and purging it from all abuses, innovations,
and superstitions[3].   By the end of the year, through the
agency of Dowsing, an outward reformation had been
thoroughly effected, but the personnel of the University
had as yet undergone no systematic "regulation."   To
this the Parliament now turned, and on January 22,
1643/4, an ordinance was issued for "regulating the
University of Cambridge, and for removing of scandalous
ministers in the seven Associated Counties[4]."

[1] Thus £22. 18s. 4d. was paid to the sequestrators in 1645 for "the
wages and other emoluments of some particular fellowes."   Trinity Senior
Bursar's Book ; Walker: *Sufferings of the Clergy*, p. 111. Walker, who makes
a mistake in the year and assigns the declaration to January 6, 1642, states
that it ordered the treasurers to "pay the incomes and revenues to the
Committee for Sequestrations," overlooking the fact that this was only so in
the case of the incomes and revenues of delinquents.   "By this declaration,"
he concludes, "the whole estates of the masters, fellows, etc., were plainly
put into his [*i.e.* Lord Manchester's] hands."

[2] That of June 5th.   See *ante*, p. 109.

[3] C. H. Cooper: *Annals*, iii, 347–9.

[4] *Acts and Ordinances of the Interregnum* (Ed. C. H. Firth and
R. S. Rait), i, 371.

A description of this ordinance, as far as it affected the Associated Counties, has already been given[1], and, as the University was included under the same provisions, it need not be repeated, The committee of sequestrators appointed for Cambridge, were empowered " to call before them, all provosts, masters, and fellowes of colledges, all students, and members of the University... that are scandalous in their lives, or ill affected to the Parliament, or fomentors of this unnaturall warre, or that shall wilfully refuse obedience to the ordinances of Parliament, or that have deserted their ordinary places of residence, not being imployed in the service of the King and Parliament."

Almost immediately after the issue of the ordinance, the Earl of Manchester, who, as holding the chief command in the Associated Counties, had been entrusted with the control of the regulation, arrived in Cambridge, and took up his quarters, together with the commissioners, in Trinity[2]. On February 24, he issued a warrant requiring Heads of Houses to send him the statutes of their colleges with the names of the members of their societies, and to certify who were then present in the University and who absent[3]. Two days later, he issued a second warrant, requiring the Heads " to give speedy advertisement viis, mediis et modis, to the fellowes, schollars, and officers " to be resident in their respective colleges on the 10th of March following, " to give an account wherein they shall be required, to answer such

[1] See *ante*, pp. 66 *et seq.*

[2] See *State Papers*, *Domestic*, vol. DXL. "A note of the charges for goods seized" from delinquent fellows : " Paid 2 porters for carrying goods to Trin. Coll. for my Lord's use...3s. od.

" Delivered in beds and bedding to Trin. Coll. for the use of the Commissioners by my Lord's Order...£10. os. od."

[3] C. H. Cooper: *Annals*, iii, 371.

things as maybee demanded by mee, or such commissioners as I shall appoint[1]."

The injustice of this latter order has been severely criticised by royalist writers, inasmuch as it was plainly impossible for those members who were far distant to return to Cambridge within twelve days[2], but the time was subsequently extended and it was not until April 3 that summonses were issued, in Manchester's name, ordering certain members of the several societies to report themselves at the Bear Inn on pain of expulsion. As a result of failure to obey this order, about sixty fellows of colleges were deprived on April 8[3].

[1] C. H. Cooper: *Annals*, iii. 371.

[2] John Walker: *Sufferings of the Clergy*, p. 112. Fuller explains the apparent injustice of the first order by saying that "because many of them were suspected to be in the King's army, twelve days were conceived for them as much as twelve months ; no time being too short for those who were willing, and none long enough for such who were unwilling." *Hist. of Cambridge*, p. 236. Neal also states that "the earl being informed that this notice was too short, the time was prolonged to the 3rd of April." *Hist. of the Puritans* (ed. 1822), iii. 96.

[3] Baker MSS. xxvii, ff. 461–2. At this point the *Querela Cantabrigiensis* describes what was known as the "Oath of Discovery." It asserts, that the sequestrators were unable to find other grounds of objection against those whom they wished to expel for their loyalty, and accordingly framed an oath which they tendered to all members of the University. This Oath of Discovery required those who took it to "accuse their nearest and dearest friends, benefactors, tutors and masters, and betray the members and acts of their several societies" (*Querela Cantabrigiensis*, p. 20). In 1654, Fuller, on reading the account of this oath in the *Querela Cantabrigiensis*, referred to Simon Ash, Lord Manchester's chaplain, for corroboration or contradiction, and Ash denied any knowledge of it, though he admitted that he might "be under mistakes through forgetfulness." Fuller's own view was that such an oath had been tendered, but unofficially (*Hist. of Cambridge*, p. 320), and in this he appears to have been very near the truth. Thomas Baker thought the so-called Oath of Discovery referred to a clause in the declaration taken by the Puritan nominees to University and college offices, in which they swore to procure "reformation by all means." "Either this was the oath of discovery," he says, "or I believe none such was tendered," and he goes on to quote Simon Ash's disclaimer (Baker's *Hist. of St John's*, ed. J. E. B. Mayor, pp. 225–6). William Cole, the antiquarian, was, however, able to correct him on this point and to offer a tolerably conclusive solution. In his transcript of Baker's history in the British Museum, he appends "a

The ordinance of January 22, 1643/4 had directed that the Covenant was to be tendered "to all persons in any of the said Associated Counties, and the Isle of Ely," but had not especially mentioned the University. On February 5, the House of Lords ordered the Earl of Manchester to take special care that it should be tendered and taken in the University of Cambridge[1], and to this date must be attributed an interesting little tract entitled *The Remonstrance of the Associated Counties to the University of Cambridge, concerning the late Covenant.* The tract is in the form of a letter addressed " to the Right Worshipfull the Master and Fellows of ——— College," and calls upon the University to set an example in refusing the Covenant, but the order of February 5 was not literally executed. The necessity of signing the Covenant was not forced upon the University as a whole[2], and it is probable that the majority of the members of King's were especially exempted through the influence of Whichcote, who became Provost in 1644[3]. In fact, although, as will be seen later, a considerable number of sequestrations were taking place, the Earl of Manchester was in no hurry to press the Covenant upon the University generally[4]. On January 18, the committee for the

MS. note entered into my copy of Fuller's *Church History*," which is in the form of a deposition signed " Ra. Tonstall." This states that "the abovesaid oath of discovery was tendered by a sub-committee of laymen, where one, whose name was Ffortune, an haberdasher of hatts, had the chaire : where I, whose name is here underwritten, being then fellow of Christs col. Camb. with several others, upon sumons, did appeare. This oath was first tendred to Mr Brearly the sen[r] of us, who alledged it to be the oath ex officio, refused to take it, and argued as above : to which the rest each excused and refused, and so dismist" (*ibid.* p. 638).

[1] *Lords' Journals*, vi, 412.
[2] Walker : *Sufferings of the Clergy*, Pt. i, p. 113.
[3] Neal : *Hist. of the Puritans*, iii, 97.
[4] An entry in the records of the Committee of Plundered Ministers, dated July 3, 1644, five months after the order to enforce the oath, states that he " had not at his going hence towards York urged the Covenant in general

Association, at Manchester's direction, ordered that no person was to be admitted to any college office until he had taken the Covenant[1], but, according to Neal, even this rule was not strictly adhered to. The form of declaration made by Lazarus Seaman on his appointment to the mastership of Peterhouse, contained a clause to the effect that he would "faithfully labour to promote learning and piety...agreeably to the late solemn, national league and covenant, by me sworn and subscribed." This clause, Neal says, was "omitted by those who did not take it [*i.e.* the Covenant], as in the case of Dr Witchcote and others[2]." It seems, in fact, that in the case of a good many moderate men, who evinced no signs of hostility to the Parliament, the oath and subscription were never pressed at all[3].

But in spite of this, a considerable number did suffer the loss of their fellowships and the sequestration of their property, as a result of the imposition of the Covenant. A small book has been preserved, in which was kept a rough inventory of the property so appropriated by the commissioners[4] and "A note of the charges for the goods seized" shows that the furniture and books, belonging to the delinquent fellow, were formally valued and conveyed away to a house especially hired for the purpose[5]. It seems probable, however, that the owners were allowed to redeem their property[6].

upon divers colledges...neither since his going hath the Committee here by commission from him pressed it upon any save upon some particular men by him named." *Record Office S. P. Dom. Int.* F. 3.

[1] Heywood and Wright : *Cambridge Transactions*, ii, 463.

[2] *History of the Puritans* (ed. 1822), iii, 106.

[3] Walker was informed, in a letter from Sir P. Sydenham, that the Covenant was never imposed in Emmanuel, the Puritan authorities supposing that the members were "all true and right to the rebellious cause" (MS. J. Walker, c. 3, fol. 17).

[4] *State Papers Domestic*, vol. DXL.

[5] "Paid to Mr James Sadler a rate for the house we lay goods in...2. 6."

[6] J. B. Mullinger : *The University of Cambridge*, iii, 280.

In the absence of reliable records, it is impossible to indicate the grounds or the occasions on which the bulk of the sequestrations took place, but it is clear that either before or after the appointment of the " Regulators," a complete change was made in the government and personnel of the various colleges. John Cosin had been declared unfit for the mastership of Peterhouse as early as January 1641/2 ; but he seems to have remained in Cambridge for more than a year, and was finally ejected on Manchester's warrant on March 13, 1643/4[1] together with Drs Martin, Sterne, Beale and Lany. Martin, Sterne and Beale had been committed to prison in the summer of 1642 for the part they had taken in sending plate to the King. The first two remained in confinement: the last named obtained an exchange, spent some time in attendance on the King, and ultimately died in Spain in 1650[2]. In May 1643, Dr Holdsworth, Master of Emmanuel and Vice-chancellor, had been seized for licensing the publication of the King's Declaration. He refused to subscribe to the Covenant and was consequently deprived of his mastership[3]. Altogether, Neal reckons that out of sixteen Heads of Houses ten were ejected by Manchester and his commissioners[4].

The six who complied were, according to him, Bainbrigg of Christ's, Eden of Trinity Hall, Love of Corpus, Brownrig of St Catharine's, Batchcroft of Gonville and Caius, and Rainbow of Magdalene. Eden died in 1645 and Bainbrigg in 1646. Three of the remaining four were afterwards ejected. Brownrig, who maintained a moderate attitude during the early days of the troubles

[1] *Cosin's Correspondence*, I, xxxii and *D.N.B.* Cosin, John.
[2] Baker's *Hist. of St John's*, ed. J. E. B. Mayor, pp. 220, 633.
[3] Cooper : *Annals*, iii, 347 ; and *D.N.B.* Holdsworth, Richard.
[4] *Hist. of the Puritans*, iii, 98.

and received a nomination to the Westminster Assembly of Divines, was deprived in 1645 for preaching a royalist sermon[1]. Batchcroft was ejected in 1649, and Rainbow in 1650: Richard Love was the sole survivor.

The list of ejections from the University, appended to Walker's *Sufferings of the Clergy*, contains 215 names, not including scholars, and for the present this must be accepted as a tolerably accurate figure. His chief source of information was the list printed at the end of the *Querela Cantabrigiensis*, which professed to include "such heads and fellowes of colledges, and other learned, reverend, and religious gentlemen...as have been ejected, plundred, imprisoned, or banished," but this he was able to supplement by the college lists with which various friends at Cambridge provided him. Thus we find in the Walker Collection, a list of the fellows, etc., ejected at Cambridge from Samuel Dod of Clare[2]; an account of the sequestrations at St John's from Thomas Baker himself[3]; a similar account for Peterhouse taken "ex Registro Veteri Collegii[4]." Even with this valuable means of checking the list in the *Querela* he was not able to make many deductions or additions. The number of names contained in that list was 195, but this was published in 1647, and a few ejections no doubt took place between then and 1650. Ejections for refusal of the Engagement Walker did not profess to include. He himself seems to have thought that his figures were tolerably complete, and in a summary at the end of the list he is content to accept 230 as a minimum, including masters, fellows and chaplains.

Characteristically, however, he endeavours to swell the list by a calculation of the probable number of

[1] *D.N.B.* Brownrig, Ralph.
[2] MS. J. Walker, c. 4, ff. 15–16.
[3] *Ibid.* ff. 42–6.   [4] *Ibid.* ff. 47–50.

ejected scholars, and here he touches on less certain ground. In the "most perfect accounts" which he had received from Oxford colleges, he had found that the percentage of ejected scholars was the same as that of fellows, and this was also the case at Queens' College in Cambridge where, according to the *Querela*, "all of each kind" were expelled. This, he thought, warranted him in calculating that, if out of a total of 355 fellows 230 were ejected, out of 700 "scholars, exhibitioners etc." more than 400 must have been turned out, which would bring the total number for the University to about 600[1].

The "Visitation Book," the record of the proceedings of the "Regulators," is unfortunately lost[2], and the chief remaining sources by which Walker's computation can be checked are stray summonses and orders of ejection issued by the Parliamentary delegates, the Admission books in the various colleges, and the records of the payment of residence allowance to fellows and scholars. The examination of these gives an approximate idea of the numbers actually ejected, and it may be instructive to take the case of one college as an example.

In Trinity, seventy-seven fellows received the "stipendium" or residence allowance in the year 1642. On April 3, 1644, the Earl of Manchester summoned seventeen[3] fellows to report themselves at the Bear Inn on the following Friday, warning them that he would "proceed to execute sentence by ejectment or otherwise,' should they fail to do so. Only two of them would seem to have obeyed the summons, for on April 8, a

[1] *Sufferings of the Clergy*, Pt. ii, pp. 162–3.

[2] Zachary Grey, in his *Examination of Neal* (vol. iii, 145), quotes from it. It was then (cir. 1737) in the possession of Rev. P. Williams.

[3] Drs Roe and Meredith, and Messrs Marshall, West, sen., Chamberlain, Willis, Barrey, Cooke, Croyden, Cowley, Wheeler, Arundell, Stacy, Sclater, Cave, Abdy, and Nicholas.

second order was issued sequestering the other fifteen[1], all of whom, with a single exception, appear to have left Cambridge in the course of that or the following year. In this, however, they were merely sharing the fate of the great majority of the society, for in 1645 and 1646 there was a wholesale disappearance of the existing fellows. Only twenty-two of the "old" fellows were present throughout the whole of 1645, and twenty-one in 1646. In the latter year, in fact, the names of all but twenty-four of the original seventy-seven had disappeared from the "stipendium" list altogether, all, no doubt, except those who were content to remain and take office under the new *régime*. Nor was this the end. Herbert Thorndike and William Wotton were deprived in 1646, and John Abdy, the only one of the fifteen fellows who seems temporarily to have evaded the sentence of April 8, 1644, was struck out of the buttery-books in October 1647. Five more fellows, Humphrey Babington, Peter Samways, Theodore Crosland, William Chamberlain and John Rhodes, were deprived in 1650 for refusing to take the Engagement[2]. Of the seventy-seven fellows who formed the resident society in 1642 only four, Robert Boreman, Francis Barton, William Bayly and Charles Rich, weathered all the storms of the period and were found in possession of their fellowships in 1660.

The extant records of ejection thus show that twenty-two fellows lost their places, fourteen in 1644, two in 1646, one in 1647, and five in 1650, but seven others appear amongst those who returned in 1660[3] and may fairly be added to the list, bringing the total to twenty-nine.

[1] *i.e.*, all except Croyden and Sclater.   Copies of these orders are in the Baker MSS. xxvii, ff. 460, 462.

[2] Baker MSS. xxxii, ff. 395–9.

[3] Sherman, Nevile, Briscoe, Crane, Price, Crawley and Parish.   Trinity College Senior Bursar's accounts and Baker MSS. xxxiii, f. 285.

Walker's list, which contains forty-four names, besides the Master, Thomas Comber, omits five of those who were ejected in 1646 and later, and adds twenty others[1]. Whether these were formally dispossessed, or whether they were only "driven from or did otherwise lose" their fellowships, to use Walker's comprehensive phrase, it is not possible to say. In any case their names disappear from the "stipendium" accounts in 1646.

Of the scholars in the various colleges it is more difficult to speak, for the residence allowance lists afford no clue as to whether the disappearance of a scholar's name were due to natural or violent causes. Walker's computation, based on what took place at Oxford, is unsound. At Oxford, all members of the University, and even college servants, were required to give an explicit submission to the authority of the Visitors on pain of expulsion, but at Cambridge no such test was imposed. The assertion, in the *Querela Cantabrigiensis*, that neither fellow nor scholar was left at Queens'[2], is contradicted by Simon Patrick, who was a sizar of the college at the time. "There were about a dozen schollars," writes Patrick, "and almost half of the old Fellows, the Visitors at first doing no more than putting in a majority of new to govern the College. The other rarely appearing were all turned out for refusing the Covenant, which was then so zealously pressed, that all schollars were summon'd to take it at Trin: Coll: Thither I went and had it tender'd to me, but God so directed me, that I telling them my age was dismiss'd and never heard more of it—blessed be God[3]."

[1] The list of fellows given in the Baker MSS. xxxiii, f. 285 agrees with Walker's list, save that Appleby and Wotton are not entered as among those who were ejected, while Baldero, Jones and Stacy are omitted entirely.

[2] *Querela Cantabrigiensis*, p. 22.

[3] Patrick's MS. Autobiography, quoted by W. G. Searle : *Hist. of Queens' Coll.*, pp. 541–2.

Patrick's assertion that the Covenant was "zealously pressed" to some extent conflicts with other evidence on the subject, noticed above, but his account suggests that age was taken into consideration in the case of scholars and that his own experience was not uncommon. The evidence, in fact, for the ejection of scholars on the scale implied by Walker is entirely lacking. Of the four chaplains at Trinity, three were expelled and one kept his place.

The abolition of music in the chapel-services threw the lay-clerks and choristers, where such existed, out of employment, but those concerned were not always deprived of their livelihood. Chambers, the Trinity organ-blower, received his customary fee of forty shillings in 1643 "for *not* blowing the organes a whole year," and again in 1645, "in lieu of his wages." On the other hand, "Jo. Browne for the Sackbut...xl. s.," which figures as an item in the chapel accounts from 1637 to 1644, is discontinued after that date[1]. The number of choristers was gradually reduced from ten to two in 1646, and in that year eight students were, by an order of the Master and Seniors, appointed to receive the profits of the vacant places[2]. From 1650 to 1658 the choristers disappear from the accounts, but five "clerici" were maintained until the Restoration. It was very much the same in King's. Henry Loosmore, the organist, and the men-choristers continued to receive their stipends. The boy-choristers, however, were allowed to dwindle in number from sixteen in 1642 to one in 1651, and in 1655 they had disappeared altogether.

The methods by which the vacant places and fellowships were filled were, of course, quite irregular. In the case of Heads of Houses the "Regulators" were

[1] Trinity Senior Bursar's accounts.
[2] Trinity Seniors' *Conclusion Book.*

naturally careful to see that none but men of a strictly Puritan type were appointed, and the elections made, under the Earl of Manchester's direction, conformed to this rule.

In the case of the mastership of Sidney Sussex, which became vacant by the death of Dr Samuel Ward in 1643, the election of the Puritan candidate, Richard Minshull, was achieved while one of the society was under arrest, and was carried through by an actual minority of the fellows[1]. This, however, took place before the beginning of the Regulation. After that date the usual method seems to have been for the Earl of Manchester to issue a mandate to the college requiring them to elect the person whom he had selected, and in some cases he carried out the ceremony of installation himself. In the course of the years 1644–1646 twelve appointments were made to masterships which had become vacant either by sequestration or death[2], and in no case, except possibly in that of Samuel Bolton, the

[1] Two candidates were put forward—Herbert Thorndike and Richard Minshull. Pope's *Life of Bishop Ward* states that at the election in the college chapel, there was a majority of one in favour of Thorndike, nine voting for him and eight for his rival, "but while they were at the election, a band of soldiers rusht in upon them, and forcibly carried away Mr Parsons [Pawson], one of the Fellows who voted for Mr Thorndike, so that the number of suffrages for Mr Mynshull, his own being accounted for one, was equall to those Mr Thorndike had. Upon which Mr Mynshull was admitted Master, the other eight only protesting against it" (Pope's *Life of Bishop Ward*, p. 14, quoted in Cooper's *Annals*, iii, 357). According to the *Acta Collegii*, it appears that Pawson's arrest took place before the election, and that Seth Ward protested against the election because Pawson was unable to vote. Ten fellows were present, and Seth Ward and three others withdrew and refused to take part in the election. Five of the remaining six then voted for Minshull, while one "suspended his vote, giveing for nobody" (Cooper's *Annals*, iii, 357–8).

[2] Lazarus Seaman (Peterhouse), Ralph Cudworth (Clare), Richard Vines (Pembroke), John Bond (Trinity Hall), Benjamin Whichcote (King's), Herbert Palmer (Queens'), William Spurstow (St Catharine's), Thomas Young (Jesus), Samuel Bolton (Christ's), John Arrowsmith (St John's), Thomas Hill (Trinity) and Anthony Tuckney (Emmanuel).

new Master of Christ's[1], could the election have been described as free.

The men who were thus placed in positions of authority in the reformed University were divines who by their attitude and conduct had rendered themselves acceptable to the Parliamentary party. A majority of them were members of the newly founded Assembly of Divines and were in possession of more or less important benefices, but they did not, as a whole, belong to the more extreme school of Puritans. The prevailing tone among them was Presbyterian, and two of the number, Thomas Young and William Spurstow, had been part authors of the celebrated *Smectymnuus*. Only in three cases[2] had the newly appointed Master been a member of the college over which he was now called upon to preside, but, with the exception of Thomas Young, who was a graduate of St Andrews University, they were all Cambridge men—six hailed originally from Emmanuel—and eight of them had held college fellowships. They numbered among them several distinguished men. Whichcote and Cudworth were prominent among the Cambridge Platonists and, taken as a whole, the colleges had no great reason to complain of the appointments even though they might justly except to the means taken to effect them.

With regard to fellowships, the action of the Parliamentary authorities was hardly less arbitrary. The committee, which met first at the Bear Inn and afterwards in Trinity, under Manchester's rule, took definite precaution to ensure the election of Parliamentary supporters. On April 10, 1644, the Earl acquainted the

---

[1] *College Hist. Series*, Christ's, p. 168.

[2] Herbert Palmer, appointed President of Queens' in 1644; William Spurstow, appointed Master of St Catharine's in 1645, and John Arrowsmith appointed Master of St John's in 1644.

Master of Corpus with the fact that he had ejected Tunstall and Palgrave from their fellowships in that college, and desired him to send in "the names of such schollars in your colledge, whom you judge most capable of fellowships, that they may be examyned and made fellows, if upon examination, they shall be approved." After the candidates had been duly examined and approved, a warrant was issued requiring the society to elect them. The newly appointed fellow then made a declaration, similar in form to that read in the case of masters of colleges[1], in which he described himself as appointed by the Earl of Manchester, and approved by the Assembly of Divines, and promised obedience to the Solemn League and Covenant[2]. The unconstitutional nature of such election was not disguised : exceptional circumstances necessitated exceptional methods. On the other hand, it appears that, by 1649 at any rate, if any exception could justly be taken against any person nominated as head or fellow of a college, appeal could be made to the Committee for Reformation of the Universities[3].

Occasionally appointments were made in an even more arbitrary manner. For example, on February 13, 1645/6, a supplementary edict for regulating the University ordered that Messrs Harrison, Culverwell, Croydon and Bradshaw were to be made Seniors in Trinity College, and empowered them to act as such, besides appointing eight others to fellowships in the same college[4]. But though the Parliamentary authorities assumed this arbitrary control while the need for "reformation" was supposed to exist, they were ready to allow affairs to resume their

---

[1] See *ante*, p. 118.

[2] C. H. Cooper: *Annals*, iii, 379, quoting Masters' *Hist. of Corpus Christi College*.

[3] *Clare College Letters and Documents* (ed. J. R. Wardale), p. 11.

[4] *Lords' Journals*, viii, 165, quoted in Cooper's *Annals*, iii, 398.

natural course as soon as this might safely be done. The same ordinance of February 13, 1645/6, while directing the election in Trinity, allowed that "other colleges in the said University of Cambridge shall choose fellows into the places now vacant by ejectment, according to their usual and accustomed manner, as if the fellows so ejected had been naturally dead, or resigned their fellowships[1]."

At the same time Parliament continued to keep the "reformation" of the University in view, and constant debates took place on the subject. On October 17, 1645, on a report from the Grand Committee for Religion, a commission was appointed "to view the laws and statutes of the University, and of particular colleges and halls there ; to consider, what is defective, or fit to be altered, in them ; and to propound remedies for the same." The commission was also to discuss the question of vacant fellowships and scholarships, and "to consider, how godly and religious preaching may be established, both in the University Church, and in other parish churches in the town[2]." The ordinance of the following February 13, as we have seen, dealt with the first of these two questions : it also directed that the various Heads of Houses should "supply the Morning Course every Lord's Day by preaching at St Marye's" and they should "maintain a constant course of orthodox and edifying sermons there." In July 1647, the attention of the Houses was called to the fact that there was a tendency on the part of some of the fellows, notably in St John's, to obstruct the peaceable government of the University[3]. From subsequent notices it would appear that the privilege of free election had been granted somewhat prematurely,

[1] *Lords' Journals*, viii, 399.
[2] *Commons' Journals*, iv, 312, quoted in Cooper's *Annals*, iii, 395.
[3] *Commons' Journals*, v, 235, quoted in Cooper's *Annals*, iii, 414.

for, on October 12, 1647, a committee was directed "to examine the information given in concerning malignants chosen fellows of St John's College, or any other college in the University of Cambridge; and the other information concerning the praying for Bishops, and using the book of Common Prayer[1]." About the same time, the Houses returned to the idea of establishing classical presbyteries throughout the country, a project which had been discussed in August 1645[2], and on January 29, 1647/8, an ordinance on the subject was issued, in which the University authorities were required to consider how the colleges might be brought into such a system[3].

But, in spite of this constant care, the University continued to evince a considerable amount of feeling in favour of the royalist cause, and at one point at any rate partisanship broke out into open violence. The date was the period of the siege of Colchester, in June 1648, and the occasion "some disgraceful expressions in the Schools against the Parliament and Army," which led to an open conflict between the supporters of King and Parliament respectively, "the Royall Townsmen readily assisting the schollers of their party." The fight ended in favour of the Parliament's friends, and Captain Pickering, who arrived on the scene with a troop of horse at the conclusion of the disturbance, issued a proclamation against those who "should presume to raise any insurrection or tumult" in the town. The Committee for Cambridge was also directed to "consider of some effectual course...to prevent the like for the future[4]."

---

[1] *Commons' Journals*, v, 331, quoted in C. H. Cooper: *Annals*, iii, 417.

[2] *Lords' Journals*, vii, 545, quoted in C. H. Cooper: *Annals*, iii, 394.

[3] *Acts and Ordinances of the Interregnum* (Ed. C. H. Firth and R. S. Rait), i, 1062.

[4] C. H. Cooper: *Annals*, iii, 423. The account of the fight is given in the *Moderate Intelligencer* for June 8-15, 1648, and also in a pamphlet entitled *Another bloudy fight at Colchester*: London 1648. Brit. Mus.

Hitherto, as the above references show, the affairs of the University of Cambridge had been under the immediate control of the Parliament acting sometimes through the agency of the local committee. In Oxford, power had been delegated, as early as July 1, 1646, to a special commission, which was to "consider of, and bring in, an ordinance for regulating of the University[1]." On May 4, 1649, the Commons, moved perhaps by the apparent need of further "reformation" revealed by the recent outbreak, ordered that it should be "referred to the Committee formerly appointed for regulating the University of Oxon to take care of the regulating of the University of Cambridge and Winchester College[2]," and this body consequently was the supreme authority until its dissolution on April 21, 1652[3].

Of the proceedings of this Committee for the Reformation of the Universities very few traces remain. Only two books of orders emanating from it are extant, and they deal almost entirely with the payment of augmentations to livings, a form of business which, in accordance with the chaotic system of administration which then obtained, the committee was at one time called upon to discharge[4]. It is clear, however, that the commissioners interfered to a not inconsiderable extent in the government of the University and colleges, and that they arrogated to themselves the power, occasionally claimed by the Crown in earlier days, of obtaining elections to scholarships and fellowships by means of a mandate[5]. It was not

E. 448 (2). Another account of the incident is given in a letter from Thomas Harley to his brother. *Hist. MSS. Com. 14th Rep.*, Duke of Portland's MSS., App., Pt. ii, p. 162. "The royall sophs were so extravagant in fearing the Parliament that the other party kicked downe the moderator and opponent and beat them all out."

[1] *Commons' Journals*, iv, 595.   [2] *Ibid.* vi, 200.   [3] *Ibid.* vii, 124.
[4] See Shaw: *Hist. of the Eng. Ch.* 1640–60, ii, 217–19.
[5] Mar. 8, 1649/50. "Whereas the Honourable Committee for Reformation of the University of Cambridge Jan. 17th 1649 did think fitt to order

uncommon either for degrees to be conferred by their order[1].

One of the most important duties carried out by the committee, in connection with the Universities, was the payment of augmentations to the stipends attached to masterships of colleges, a proceeding which had not been necessary in former times owing to the fact that Heads of Houses were generally in possession of other preferments. By the ordinance, passed on June 8, 1649, dealing with the maintenance of preaching ministers, an annual sum of £2000 was set aside for this particular purpose, out of the revenue arising from tenths and first fruits[2]. The intention of the committee seems to have been to raise all masterships to the annual value of £200, and their records show that in the years 1650–1 the whole of the £2000 was granted in an equal proportion between the two Universities[3].

Before the dissolution of the Committee for Reformation, Cambridge was destined to be subjected to an inquisition of a different kind. On October 12, 1649, Parliament decided that the obligation of signing the Engagement to be faithful to the Commonwealth as then established, without a King or House of Lords, should be extended from members of the House of Commons to all civil officials and to all graduates and officers in the University as well as to the colleges of Eton, Winchester

that Mr Robert West, and Mr Walter Catstrey have their time allowed them from their first admittance into the several universities and that they take their seniority in Trinity College accordingly, We the Masters and Seniors of the same Colledge do accept this order and submit unto it." (Trinity Seniors' *Conclusion Book.*) On Oct. 29, 1650 the Masters and Seniors accept the order of the committee appointing six fellows in place of those who had been removed. The "Protocollum Books" at King's record similar instances.

[1] Several instances in Grace Book H in University Registry.

[2] *Acts and Ordinances of the Interregnum* (Ed. C. H. Firth and R. S. Rait), ii, 145.

[3] The grants are to be found scattered about in the book of orders

and Westminster[1]. On December 20 following, it was accordingly tendered at Cambridge, but a general reluctance to subscribe was evinced. Only seventy-nine gave their signatures, and a considerable number of the remainder, led by Drs Collings, Lane and Rainbow, joined in presenting a document in which they undertook to live peaceably, and desired that this might be considered as their submission[2]. But the Parliament, having once embarked on their course, pursued it to its logical conclusion, and on January 2, 1649/50, an ordinance was passed imposing the Engagement on the country at large[3]. With this before them, the University could hardly have expected to obtain exemption, but the final blow was deferred until the middle of the year, when, on

belonging to the Committee for Reformation of the Universities, now among the Sion College MSS. The payments were as follows:

CAMBRIDGE.	£	OXFORD.	£	s.
Ralph Cudworth of Clare ...	100	Dr Langbaine of Queen's	63	10
John Arrowsmith of St John's	100	John Saunders of Oriel ...	92	0
Anthony Tuckney of Emmanuel	100	Paul Hood of Lincoln ...	63	0
John Worthington of Jesus ...	90	John Wilkins of Wadham	63	10
Samuel Bolton of Christ's ...	50	John Conant of Exeter ...	92	0
Thomas Horton of Queens' ...	50	Thankfull Owen of St John's	90	0
John Bond of Trinity Hall ...	53	[Henry Langley] of Pem-		
William Dell of Gonville and		broke	100	0
Caius	60	Tobias Garbrand of Glou-		
Richard Love of Corpus ...	70	cester Hall	50	0
John Sadler of Magdalene ...	47	Daniel Greenwood of B. N. C.	90	0
Sidrach Simpson of Pembroke	70	George Bradshaw of Balliol	92	0
Richard Minshull of Sidney ...	40	Robert Harris of Trinity ...	20	0
John Lightfoot of St Catharine's	90	Michael Roberts of Jesus...	92	0
Lazarus Seaman of Peterhouse	80	Joshua Hoyle of University	92	0
	£1000		£1000	0

The payments were actually made by the Trustees for Maintenance on the order of the Committee for Reformation of the Universities. See an order in the Sion College MS. f. 732.

[1] Gardiner: *Commonwealth and Protectorate*, i, 176.
[2] *Theologian and Ecclesiastic*, vii, 283.
[3] *Acts and Ordinances of the Interregnum* (Ed. C. H. Firth and R. S. Rait), ii. 325.

June 21, the Committee for the Reformation of the Universities was directed to inquire what officers and members of the various colleges had refused subscription and to eject those who continued to do so[1].

The consternation in Cambridge caused by these orders is reflected in the correspondence of the time between William Sancroft and his friends. As a member of Puritan Emmanuel, Sancroft was one of those who had hitherto been absolved from the necessity of a definite statement of their principles. There were at that time in the University many who, while heartily disapproving of the Parliamentary government, had retained their places by means of quiet behaviour and a politic compliance with the new order; the majority also of those who had gained places in the University in the early years of the Regulation were Presbyterians, and many of them had disapproved of the subsequent course of political events. Neither of these parties were prepared to sign a declaration which not only pledged them to the support of the existing government, but also implied approval to its past actions. If the Engagement were rigidly enforced, therefore, it was clear that either principles or preferment must be sacrificed. A glimmer of hope was distinguished by some in the influence of Cromwell, who was supposed to favour a connivance of non-subscribers, but Sancroft distrusted his sincerity.

"The Commissioners[2] sit this week," he writes in a letter to his brother, dated July 10, 1650, "and what they will do, I know not. Some assure me, that Mr Cromwell, when he was here on Saturday was seven night, (in his passage towards the north), told the vice-chancellor and doctors, who sneaked to the Bear to wait upon his mightiness, that there should be no further

[1] C. H. Cooper: *Annals*, iii, 433.
[2] The Commissioners for the Reformation of the University.

proceedings against non-subscribers; that he had desired the committee of regulation above to petition the house, in his name, that we might be no further urged. But we know his method well enough, namely, by courteous overtures to cajole and charm all parties when he goes upon a doubtful service; and as soon as it is over to his mind, then to crush them[1]."

Sincere or not, however, Cromwell was unable to obtain exemption for the University. The committee sat again on September 13 and summoned non-subscribers to attend. Sancroft disregarded his summons, but learnt that "the business was to angle for more proselytes....It seems," he writes, in another letter to his brother, "the gentlemen think that their victories resolve our cases of conscience to their advantage; and that it is but to rout the coward Scots, and all our arguments are answered. But I hope God will enable us to let them see they are deceived[2]." As time went on, and the University remained firm, the committee had recourse to severer methods. On November 17, Sancroft wrote that many had lately been turned out, " Dr Young of Jesus, Dr Syms too of Katharine Hall, and Mr Vines of Pembroke hall, and some fellows of several colleges." He himself had again been "returned as a refuser," but he had been told that he had "some secret friend" who did him good service[3]. The penalty of persistent refusal did not in fact overtake him until the following year.

Shortly afterwards Sancroft left Cambridge, and the course of events can be traced in a series of letters to him from Samuel Dillingham of Emmanuel. " The storm is not yet risen," writes Dillingham in an undated letter, "all is quiet; and men have time to study how to shift

[1] H. Cary: *Memorials of the Civil War*, ii, 224.
[2] *Ibid.* ii, 233.   [3] *Ibid.* ii, 234–6.

not off, but with the subscription : so degenerated are we from all spirit and courage, which should carry us on to an unanimous opposing the stream of things, that we think it bravely done if we can make ourselves believe, by any manner of evasion, that our consciences are kept entire, and the Engagement subscribed[1]." To Dillingham, the imposition of the Engagement appeared as a divine judgment on the compliant attitude of the University towards the Puritan rule. What he anticipated was a further lapse in the same direction, for he saw "the generality nearer and nearer every day resolved to shift[2]." In December, the committee seems to have made a more determined onslaught. "Some have subscribed that were never dreamed on ; others quite contrary," wrote Dillingham. Several papers had been handed in to the committee containing the arguments of those who refused the Engagement. On the other hand, "Trinity Hall swallowed it roundly, all but their divine, Mr Owen, and Mr Clark." He was surprised to find how many were able to give an equivocal submission, and "thought themselves only bound negatively, and but so long till a party should appear against the present power." Such an attitude he was unable to understand, affirming that for his part, if he subscribed at all, it would be "to the full intention of the urgers," or he would think himself "in the briars, turn things how they will." Yet even with these mental reservations, the number of subscribers was but sixty-six, while "there were nearer six hundred refusers, if they may be so called, who make account they have not yet given their final answer[3]."

Several leading men, however, had suffered expulsion. Rainbow was deprived of the mastership of Magdalene in August 1650. Richard Vines of Pembroke, William

[1] H. Cary: *Memorials of the Civil War*, ii, 239.
[2] *Ibid.* ii, 242–3. [3] *Ibid.* ii, 244–9.

Spurstow of St Catharine's, and Thomas Young of Jesus, three of the Presbyterian Masters appointed in 1644 and 1645, also lost their places[1]. Even Richard Love was suspended[2]. A more significant indication of the changing times was the fact that on November 27, 1651, the Earl of Manchester himself was deprived of the chancellorship for refusing to take the Engagement[3].

Sancroft waited on in expectation of the end until April in that year. On March 23, a friend at St John's, one Henry Paman, had written to inform him of the contradictory reports that were current as to his fate. "The news from London," he told him, "says your business is treated, and you are given to us now upon a surer foundation than we could possibly hope to enjoy you. For when your fellowship was asked, the petitioners were answered, that they might as well think to remove a mountain as Mr Sancroft." At the same time, it had been given out that he had subscribed[4]. Neither statement was true. On April 10, the Committee for the Reformation of the University issued an order warning the Senior Fellow of Emmanuel that if Sancroft had not subscribed the Engagement within a month, the committee would nominate another to his place[5], and in the appointed time, the order took effect.

With the imposition of the Engagement the work of the Committee for Reformation practically ceased, and on April 21, 1652, it was formally dissolved[6]. In another year, almost to a day, the power of the Long Parliament, its creator, was at an end[7]. Henceforward, the destinies of the University were virtually in the hands of Cromwell.

[1] C. H. Cooper: *Annals*, iii, 439.   [2] H. Cary: *Memorials*, ii, 235.
[3] C. H. Cooper: *Annals*, iii, 448.   [4] H. Cary: *Memorials*, ii, 252.
[5] *Ibid.* ii, 269.   [6] C. H. Cooper: *Annals*, iii, 449.
[7] The Long Parliament was dissolved by Cromwell on April 20, 1653. Gardiner: *Commonwealth and Protectorate*, ii, 263.

Cromwell's connection with Cambridge dated from the time that he had been returned to the Long Parliament as one of the two members for the borough, but his relations with the members of the University had not been calculated to win the confidence of those who either openly or secretly supported the royalist cause. It was he who had intercepted the college plate destined for the King, and it was he who, as the commander of the troops in the district, had been entrusted with the arrest of offenders. It was even suggested that he had encouraged the soldiers in their violent behaviour on the occasion of the Latin sermon in the University Church[1]. It was not surprising, therefore, that the promise of his good offices at the time of the Engagement should have been misconstrued, or that Samuel Dillingham, in a letter to Sancroft, should evince his hatred by covering a sheet with malicious references to Cromwell's personal appearance[2]. In recent years, however, there could be no doubt that his attitude towards the University had been favourable. On July 1, 1652, he had issued an order to the officers under his command, charging them not to quarter any troops in the Cambridge colleges, or to offer any injury or violence to any of the members of the University[3].

His favour was the more valuable because there was a noticeable tendency among the more violent sectarians to attack Universities as institutions. The "Barebones" Parliament seriously considered the question of suppressing all places of learning as unnecessary[4], and various wild proposals of a similar kind were in the air. The line taken by most of these reformers was that learning was a hindrance to true religion. Thus a man

[1] John Walker: *Sufferings of the Clergy*, p. 110.
[2] H. Cary: *Memorials*, ii, 226-7.
[3] C. H. Cooper : *Annals*, iii, 452.   [4] *Ibid.* iii, 453.

named Samuel Hering proposed that two colleges should
be set apart for those who wished to apply themselves
"to the studdy of attaining and enjoying the spirit of our
Lord Jesus." The Scriptures and "the works of Jacob
Behmen, and such like, who had true revelation from the
true spirit" were to constitute the entire literature, and
provide a course of study which "would confute and
confound the pride and vain-glory of outward humane
learning, stronge reason, and high astrall parts, and
would shew men the true ground and depth of all things[1]."

Other writers, who were not prepared to go quite as
far as Hering, also advocated changes which amounted
to an entire revolution in the nature of Universities.
Prominent amongst these was William Dell, Master of
Gonville and Caius College, who wrote two or three
pamphlets on the subject of University reform, partly in
answer to Sidrach Simpson, the Master of Pembroke.

It would be a mistake to represent Dell as an enemy
to all forms of learning, though his antagonists were apt
so to regard him. He himself disclaimed such a position.
"I am not against Humane Learning upon all accounts,"
he wrote, "but do allow Humane Learning (so it be sober
and serious) in its own place and Sphear, as well as other
Humane things: but I do oppose it as it is made another
John Baptist, to prepare the way of Christ into the
world, or to prepare the world's way to Christ: And
also, as men make it necessary, for the true knowledge
of the Scriptures; yea, the very Unction for the
Ministry[2]."

His attack was directed against the existing system
of education, which made the intellect rather than the
spirit the avenue towards a right understanding of the

[1] C. H. Cooper: *Annals*, iii, 454, note.
[2] Dell: *A Plain and Necessary Confutation of divers gross and Anti-
christian errors* etc. (1654), Preface.

Christian faith. He attacked also degrees and titles in the Universities and ecclesiastical orders in the Church, as the paraphernalia belonging to the same system and as things by which men "are not able to discerne Antichrist, but rather are the more ready to be overcome by him[1]." It was with this purpose that he "adventured, through the inspiration of the Almighty, to undertake openely and plainly against the Clergy and Universities, which in their present state, are the residue of the hour and power of darkness upon the Nations[2]."

In some remarks on "The Right Reformation of Learning," Dell gives his views on a suitable curriculum for the Universities. The study of profane classical authors was to be discouraged, but Physic and Law should form part of the course, and "the Mathematicks especially are to be had in good esteem...as Arithmetick, Geometry, Geography, and the like, which as they carry no wickedness in them, so are they besides very useful to humane Society, and the affaires of this present life[3]."

Another writer who took a similar line was John Webster, also a Cambridge man. Wood describes him as a man who "was very well known to be one who endeavoured to knock down learning and the Ministry both together[4]," but he himself, like Dell, posed as a reformer. "Humane knowledge," he admitted, "is good, and excellent, and is of manifold and transcendent use, while moving in its own orb ; but when it will see further than its own light can lead it, it then becomes blind and destroys itself[5]." The Scriptures, he contended, should not be "torn with the carnal instruments of man's wit and reason, nor modell'd, or methodized as an humane

[1] Dell: *The Tryall of Spirits* (1653), p. 60.
[2] *Ibid.* Preface.
[3] Dell: *A Testimony from the Word*, etc. p. 27.
[4] A. Wood: *Hist. of Oxford*, iii, 657.
[5] John Webster: *Examination of Academies*, p. 3.

art or science, but laid aside in Scholastick exercises, as a sacred and sealed book[1]."

Views of this kind were not very uncommon amongst the more advanced Independents, and proceeded from a jealousy of the clergy, whether Episcopalian or Presbyterian, and from a growing distrust of theological learning, bred of a long experience of religious controversy. Even Cromwell himself seems .to have sympathised with their desire to encourage the "things of the spirit" rather than the mere acquisition of knowledge, when he referred to the "very great seed" for the ministry "in the youth now in the Universities; who instead of studying books, study their own hearts[2]." The attacks, however, had no concrete result, and the Universities were allowed to continue until the end of the Interregnum without undergoing any further "reformation."

At the same time, the Government was careful to keep a constant control over the Universities. On September 2, 1654, the Protector and Council passed an ordinance appointing visitors for both Universities and "the schools of Westminster, Winchester, Merchant-Taylor's School, and Eaton Colledge and school[3]." On April 28, 1657, a proposal was brought forward in Parliament to confirm the ordinance for regulating the Universities. Some objection was raised on the ground that such a confirmation would be an invasion of the rights of the Protector and of the statutable visitors, but it was finally decided to confirm the ordinance for six months[4].

[1] *Examination of Academies*, p. 97. For a full account of the writings of Dell and Webster see Mullinger's *Hist. of the Univ.* vol. iii, pp. 448 *et seq.*
[2] Speech on Sept. 17, 1656. Carlyle's *Cromwell's Letters and Speeches* (Centenary Edition, 1902), iii, 296.
[3] *Acts and Ordinances of the Interregnum* (Ed. C. H. Firth and R. S. Rait), ii, 1026. Scobell: *Acts and Ordinances*, ii, 366.
[4] C. H. Cooper: *Annals*, iii, 467.

Towards the end of the Interregnum, a last attempt at reform was made in a scheme to remodel the Universities on the Dutch system with three colleges in each, devoted respectively to divinity, law, and physic[1].

The general effect of the Puritan rule upon the University is not easy to summarise, since the history of the various colleges was by no means uniform. As a result of the exodus of some, during the early stages of the war, and the forcible expulsion of others, the colleges were deprived of a great number of their former members, and it was natural that those who took their places should be chiefly men of a Puritan stamp. In the case of those who were to hold any office or place of authority, this was necessarily so, but it was true also, to a less extent, of those who entered the University in the ordinary course as undergraduates. With regard to the former, royalist writers have endeavoured to throw contempt upon the Puritan nominees, but the general standard was by no means low, and though there was a certain number of extremists like William Dell, the Master of Gonville and Caius, men like Whichcote of King's, Lightfoot of St Catharine's and Worthington of Jesus were worthy of the best traditions of their University. With regard to the rank and file, a good deal depended upon the influence of the Heads, but several colleges entirely changed their character during the period. Peterhouse, for example, which had been essentially royalist in sympathy, attracted, under the mastership of Lazarus Seaman, a considerable number of men from the opposite party[2]. At the same time, the metamorphosis was neither as complete nor as marked as has sometimes been represented. The

[1] C. H. Cooper: *Annals*, iii, 475.
[2] *College Hist. Series*, Peterhouse, p. 123.

royalist connection was not entirely severed, as the outbreak in 1648 and similar occurrences show, and the University continued to contain men of widely divergent views. It is even remarkable that the bitter party feeling engendered by the Civil War went no further towards breaking old ties, and that, just as Oliver Cromwell sent his son to St Catharine's in 1640, in the days of the supremacy of Laud, so in 1649 John Cosin could send his son to the college from which he had himself been ejected[1].

The most noticeable change in the college societies was the gradual disappearance of clergymen. In 1652 there was only one fellow of King's in orders and in 1653 there were none[2], and in St John's it was found necessary, in February 1649/50, to make a decree that "few of the fellows being in Orders" all M.A.'s should officiate in chapel in turn "and not only Ministers, as heretofore, when the Liturgie (now taken away by publicke authoritie) required the pronouncing of Absolution by them alone[3]."

In Trinity the statutes required that a certain number of fellows must be ordained within seven years of election, a state of affairs which gave rise to some little difficulty. On June 17, 1650, however, the Seniors gave their opinion that as bishops had been abolished, and the ordaining power of Classical Presbyteries discontinued, no person could legally be ordained and that the statute was therefore void. Upon this, one William Croyden made a statement to the effect that he was ready to be

---

[1] *College Hist. Series*, Peterhouse, p. 128.

[2] For this and many other details relating to King's I am indebted to Mr F. L. Clark of the King's College Office, who kindly showed me his transcripts and extracts of the College Records.

[3] From the St John's *Plate Book*, extracts of which have been published by Mr R. F. Scott, in the *Eagle* magazine, under the title "Notes from the College Records."

ordained, but since that was not possible, he would "use the utmost of my guifts and abilities for the Propagation of the Gospel of Jesus Christ in Trinity College whilst fellow there, and for the Outward Call, I shall be ready to seek and embrace it as it shall be held out by Parliament[1]."

Of the moral welfare of the members of the University the Puritans showed themselves very careful, and there can be no doubt that they endeavoured to introduce a severer code of manners as well as stricter moral and religious life. Customs which were regarded as unduly frivolous and tending towards corruption were suppressed. Such were the "Salting nights" at Trinity which were "wholly layd aside" by an order of July 17, 1646, the Sophisters being directed to "carry themselves in all civilitie and without any noyse or humminge" on those occasions[2]. At the same time the authorities were careful to remove any evil influences from the town, and the *Acta Curiae* contain several references to proceedings against inn-keepers for allowing scholars to drink or gamble in their houses.

Within the colleges strict attention was paid to the scholars' moral well-being. Akehurst, tutor of Trinity, who is described by one of the more distinguished of his pupils as a "flourishing instrument" and "a gracious savoury Christian," was solicitous of the company kept by those under his charge, would "sometimes read lectures" to them and had prayers "in his chamber every night[3]," a practice which seems to have been general[4], and several writers have testified to the measure

---

[1] Trinity Seniors' *Conclusion Book.*   [2] *Ibid.*

[3] J. Hunter: *Life of Oliver Heywood,* p. 45.

[4] In the St John's *Plate Book* is an order that all B.A.'s and undergraduates "shall duly and constantly attend their Tutor's prayers at eight of the clock every night." Printed by Mr R. F. Scott in "Notes from the College Records." The Emmanuel "Admonition Book" contains a record of the

of success which attended the system. Neal, indeed, says that "vice and profaneness was banished, insomuch that an oath was not to be heard within the walls of the university[1]," and Thomas Baker, who was by no means prejudiced in the Puritan's favour, admits that the government of St John's under Arrowsmith and Tuckney was "so good and the discipline...so strict and regular, that learning then flourished, and it was under them that some of those great men had their education that were afterwards the ornaments of the following age[2]."

At the same time, it would be a mistake to suppose that the Puritans introduced an Utopian age in morals and religion or that all the undergraduates of the time were like Oliver Heywood. The authorities in the period which immediately preceded the Civil War, if their methods were different, were as bent on "reformation" as the Puritans themselves, and edicts directed towards the improvement of manners were as common at the one date as at the other. A royal order, for instance, of March 4, 1628/9, directed against the employment of women in the colleges in contravention of the statute *de modestia morum* of 1625, condemns those inn-keepers and others who had women on their premises and encouraged scholars "to misspend their time, or otherwise misbehave themselves, or to engage themselves in marriage without the express consent of those that have the gardiance and tuition of them[3]." Occasionally strict measures were employed to check the sporting proclivities of the lighter-minded students. For example, in 1634, the Vice-chancellor issued an order to

admonition in 1639 of an undergraduate "for his negligence at chappell and his Tutor's prayers," which suggests that the custom was not new.

[1] *Hist. of the Puritans* (1822), iii, 105.

[2] J. B. Mullinger: *Hist. of S. John's College*, p. 135.

[3] *Miscellanea Historica MSS. in the University Registry*, vol. xiii, No. 21.

the constables of Chesterton and other neighbouring villages, requiring them to apprehend and bring before him any of those scholars who had been in the habit of resorting "unto your towne and fields about you with fowling and birdinge peeces, stone bowes and Crosbowes and doe shoote at fowle and other game contrary to the Lawes of this Land and the expresse command of his Majestie[1]."

As to the second point, there is abundant evidence that some at least of the undergraduates of the Puritan period were very much like the undergraduates of any other period, prone to exuberance of spirits and a disregard of constituted authority, and it is possible to find many instances to illustrate the manners of the day. Thus we find the Proctor charging five members of the University in the Consistory Court for "that they...att night in Christ's Greene did plat at footeball and carried themselves very uncivillie towards him," or again that Thomas Pearne of Peterhouse was suspended *a gradu suscipiendo* for "that contrary to all civilitie and good manners of the University he did this day blow a horne in the sophisters schooles when they were hudling and thereby did cause disturbance and uncivill actions in the said schooles[2]." In Emmanuel several scholars were admonished "for playing at cards in the Colledge[3]," and the entries in Worthington's diary show that the intervention of the Vice-chancellor was still required to suppress immorality[4].

But while the Puritan rule was strict in the matter of morals and religion, it has been the custom to regard the period as one in which scholarship was almost, if not

[1] *Miscellanea Historica MSS. in the University Registry*, vol. xii, No. 46.
[2] *Acta Curiae* in University Registry. Entries for April 17 and December 19, 1657.
[3] Emmanuel College "Admonition Book."
[4] Heywood and Wright : *Cambridge Transactions*, ii, 597–603.

entirely, neglected[1]. There is substantial truth in this view, for the whole tendency of the time was to place profane learning in a position of secondary importance, but the extreme views of a man like Dell were not typical of the University as a whole, and it would probably be more true to say that the character of the studies was changed than that they were suspended. While Heywood's tutor prayed with his pupils "every night," it was only "sometimes" that he read lectures to them, and Heywood himself admits that his "time and thoughts were more employed in practical divinity" and that "experimental truths were more vital and vivifical" to his soul[2], but occasional orders in college records relating to the better observance of "acts" and "exercises" and for the prevention of neglect of studies show that the authorities were not entirely careless of this side of college life[3]. An interesting letter, written by Sancroft on January 17, 1663, after his return to Emmanuel, illustrates very well the effect of the Puritan period in this respect as it appeared to him. He rejoices, he tells his correspondent, Ezeckiel Wright, that there is "a general outward conformity to what is established by law, and, I hope, true principles of duty and obedience deep laid within, and a cheerful readiness to take off all the instances of that former singularity which rendered us heretofore so unhappily remarkable."

On the other hand, the state of learning in the college presented a less satisfactory prospect.

"It would grieve you," he writes, "to hear of our

[1] "The former studies of the University would appear, indeed, to have been almost entirely suspended." J. B. Mullinger: *Cambridge in the Seventeenth Century*, p. 180.

[2] J. Hunter: *Life of Oliver Heywood*, p. 46.

[3] For example, orders of January and May 1654 in the S. John's "Plate Book," printed by Mr R. F. Scott in "Notes from the College Records." Cf. *College Hist. Series*, Emmanuel, p. 103.

public examinations; the Hebrew and Greek learning being out of fashion everywhere...and the rational learning they pretend to being neither the old philosophy, nor steadily any one of the new. In fine, though I must do the present society right, and say, that divers of them are very good scholars, and orthodox (I believe) and dutiful both to king and church; yet methinks I find not that old genius and spirit of learning generally in the college that made it once so deservedly famous[1]."

In one noticeable direction, at all events, the Parliament, as well as the University authorities, showed their appreciation of academic institutions, and that was in respect of the new University library which had been started by the Duke of Buckingham in 1628 when he held the post of Chancellor[2]. On March 24, 1647/8, the Commons voted £2000 to the library, and a collection of books "in the Eastern languages" was bought from George Thomason for the sum of £500 and presented to the University at the same time[3]. On October 10, 1646, a Grace was passed to authorise the expenditure of thirty or forty pounds on printing Arabic books[4], and on February 20, 1652/3, a scheme was floated "for the raising of a competent maintenance for the Keepers of the University Library that soe it may forthwith become of publicke use[5]."

On the side of material prosperity, the University did not suffer as much as at one time seemed probable. There was a natural falling-off in the number of admissions during the first three years of the war and practically all

---

[1] D'Oyly: *Life of Archbishop Sancroft*, i, 126, 128.
[2] Heywood and Wright: *Cambridge Transactions*, ii, 357–61.
[3] C. H. Cooper: *Annals*, iii, 421.
[4] *Grace Book* H (University Registry).
[5] *Acta Curiae* (University Registry). Under this scheme every college was to make a quarterly payment of two shillings and sixpence for the Master and one shilling for every fellowship.

the colleges were affected to a greater or less degree[1]. In Pembroke the admissions fell from seventeen in 1641 to six in 1642, and for the two following years there is no record at all, but the numbers in this college seem to have been subject to mysterious fluctuations throughout the whole period[2]. Generally speaking, the number of admissions began to rise again about 1646, though in some cases, notably that of Trinity Hall, the recovery was longer deferred[3].

It has already been noticed that the danger to be anticipated from the sequestration of college property was averted as soon as it became known, and on April 11, 1645, on a representation from the University that the colleges were reduced to necessity through the decrease in rents, Parliament passed an ordinance granting exemption from taxation[4]. The records of revenues are an uncertain guide to the actual financial condition of a college at any given date, since estates were generally let at a low rack rent, and the income was largely derived from fines accruing at irregular intervals. The rents themselves also were commonly paid partly in wheat, partly in malt, and partly in money, but it is clear that college property, like other landed property, had suffered very heavily during the early years of the war. No dividend seems to have

---

[1] See *College Hist. Series*, Peterhouse, p. 119; Jesus, p. 115; Trin. Hall, p. 141; Christ's, p. 165; S. John's, pp. 85, 126.

[2] The numbers, as appears from the college "Admission Book," were as follows:

1645 : 18	1648 : 13	1651 : 5	1654 : 22
1646 : 28	1649 : 9	1652 : 9	1655 : 6
1647 : 13	1650 : 9	1653 : 10	1656 : 16

[3] *College Hist. Series*: Trinity Hall, p. 141. J. B. Mullinger: *The University of Cambridge*, iii, Appendix E.

[4] C. H. Cooper: *Annals*, iii, 386. In 1645 the Senior Bursar of Trinity entered £139. 10s. 8¼d. for "abatements of rents for taxes by ordinance of Parliament under the hands of Collectors and Tenants, as also the remaynder of rents, to be demanded of Tennants which the Bursar did take upon him at the Audit 1644 as appears in the rentall."

been declared in Trinity from 1644 to 1647, and some of the colleges were reduced to a position of extreme difficulty. In King's it was necessary to suggest economies in the style of living, and a paper was drawn up on December 20, 1644, proposing certain "courses" "that the college may continue together." All "knacks" were to be taken away, and all second dishes "except such as were usuall on Fishdayes, and those onely single, and the Lyngs exchanged for Haberdine." The diet was to be "first and chiefly provided for and the College debts discharged, before any wages, sealing, dirge, lyvery money, or servitors' money be expected," and the Provost expressed his readiness to receive £35 a quarter in lieu of the various payments and allowances due to him, "the rest to abate for the present, and after to receive in proportion with the fellowes as the Colledge shall be able." In 1646 the finances of the college began to recover and some of the junior members of the society appear to have thought that such rigid economy was no longer necessary, since they put forward a paper of "Proposals...for increasing Stipends," dated November 2, 1646. They desired that the officers of the college should pay "all arrearages, viz: wages, sealing, livery, and the rest of that kinde, as alsoe for abatements of commons and bread and beere, or make it appeare, that they have not in their hands sufficient monies to doe it." In any case so much should be paid as the funds could provide, and in the meantime no money should be disbursed "but what is deemed necessary by the company and not on works of ostentation." The uncertainty of the times led them to attack the idea of future provision, and to adopt what at any other period would seem an extremely improvident attitude. They proposed "that there be noe thought entertained or consented unto, that what we have for these 3 years pinched out of our bellies should be stored up, for we know not whom, nor against what time, since its very unreasonable to provide for future debts, and wants, and neglect the present[1]." Such stray extracts illustrate to some extent the financial difficulties and general feeling of insecurity.

In the two previous years, that is to say in 1644 and 1645, it had been found necessary to sell some of the college plate, and £510. 18s. 1d. was received in the course of those years "pro vasis argenteis venditis diversis temporibus[2]." Corpus also were obliged to sell plate in 1648 and 1656 and to consider the advisability of keeping some of their fellowships vacant[3].

Here again, however, as in the case of the number of admissions, the close of the first Civil War generally saw a marked recovery, and under the Commonwealth and Protectorate the state of the colleges was usually prosperous. The price of wheat, which had risen to an average of fifty-nine shillings a quarter in 1648, fluctuated between fifty-four shillings and twenty-one shillings in the ten years between 1650 and 1660, and the college revenues generally returned to the level of the years immediately preceding the war.

Not much is heard of the Universities during the closing years of the Interregnum. On May 21, 1659, the Commons resolved that the Universities should be "so countenanced and reformed, as that they may become the nurseries of piety and learning," and on January 23, 1659/60, they issued a declaration in which they undertook to uphold the public universities and schools of the land[4]. A similar spirit was evinced in a petition to

---

[1] The originals of these papers are amongst the college records.

[2] King's College " Mundum Books."

[3] R. Masters: *Hist. of Corpus*, p. 149. Trinity appears from the Senior Bursar's accounts to have borrowed money in 1646.

[4] C. H. Cooper: *Annals*, iii, 474–5.

Monk on January 30 of the same year by the borough of Leicester, in which a desire was expressed that the true Protestant religion might be defended, and the two Universities preserved[1].

[1] *Cal. of S. P. Dom.* 1659–60, p. 336. See a similar petition from the county of Oxford, *ibid.* p. 361.

CHAPTER V

THE PURITAN VISITATION OF OXFORD UNIVERSITY

To the student of the religious controversies in the first half of the seventeenth century, the history of Oxford during that period has a peculiar interest. In the first place, the state of England generally, with regard to ecclesiastical affairs, was reflected there. The same parties were represented, and the same questions were in dispute. In the second place, the academic isolation of the University enables one to observe those questions separated to some extent from their political setting. Again, as a result of Laud's close connection with it, Oxford had been the centre of the most important religious movement of the time. Not only do we see the Laudian school of thought in the place where perhaps it had the greatest hold, but also we see in full prominence its relation on the one hand to the Puritanism of men like Cheynell and Henry Wilkinson, and on the other to the moderate churchmanship of Abbot and Prideaux.

The same applies, though not quite in the same way or to the same extent, in regard to the history of the Puritan Visitation of the University. As before, there is the partial isolation from political surroundings, and, as a result, a clearer view is obtained of the characteristics of those widely differing types which were all included under the name of Puritan. As before, there is the opportunity of observing a system in working. Perhaps nowhere else had the Presbyterians at first, and Cromwell later, a better opportunity of showing their principles in practice, and in this one of the chief points of interest of the subject may be said to lie.

The state of affairs at Oxford, during Laud's Chancellorship[1], was not unlike that at Cambridge, during the same period, except that the tendencies of the time were more clearly marked. The conflict between the old Protestantism and the new order which Laud was endeavouring to superimpose upon it, found expression in the pulpit, and " what one person delivered this, another would speak to the contrary the next, Sunday. So it was also in disputations and common discourses," writes Wood, " meerly occasioned by the Chancellor's favouring a party in the University, which the generality would strive to oppose and exasperate[2]." Proceedings against preachers for acting in defiance of the King's declaration of 1628, by indulging in a "curious search" on points of doctrinal controversy, are frequent during these years— more frequent, indeed, than at Cambridge, just as the power of Laud's party to carry their way was stronger.

But though, at the end of the period of Charles' personal rule, the "Anti-Arminian" party, as Laud's opponents were sometimes called, was in a state of comparative subjection, opposition was by no means dead, even in Oxford. From outside, of course, attacks began as soon as the Short Parliament was called, and, according to Wood, a report was soon circulated that the University was infected with popery. This arose from the fact that the Mass had been celebrated in the Mitre Inn, which was kept by one Charles Green, a Roman Catholic recusant, but the rumour was of sufficient

---

[1] He was elected in 1629.
[2] A. Wood : *Hist. of Oxford* (ed. Gutch 1796), ii, 382.

importance to cause the Heads to make a formal declaration, in December 1640, that they knew of no one in the University who was that way inclined[1]. The succeeding attack on Episcopacy and on the King's power consolidated the conservative feeling in the University, and probably disposed many to take the royalist side who had been at best lukewarm supporters of Laud's reforms. On April 24, 1641, Convocation, moved by the revolutionary demands of the party of reaction, followed the example of other bodies in sending up a petition in favour of Episcopacy and cathedrals[2], while another was drawn up by the graduates of the University[3]. The former was followed by an " Answer " from the Puritan standpoint, in which the reasons adduced in the petition were attacked, and the abolition of episcopal government shown to be justified by the idleness and corruption of the clergy[4].

Oxford, however, was soon called upon to give more practical expression of its loyalty. Like Cambridge it complied with the King's request for money at the beginning of July, 1642, and like Cambridge it incurred the displeasure of the Parliament for so doing. On July 12, Parliament issued an order forbidding the colleges, under heavy penalties, to pursue the "wicked and unlawfull course" of sending plate or treasure to the king, and directing them to deposit such property in "some safe place, under good security, that it be not employed against the Parliament." At the same time, four Heads of Houses, Fell, Prideaux, Frewen, and Potter, were to be apprehended for their share in the conspiracy, and especial care taken to " hinder and withstand the carrying

[1] A. Wood: *Hist. of Oxford*, ii, 425.
[2] *King's Pamphlets* (Brit. Mus.), E. 156 (22).
[3] A. Wood : *Hist. of Oxford*, ii, 432 ; Rushworth, iv, 270.
[4] *King's Pamphlets*, E. 160 (10).

away of any such plate and treasure[1]." Prompt as the Parliament had been, they yet failed of their object. The colleges had not, indeed, despatched their plate, and probably had not intended to do so, but a "very considerable summe of money" found its way to Beverley, for which the King returned a letter of thanks, dated June 18. The same letter empowered the University authorities to refuse obedience to the Parliamentary order for the arrest of the four Heads[2].

In the next month, the course of events carried the University a step further, for on August 9, Charles proclaimed the Earl of Essex and his officers as traitors, and the Civil War was virtually begun. " Immediately after," says Wood, "the University began to put themselves in a posture of defence[3]," and a corps of volunteers was quickly raised, whose military exercises were performed in and around the city to the admiration of the loyal inhabitants. "Here is every day training of schollars," says a contemporary news-letter, "so that now our schollars have exchanged exercising with their bookes in study, for the practise of their armes in the field[4]."

The corps numbered about five hundred, composed, says Wood, of graduates and undergraduates alike. "There were some divines also, and a Dr of Civil Law of New College named Thomas Read who served with a pike[5]." The writer of the news-letter just quoted, who viewed these proceedings from a hostile standpoint, alleges that the martial front of the volunteers was turned into a panic on the news that the enemy were

---

[1] *Commons' Journals*, ii, 669.

[2] Printed copy of the letter in *King's Pamphlets*, E. 108 (36).

[3] A. Wood : *Hist. of Oxford*, ii, 442.

[4] *True Newes from Oxford*, London, published Aug. 29, 1642. *King's Pamphlets*, E. 114 (31).

[5] A. Wood : *Hist. of Oxford*, ii, 443.

at hand, but the first military force to appear was a small body of some two hundred royalists, under the command of Sir John Byron, who reached Oxford on August 28.

The arrival of royalist troops in the city at once discovered the broad division of opinion between the townsmen and the University. On the one hand, the former received the royalist soldiers sullenly, and complained of their behaviour in seizing provisions and offering violence to those who opposed them. Even some of the University men, according to a contemporary account, were disgusted "insomuch that some of the scholars (as it is reported) that trained for them are now gone to Abington, to combine with those that intend to oppose them[1]." It is probable, however, that the presence of the royalist force caused more embarrassment to the seniors in the University, the Heads of Houses and others, than it did to the more lively spirits in the ranks of the volunteers. It is clear, from the action of the University authorities, during these early days of the war, that, however loyal they might be to the King, they were anxious, as far as possible, to stand apart from the conflict, and not to incur the enmity of the Parliament by a too close identification of themselves with the royal cause. In view of the hostility of the townsmen and the rumour of an attack from the Parliament's forces, they "began to think of some other course[2]," and to desire that Byron's "protection" might be removed. Partly for this reason, and partly because of his own weakness in numbers, Byron accordingly rode out of Oxford on September 10, taking with him about a hundred volunteers from among the members of the University. On the

---

[1] *University Newes, or the unfortunate proceedings of the Cavaliers in Oxford*, London, 1642. *King's Pamphlets*, E. 116 (27).
[2] A. Wood: *Hist. of Oxford*, ii, 448.

next day[1], Dr Pink, Warden of New College and Pro.-Vice-Chancellor, repaired to the Parliamentary force at Aylesbury, to endeavour to arrest the threatened attack, and to represent that the royalist forces were gone. Lord Saye, to whom his mission had been directed, was not present, and he received rough treatment from the officers in command and "was clapt there in hold for being a ring-leader to the Schollers of Oxford in their exercise of armes, and also entertaining the Cavalliers in Oxford," and was sent a prisoner to London[2].

About the same time[3], the Vice-Chancellor addressed a letter to the Earl of Pembroke, who had succeeded Laud as Chancellor in 1641, and was now engaged on the side of the Parliament. The letter prays for the Chancellor's protection against the forces which threaten the University, and goes on to excuse what had taken place. "Sir John Byron," it runs, "with his Regiment of Troopers (who have been a few dayes here without the least dammage or grievance that I know of to any man) we shall (I doubt not) soon prevail withal to withdraw from us, if he may with his safety return back to His Majestie, (who of his own gracious care of us sent him hither)[4]."

But no comfort was forthcoming from this quarter. In his reply, dated September 13, Pembroke wrote : " If you had desired my advice and assistance in time I should willingly have contributed my best endeavours for safety and protection, but your own unadvised Counsells and Actions have reduced you to the streights you are now in, and in discretion you might have foreseen, that the

[1] Wood says on Sept. 9, see *ibid*.

[2] *A True Relation of the late proceedings of the London Dragoneers, sent down to Oxford. King's Pamphlets*, E. 118 (39).   Wood, *ut sup*.

[3] The printed copy of the letter is dated Sept. 12.

[4] Rushworth, Vol. v, p. 11.

admitting of Cavaliers, and Taking up Arms, could not
but make the University a Notorious mark of oppositions
against the Parliament, and therefore to be opposed by
it. If you had contained yourselves within the decent
modest bounds of an University, you might justly have
challenged me, if I had not performed the duty of a
Chancellour." He advised them to dismiss the cavaliers,
surrender the delinquents to the Parliament, and put
themselves "into the right posture of an University[1]."

A detachment of Parliament troops entered Oxford
on September 12, and Lord Saye followed with a larger
force two days later. On the whole, the University
escaped lightly. The barricades and works, which had
been thrown up in the first days of the martial prepara-
tion, were destroyed, and a contemporary version
describes how the improvised defences, which some of the
scholars had devised to retard the progress of the enemy,
were demolished, sometimes with accompanying damage
to the fabric of the colleges[2]. A strict search was made
for arms and ammunition, but the only college plate
which they seized was that belonging to Christ Church
and University, and that apparently only because it had
been hidden. Some "Popish books and pictures" were
burned, and a shot was fired at the image of the Virgin
over St Mary's door, but otherwise little damage appears
to have been done[3].

---

[1] *A letter sent from the Provost Vice-Chancellour of Oxford, to
the Right Honourable, the Earle of Pembrooke and Montgomery,* with
his answer, Sept. 12, 1642. *King's Pamphlets,* E. 116 (38). Printed in
Rushworth, vol. v, p. 13. His failure to protect the University on this
occasion was afterwards one of the charges brought against Pembroke in
October 1643, when the University elected the Marquis of Hertford in his
place. A. Wood: *Hist. of Oxford,* ii, 468–9.

[2] *The Cavallier's Advice to His Majesty,* London, Sept. 16, 1642. *King's
Pamphlets,* E. 117 (15).

[3] *A True Relation of the late proceedings of the London Dragoneers.
King's Pamphlets,* E. 118 (39). *A Perfect Diurnall of the passages of the*

The important question was whether Oxford should be garrisoned for the Parliament. The place was of obvious strategic importance, and the opinion of Lord Saye's supporters was that it should be held. Bulstrode Whitelock was spoken of as commander and there was a promise of a thousand volunteers to be raised in the district. The townsmen, who were generally favourable to the Parliament's cause, "were very forward to engage, so Whitelocke might be governor[1]."

Saye, however, decided not to garrison the city, partly, says Wood, because he thought the King would not, as the Parliamentarians feared, make use of it as his base, and partly through "favour to the University and country." The attitude of the former was the main factor which caused him apprehension. The University men were not strong enough to offer any violent opposition at the moment[2], but their conduct in the past had been unmistakable, and, before he left Oxford, Saye summoned the Heads and endeavoured to extract an assurance from them that they would abstain for the future from acts of hostility towards the Parliament. The Heads expressed their desire that the city might be spared from military occupation by the Parliamentary troops, "since the very name of a garrison would keepe off the Schollers that were gone and drive the rest after[3]." They assured him, says Wood, "that the University was enabled well enough to govern their own body[4]," but a promise of neutrality, even if they gave one, would have been an

Souldiers that are under the command of Lord Say in Oxford. King's Pamphlets, E. 122 (13). Wood: Hist. of Oxford, ii, 450 et seq.

[1] Wood: Hist. of Oxford, ii, 453.

[2] The Parliament troops nevertheless thought it well to take precautions. "All the Dragoneers of Captaine Wilson's Company went armed to Church, because of the enmity they saw in the Towne and Schollers." A True Relation. King's Pamphlets, E. 118 (39).

[3] A Perfect Diurnall. King's Pamphlets, E. 122 (13)

[4] A. Wood: Hist. of Oxford, ii, 453.

empty formality, as they must have known and as events proved.

The bulk of the Parliamentary troops departed on September 28, but soldiers were constantly pouring through Oxford during the following month, and after the battle of Edgehill, on October 23, a sudden change was given to the aspect of affairs in the city by the arrival of the royalist army. In another month, Oxford became the King's permanent headquarters, and although the actual siege did not begin until May 1645, it continued to be the centre of the royalist cause from that time forward to its surrender on June 24, 1646.

The details of that period belong rather to the military and political history of the time ; and its effect on the University can be soon summarised. The academic life was, of course, practically suspended. Schools were turned into arsenals, and colleges into quarters for the personnel of the Court[1], and while scholars performed the soldiers' functions, soldiers occupied the scholars' rooms, and even proceeded to degrees by mandate from the King. The latter practice, indeed, became so common that, on a petition from the University representing its dangerous consequences, Charles gave order that it should cease. A large number of the members of the colleges naturally volunteered for service in the army and out of a hundred students of Christ Church, twenty are said to have been officers in the King's service[2], but all able-bodied male inhabitants were expected to take their share in working on the defences, and the colleges were called upon, not only for service, but for money. Early in January 1643, the mint was transferred from

---

[1] Mr H. W. C. Davis in his history of Balliol (*Oxford College Hist. Series*) gives an amusing account of the disorganisation which attended the advent of the ladies and gentlemen of the Court to academic surroundings.

[2] A. Wood : *Hist. of Oxford*, ii, 478.

Shrewsbury to Oxford and established at New Inn Hall, and on January 10, a royal order was published requiring the colleges to bring in their plate, an order which was, of course, obeyed. Promise of repayment at a fixed rate was made, but it is hardly necessary to say that it was never fulfilled, and the colleges were forced to be content with formal receipts to be preserved as testimony to their loyal conduct[1].

Loyally as the colleges supported the King, their generosity cannot be regarded as entirely spontaneous, and it is probable that the University authorities would gladly have escaped the honour of having the royal headquarters in their midst. Naturally, the colleges suffered in point of material prosperity, even more heavily than those of the sister University during the course of the first Civil War. Revenues fell generally, and at All Souls in September 1645 it was found necessary to decree "that there should be but one meal a day between this and next Christmas, and longer if there shall be occasion[2]." Admissions literally ceased in some colleges, and the number of graduations in the whole University sank to fifty[3]. When Oxford was surrendered to Fairfax, little more than the semblance of a University remained.

Under these circumstances it was inevitable that some reorganisation should be attempted. It was inevitable also that the reorganisation should not be left to the University, but should be carried out by the party which had seized upon the government of the country.

The Parliamentary leaders, much as the more enlightened amongst them might wish to restore the

[1] A list of the college contributions of plate is printed from the Tanner MSS. in Gutch's *Collectanea Curiosa*.
[2] *College Hist. Series*, All Souls, p. 120.
[3] *College Hist. Series*, Wadham, pp. 55–6. There were no admissions in Wadham in 1645. In Trinity, admissions fell from an average of twenty-five to three in 1643, and ceased in 1644–5. *College Hist. Series*, Trinity, p. 130.

efficient working of the University, were not prepared to content themselves with a mere restoration. Oxford had not only been the headquarters of the royalist cause, it had also been the centre of that new school of religious thought which had, in the estimation of many, been a chief, if an indirect, cause of the war. Besides uprooting the seeds of political disaffection, therefore, the Parliament was concerned to attempt a thorough reformation of the religious life of the University, and a complete overthrow of that Laudian *régime* which had been in full working at the outbreak of the war. But though the political and religious motives were thus closely connected, it is important that they should not be confused with one another. It was inevitable from the nature of the case that much of the reforming policy of the Visitors, even when directed to religious ends, should assume a political aspect, but it is nevertheless true that they desired to further what they believed to be the proper form of worship in the University.

It has been the custom among a certain number of royalist writers to represent the surrender of this great stronghold of the King's army as premature and unnecessary, but the criticism is unwarranted. Sir Thomas Glemham, the Governor, would no doubt have maintained a longer resistance had it not been for the apparent hopelessness of the cause and the importunities of the royalist ladies and gentlemen resident within the walls who, says Clarendon, "bore any kind of alarum very ill[1]," but the official narrative in the Clarendon MSS. states that, when the surrender was made, there were only provisions for twelve days and not enough powder to resist a storm[2]. In any case, the fall of the city was inevitable, and it is not clear that the King's cause would have been materially

---

[1] Clarendon : *History of the Rebellion* (ed. Macray), iii, 25.
[2] S. R. Gardiner : *Civil War*, iii, 109.

furthered by so short a postponement as would have been possible, while the interests of humanity were served and better terms secured by its taking place when it did.

In spite of Fairfax's avowed wish to soften the lot of the vanquished[1], the condition of the conquered city after the entrance of the Parliamentary army presented an unhappy picture. Among Fairfax's soldiers there were many of those rough religious fanatics who were the special object of detestation to the royalist churchman. Many of these, if we are to credit Wood's account, invaded the pulpits and public schools and poured forth unchecked their attacks on "human learning[2]."

The fate of the University had been provided for in the Treaty of Surrender. The "ancient form of government" was secured to its members "subordinate to the immediate authority and power of Parliament," and that authority and power were at once put in force. Beyond this, the fabric of the colleges was preserved from spoil, and an indemnity from "sequestration, fines, taxes, and all other molestations" was granted for "anything relating to this present war or to the unhappy differences between his Majesty and the Parliament." At the end of the article was inserted a proviso that the foregoing should not extend to "any reformation there intended by the Parliament," nor give the University liberty "to intermeddle in the government[3]."

It will be necessary to revert to these terms later in connection with the powers of the Visitors. For the present it is enough to point out that, while the just rights of the University were apparently safe-guarded, the vague wording of the final proviso left the Parliament

---

[1] Burrows : *Register of the Visitors of the Univ. of Oxford* (Camden Soc.), lv.
[2] A. Wood : *Hist. of Oxford*, ii, 488.
[3] Burrows : *Register of the Visitors*, lvi.

complete latitude in any reforms which they might see fit to enforce.

But though the intended reformation was foreshadowed in the Treaty of Surrender of June 24, 1646, the actual Visitation was not ordered until nearly a year afterwards, that is to say on May 1, 1647. The interval was partly occupied with an attempt to prepare the way for the contemplated reformation by the appointment of seven Presbyterian Divines whose sermons were intended to dispose the University to a "reconciliation with the Parliament and their proceedings[1]."

That the Parliament should have hoped for any favourable result from such a course, shows that they had underestimated the difficulty of the task that was before them. Far from reducing the hostile portion of the University to a better temper, the ministrations of these seven Divines probably did much to inflame its resentment, and it is in this light that later royalist writers seem to have viewed the undertaking. Wood thus trenchantly sums up the characteristics of the Preachers : "Cornish and Langley, two fooles : Reynolds and Harrys, two knaves : Cheynell and rabbi Wilkinson, two madmen[2]." They were not, however, such contemptible characters as this summary suggests. Robert Harris, afterwards appointed President of Trinity by the Parliament, Henry Wilkinson, afterwards made Head of Magdalen Hall by the same authority, and Francis Cheynell were Puritans of the violent and bigoted type, but were not devoid of ability. Edward Reynolds and Edward Corbet, on the other hand, were men of a more moderate school, who had been forced into active opposition by Laud's reforms. The former was to be the first Vice-Chancellor under the Puritan rule, an office which

---

[1] Walker : *Sufferings of the Clergy*, Pt. i, 125.
[2] A. Clark : *The Life and Times of Anthony Wood*, i, 131.

he lost owing to his refusal to accept the Engagement. His inclinations were towards the Presbyterian form of government, but he conformed after the Restoration, and ultimately became Bishop of Norwich. Corbet found his position at Oxford "little to his liking," and though he was appointed a Visitor, he rarely appeared in that capacity[1]. Henry Cornish and Henry Langley, one afterwards appointed Canon of Christ Church, and the other Master of Pembroke, do not come to the front in the subsequent history of the University, and not much is known of them.

From the first the work of the Presbyterian Divines was complicated by the interference of other and unofficial preachers of the "Independent Principle." Foremost among these was William Erbury, a regimental chaplain in the Parliament's army[2] who took upon himself to enter the lists in opposition to the Presbyterians.

Erbury's discourses were delivered in a meeting-house opposite Merton, while the official Preachers held their sessions "in an house in S. Peter's parish in the East, in the house on the west side of the Inn called the Saracen's Head vulgarly called the 'Scruple House,' or 'Scruple Office,' to which all doubting brethren had liberty to repair for resolution and easement of their hardned consciences[3]." The conflict began by Erbury invading the citadel of his opponents, in company with a band of his soldier supporters, and openly denying their right to be considered true ministers of Christ. A public disputation or conference was agreed upon, and was accordingly held, before a numerous audience of

[1] See the accounts of these five Preachers in the *Dictionary of National Biography*.

[2] Erbury had been educated at Brasenose, had been ordained, but had been deprived of his living in Wales on account of his heterodox views. See the account of him in the *Dictionary of National Biography*.

[3] A. Wood : *Hist. of Oxford*, ii, 491.

University men and others, on November 12 and 19. His attacks were somewhat embarrassing to the Presbyterian Divines who, according to one account written from a royalist point of view, were worsted in the encounter and failed to prove that they had their "commission from God[1]." Erbury, at all events, was satisfied of his victory, and consented to a further disputation, which took place in the University Church on January 11, 1646/7. On this occasion the discussion was concerned with the dogmas of the Christian faith, and Francis Cheynell was the champion on the opposite side.

Erbury's own religious views are difficult to fathom. His opinions were undoubtedly tinged with mysticism, but at times they seem to amount to a denial of the divinity of Christ. At this period, he would have described himself as a "seeker," and his confession of faith, as expressed at the conference, besides numerous other religious pieces, are available for those who are curious to read them[2].

On the other hand the Preachers also claimed to have prevailed, and in their official report to the Parliament on March 26, 1647, they express satisfaction with what they had accomplished.

"They found the University and City much corrupted," they wrote, "and divers hopefull men in both, very much unsetled; they perceived that it was not possible to instruct, convince, reforme, and settle even ingenuous men, unlesse there were some private exercise allowed in which they might have some friendly

---

[1] *A Publicke Conference betwixt the Six Presbyterian Ministers and Some Independent Commanders. King's Pamphlets*, E. 363 (4). *A True Relation of the late Conference. Ibid.* E. 363 (6).

[2] *Nor Truth, nor Errour, Nor Day, nor Night; But in the Evening There shall be Light. Being the relation of a Publicke Discourse in Maries Church at Oxford.* London, 1647.

conference[1]." Their object was "to nourish, continue, and increase communion between the Saints, that there might be a spirituall and happy exchange of gifts, graces and experiments between Ministers and strong Christians, that both might be better enabled to bear the heaviest burthens and the manifold infirmities of weak Christians[2]."

"The Ministers saw it necessary to lay downe the first principles of the doctrine of Christ, namely the foundation of repentance from dead works, and faith towards God, and accordingly they did clearly explain the doctrins of Justification and Regeneration, they did set open the treasures of the covenant of Grace, and shew unto the people by what means they might get an interest in Christ[3]."

"The success of our Christian conferences," they continue, "whether more private or publique, was undeniably great....Divers Scholars, and some of them Fellows of Houses, did blesse God that ever they saw those Ministers in Oxford....Mr Earbury was (as we are assured) much offended, whether because his Auditory decreased, as his errors were refuted, we shall not now examine, and he stirred up the spirit of the Parliament Soldiers against the Ministers[4]." A tedious account of the disputation with Erbury follows, too long even to epitomise.

"We shall not stand to make generall observations upon all Mr Earbury's dictates," the Divines conclude, "but the designe is evident, the Magistracy and Ministry of this Kingdome are both aimed at[5]."

[1] *An account given to the Parliament by the Ministers sent by them to Oxford. King's Pamphlets*, E. 382 (1), p. 3.

[2] *Ibid.* p. 6.   [3] *Ibid.* p. 4.   [4] *Ibid.* p. 12-13.

[5] *Ibid.* p. 50.   For another account see *Truth triumphing over Errour and Heresie. Or a relation of a Publick Disputation at Oxford. King's Pamphlets*, E. 371 (7).

In the end, however, the Divines had found it necessary to have Erbury removed from Oxford by the authority of Fairfax, and from a wider point of view it may be doubted whether the effect of their work had been as favourable as they imagined. Their contest with the Independents had excited ridicule amongst the Royalists, and their ministrations had not tended to conciliate opposition or to dispose the University to bow to the authority of Parliament. Nothing had been gained by the postponement; and something more than time had been lost.

At last, on May 1, 1647, an ordinance was passed appointing Visitors and investing them with power[1].

The Visitation of Oxford University was conducted by three separate boards of Visitors[2]. The first, appointed on May 1, 1647, was Presbyterian in character, though it included men of very diverse types and opinions. Reynolds, as the first Vice-Chancellor appointed by the Parliament, was practically the head of it. The second board was appointed in June 1652, but was more or less temporary. It included Goodwin and Owen as its leading members, and its prevailing tone was Independent, although Conant probably exerted a certain influence in the way of moderation. The third and last board was appointed in January 1653/4 and contained members from both parties. Goodwin, again, was the nominal head, though Conant, especially after he became Vice-Chancellor, was the virtual leader. The last two boards were, of course, appointed under the direct influence of Cromwell, who had succeeded the Earl of Pembroke as Chancellor of

---

[1] *Acts and Ordinances of the Interregnum* (Ed. C. H. Firth and R. S. Rait), i. 925.

[2] Walker, who had himself never seen the Register, fails to distinguish between the three boards in his account of the Visitation. See *Sufferings of the Clergy*, Pt. i, 122–144.

the University, and possibly for this reason the presence of the more bigoted Independents was counteracted by a leaven of broad-minded men. Taking the years 1647 to 1660 as a whole, the tendency was, says Professor Burrows, for the University to fall under the moderate section of the Presbyterians[1].

The first board consisted of twenty-four members, of whom fourteen were laymen and ten clergymen. Five were to form a quorum, and it was but rarely that a greater number took part in the business. The work was, in fact, soon left to the clerical element in the committee, although Sir Nathaniel Brent, the Warden of Merton, had been elected chairman. This fact, besides being calculated to excite particular resentment, was open to a valid objection at the hands of the University. In October 1641 the Parliament had passed an act prohibiting any person in orders from exercising any temporal authority by virtue of any commission[2], and this enactment was very naturally cited as a bar to the presence of clergymen amongst the Visitors. The objection, of course, was not insuperable at a time when the entire constitution of the country was about to undergo a process of change, but it added to the difficulty of the Visitors' position.

The powers conferred upon the Visitors should be considered by the side of the Treaty of Surrender. It has already been remarked that the studied vagueness of the terms contained in the latter document gave ample scope for radical reform, and therefore there was nothing contrary to the Treaty in authorising the Visitors to inquire upon oath "concerning those that neglect to take the Solemn League and Covenant and the Negative Oath," or "oppose the execution of the ordinances of Parliament

[1] Burrows: *Register of the Visitors*, p. xxxii.
[2] *Commons' Journals*, ii, 293.

concerning the Discipline and Directory." The strict
enforcement of the Presbyterian form of worship had
been the policy followed by the Parliament throughout
the country, and Oxford had no reason to expect to
escape it. Similarly, the interference with University
and college statutes and with elections to college offices
and fellowships could be justified by reference to the
saving clause in the Treaty. On the other hand, in
ordering an inquiry to be made concerning those who
had taken up arms against the Parliament, it is doubtful
whether the Government was acting within the provisions
of the terms of surrender. Professor Burrows, indeed,
explains that "these persons...had not been specified in
the exemptions mentioned in the Treaty of Surrender,
because all such persons had been *ipso facto* expelled and
granted a safe-conduct out of the city at its capture[1],"
and this is no doubt true if the intentions of the Parliament extended only to those who were literally in arms
against them. But that a wider application was contemplated is suggested by a supplementary ordinance of
September 24, wherein the Visitors were empowered to
inquire, not only concerning those who had been in arms,
but also concerning those who had been in any way
concerned in the war, either in their own person or by
their advice[2]. It is hardly possible to suppose that this
additional power referred only to actions subsequent to
the surrender, but if this is not the case, then it was
undoubtedly in contravention of the indemnity clause of
the Treaty, by which members of the University were
guaranteed against sequestration and "all other molestation" in respect of anything connected with the war or
the "unhappy differences" with the King. It might, of
course, be urged on the other side, that, in view of the
unexpected opposition with which it had to deal, the

[1] Burrows : *Register of the Visitors*, p. lxii.   [2] *Ibid.* p. lxv.

interests of the Visitation demanded more stringent measures than had at first been deemed necessary, and therefore the indemnity clause as hindering the reformation "intended by the Parliament" could legitimately be set aside, but, if each specific condition made in the University's favour could be nullified by one vague proviso, the practical value of the Treaty was very small. The exigencies of the case demanded a certain elasticity in the conditions, but, even when allowance has been made for this, the fact remains that the advantages actually obtained by the University bear no very distinct resemblance to those outlined in the Treaty.

Parliament, at any rate, was determined on carrying through the work which lay before it. Just as, at an earlier date, the county sequestration committees had been urged to activity, so now the London Committee which was entrusted with the regulation of the University, in conferring these ample powers upon the Visitors, expressed the hope that they would "act vigorously[1]."

This was in September 1647, and from this time onward the work of the Visitors continued more or less unchecked. The actual inauguration of their sittings had taken place in the previous May, but it had been made inauspiciously. In the first place, a mutiny of the garrison had alarmed the Visitors and delayed their arrival in Oxford[2], and, in the second place, their first engagement with the University authorities resulted in a moral victory for the latter.

The Visitors had fixed upon June 4 for a Convocation to take place. The members of the University assembled in obedience to the citation, but the Visitors were detained by a long sermon in the University Church, and at the hour appointed by them for the meeting had

[1] Burrows: *Register of the Visitors*, p. lxvi.
[2] S. R. Gardiner: *Civil War*, iii, 314.

not yet put in an appearance. Taking advantage of their unpunctuality, the Vice-Chancellor, Dr Fell, dissolved the Convocation and dismissed the members before the Visitors had arrived[1].

About the same time, the University passed a series of resolutions stating their own position with regard to the Visitation. This work, entitled the "Judgment of the University," had been drawn up by Robert Sanderson, afterwards Bishop of Lincoln, and Dr Zouch. The case for the University was well and moderately defined and their reasons for refusing the demands of the Visitors clearly stated[2].

So far the Visitors had not appeared to great advantage. Their authority had been openly flouted and no headway had been made. For the four following months nothing further was done, but this was not due to a sense of defeat[3]. More weighty causes in the political affairs of the Kingdom at large were at work to hinder their progress[4]. On June 4 the King had been seized at Holmby House, and the chief interest of the nation became centred in the possibility of a compromise. When, at length, Parliament was enabled to turn its attention to Oxford, they saw that, if the Visitors were to proceed with their work, they must be invested with larger powers. The result was the passing of the additional ordinances of September mentioned above.

Reinforced by their new powers and urged on to "vigorous" action by the London Committee, the Visitors at once set about clearing the University of those who would not submit to the new *régime*. For this purpose

---

[1] The incident is described in *A letter from a Scholar at Oxford to his friend in the Country*. Pr. 1647.

[2] Burrows: *Register of the Visitors*, p. lxiv. The "reasons" were repudiated in a petition from the Puritan members of the University.

[3] Walker: *Sufferings of the Clergy*, Pt. i, 128.

[4] Burrows: *Register of the Visitors*, p. lxv.

they sat daily to receive "informations," and, to further expedite matters, appointed forty-three delegates to report upon the members of the respective colleges.

These "spies and informers," Walker says, could be "none but persons of the basest spirits" since no others would have engaged themselves in "so vile a service," and inasmuch as they were afterwards rewarded "with the fellowships of such as were ejected," some light may be thrown on the "characters of those who succeeded the loyalists[1]."

The assertion that the delegates undertook the work with a view to succeeding to the places of those whom they were instrumental in expelling is not, however, supported by the facts. Of the forty-three delegates, thirty-four were members of colleges, and nine of halls. Of the thirty-four members of colleges, only eleven were not already fellows ; so that the charge can only justly be applicable to twenty, or less than half of the total number. As a matter of fact, fifteen of these did afterwards obtain fellowships[2]. But the general purpose and character of the delegates does not seem to justify the term "spies." They were intended to act with regard to the individual colleges as the Visitors themselves acted with regard to the University as a whole, that is to say, to see that the conditions demanded by Parliament were fulfilled. In any case, the method afterwards pursued by the Visitors in demanding a submission from each individual, rendered the service of informers unnecessary. There is no real resemblance between these agents and the informers engaged by the county committees[3]. We find little trace in the Visitors' Register of citation for

---

[1] Walker : *Sufferings of the Clergy*, Pt. i, 129.

[2] These facts about the delegates can be traced in Professor Burrows' edition of the Register.

[3] See *ante*, pp. 67–8.

specific offences[1], as a result of information, which is the
characteristic of the proceedings of the sequestration
committees, nor, on the whole, would the character of
the delegates have been consistent with such work.
Two or three of them do not seem to have been more
than luke-warm supporters of the party who appointed
them, and several more, such as Conant, who was
afterwards Vice-Chancellor, and Robert Crosse, were
men of some eminence. On the other hand, it is certain
that spies and informers existed under the rule of the
Visitors, and it is likely enough that there were place-
hunters among the delegates.

The summonses which the Visitors now began to
issue to the Heads of Houses and others drew from the
University further protestations of their inability to
recognise the legality of the Visitation. To settle the
question finally the London Committee found it necessary,
in November, to summon the recalcitrant members before
them to be rated for their obstinacy by the Chancellor,
the Earl of Pembroke. Some of the more violent
members of the committee were in favour of summary
methods, and the Earl of Manchester's proceedings at
Cambridge were cited as an example. Sir Henry
Mildmay gave it as his opinion "that had they at first
took the same course with the University of Oxford which
an honourable person there present...did with Cambridge,
Oxford by this time had been in a good condition as

[1] There are, indeed, some instances. See, for example, the case of
Henry Tozer, sub-rector of Exeter, in Burrows' *Register of the Visitors*, p. 13,
and Walker, *Sufferings of the Clergy*, Pt. i, 131. A further instance is found
in the case of John Greaves of Merton. In this case, another fellow of the
college, John French, seems to have claimed the honour of having procured
Greaves' expulsion, for a return on p. 282 of the Register (Burrows' edition)
states in answer to "the humble petition of Mr John French" that Mr Greaves
"was not put out of his fellowship...by any articles or voluntary information
exhibited against him by Mr French."

her sister[1]." It was principally through the intervention of Selden that a legal hearing, with the advantage of counsel to assist them, was granted[2]. Several well-known Parliamentarians besides Selden took the part of the University, but the issue was a foregone conclusion, and the denial of the Parliamentary authority was decided to be "high contempt." Following upon this, several of the chief University authorities were formally deposed, but inasmuch as the orders of the committee were still disregarded, the situation remained practically unchanged. It was not until February 18 that the committee took the step of appointing its own nominees to the offices which they had declared to be vacant.

The solemn entrance of the detested Chancellor into Oxford for the purpose of installing the new officials was a signal for the effusion of much derision and bitter satire from the local royalist pamphleteers[3]. No doubt there was little to command respect in the person of the Chancellor or in his manner of proceeding, but his visit was at least effective from the point of view of the Visitors. After his departure in April 1648, they at once began a wholesale citation, not only of Heads of Houses, but of the whole body of the University also, with a view to the summary ejection of those who refused to submit to their authority. Yet the decision of each individual case was not so simple as it would appear, for it was found that the direct question : " Do you submit to the authority of Parliament in this present Visitation?" was capable of many indirect forms of reply.

As early as November, 1647, the Delegates of the University had held a meeting in Hart Hall for the

---

[1] A. Wood : *Hist. of Oxford*, iii, 543.

[2] Burrows : *Register of the Visitors*, p. lxxi.

[3] See for example *Lord have mercy upon us, or the Visitation at Oxford;* *Pegasus or the Flying Horse from Oxford*, by Thomas Barlow; and *Halifax Law translated to Oxford*, etc.

purpose of drawing up a paper of "directions," so that
"whosoever was called before the Commissioners might
know how to answer." One of the most striking of these
directions was that the examinee should "be sure to
answer to no question positively yea or no," but should
gain time by questioning the commissioners' authority,
or by referring to the official answers given by the University[1]. This procedure was not merely due to vexatious
obstruction, but was justified by the fact that the character
of the Visitors' authority was absolutely unknown to the
University and college statutes. Royalists were, no
doubt, ready to make use of the dilemma, but the dilemma
itself was a real one. "'Tis apparent to us," runs a
published letter of the period, "that as the state of things
now stands, we have an easie, tho' unhappy choice
proposed to us, viz. : Whether we will prefer the preservation of our Estates, or of our Soules by admitting perjury
or ruine[2]."

The evasive replies which the members of the colleges,
acting in accordance with the "directions," returned
caused the Visitors some embarrassment, but on referring
for guidance to the London Committee they were instructed
that the following forms of answers were to be treated as
no submission : "Profession of ignorance," "referring to
the answer of their several Houses," "saying that they
cannot, dare not, or do not, submit without giving a
reason," and "submitting to the authority of the King
and two houses of Parliament[3]." Many, of course,
scorned to elude the consequences of a flat denial, but it
does not seem that those who gave the bravest answers
were always the steadiest to their principles.

---

[1] A. Wood : *Hist. of Oxford*, iii, 532.

[2] *The case of the University of Oxford...in a letter sent from thence to Mr Selden*. Published May 18, 1648. *King's Pamphlets*, E. 443 (19).

[3] Burrows : *Register of the Visitors*, p. lxxxv.

The six instances of bold replies which Walker quotes[1] are at all events unhappily chosen. " Jo. Pistwich " (probably a mistake for Prestwich), Carrick and Whitehall all afterwards submitted, and the answers attributed to the first two are not those which are given in the Register. The answer of "the young gentleman of Trinity College" does not appear. Possibly he gave the common reply that he would submit if the Visitors could show a commission from the King. Such tactics, however, did not have the effect of averting the fate of those who employed them, unless they were followed by a full submission, and the sufferers had to content themselves with the thought that they had at least been true to the principles of their cause. "Howsoever we may suffer for it," runs a contemporary letter, "I believe what we have done will be of some use and advantage to ye King's whole businesse. Whereas if we had submitted to them as Visitors being made so by ye 2 houses without ye King, we had as much as in us lies decided ye maine question in favour of them against his Majestie[2]."

The fate of such comparatively unknown persons as those just mentioned is less interesting than that of the leading men in the University, the Heads of Houses and the Professors. Here also a tolerably clean sweep was made, but a few survived[3]. Besides Hood[4], the Rector of Lincoln, and Langbaine, the Provost of Queen's, who, according to Walker, were the only Heads spared by the Visitors, four others, Laurence of Balliol, Hakewill of

[1] Walker : *Sufferings of the Clergy*, Pt. i, 136.
[2] Clarendon Papers (Bodleian) 2636.
[3] *Ibid.*
[4] See passage in a letter from Dr Payne to Sheldon, Feb. 4, 1649/50, " I suppose you have heard...that Dr Hood, though articled against by some of his own fellows, is yet in possession, the business being referred to the Oxford visitors, who are his friends." Quoted in *Theologian and Ecclesiastic*, vi, 167–8.

Exeter, Saunders of Oriel[1] and Sir Nathaniel Brent of Merton submitted sooner or later and retained their places, though the last-named, as himself a Visitor, need hardly be reckoned. Of the Professors and Readers, thirteen were displaced and three submitted. "If this world goe on," says a contemporary tract, "'twill bee a shame to bee out of prison or in a Fellowship[2]."

Both in the general account of the Visitation in Part I of his book, as well as in a long note appended to the "Oxford List" in Part II, Walker gives a considerable amount of attention to the question of the numbers of those who were ejected. Statistics of this kind are always liable to be deceptive, and in this case, where no certainty can be attained and much must necessarily be left to conjecture, little help is to be derived from them. Still, it may be worth while to compare Walker's computation with the lists given at the end of Professor Burrows' edition of the Register.

The impossibility of drawing up an exact list is at once frankly admitted by Walker, and Professsor Burrows, though able to attain greater accuracy, has still to be content with more or less approximate figures. The actual list in Part II of Walker's book contains 573 names, but about 250 of these Walker admits, either explicitly or implicitly, to be doubtful, so that we may take the number of certain expulsions, as given by him, to be roughly 320. The figure which elsewhere in his book he himself accepts as probable is 400, and he arrives at this in the following way[3]. The total number of those ejected, as given by Wood, and in the Register and in a tract

---

[1] In the case of Saunders, Walker followed the original Latin edition of Wood's *History of Oxford*, which did not mention that Saunders was afterwards reinstated. This mistake was rectified in Gutch's translated edition (iii, 588).

[2] *Pegasus or the Flying Horse from Oxford*, p. 6.

[3] See Walker: *Sufferings of the Clergy*, Pt. ii, 138.

entitled *Oxonii Lachrymae*, he takes to be roughly 640, but as he was only concerned with those on the foundations, he makes a reduction of a fifth for commoners, which brings the total to about 500. A further reduction of 125 is then made on account of those who subsequently submitted and either retained or were restored to their places. The total of 375 thus arrived at he then proceeds to check from another source, that is to say from the number of elections to the foundations. The number given in the Register is 396, and practically all of these, Walker thinks, were made to vacancies caused by expulsion. He makes a reduction of 40, however, for the few cases in which the election was made to a vacancy caused "regularly" by death or resignation. But, inasmuch as the power to make their own elections was, after a certain time, restored to the colleges, the Register would only include the elections made before such power was restored and not the total number. In view of this, he feels himself justified in adding an extra fifty, so as to bring the total up again to about 400.

In the Introduction to his edition of the Register, Professor Burrows accepts this figure as the most satisfactory that it is possible to obtain[1], but in the explanatory preface to the index of names he sees reason to reconsider this[2]. He shows that the "total number of expulsions... falls below this figure," and that a large proportion even of this reduced total were not on the foundation. In his general summary[3] of the number of expulsions and submissions, he divides the names that appear in the index into four classes, the first composed of those who were certainly expelled, not only for non-submission but for any cause, whether connected with the Visitation or

[1] Burrows : *Register of the Visitors*, p. xc.
[2] *Ibid.* p. 470.
[3] *Ibid.* p. 571.

not, the second of those whose expulsion is doubtful, the third of those who certainly submitted, either at once or ultimately, and the fourth of the cases in which there is a strong probability of expulsion. The numbers in each class are founded on a careful examination of the Register and a comparison of the various lists of expulsions and submissions.

According to this classification, 374 certain cases of expulsion appear and 141 doubtful cases, but this includes commoners, which Walker's computation did not profess to do. On the whole, therefore, if we disregard the doubtful cases in both accounts, Walker's 320 does not appear very extravagant beside the 374 of Professor Burrows, even though the latter contains a considerable proportion of commoners and a certain number of cases in which the expulsion was the result of irregularity or misdemeanour unconnected with the particular work of the Visitors.

The bold front which the University offered at first in refusing to acknowledge the authority of the Visitors was not, as we have seen, maintained to the end, and many of those who had begun with defiance finished with submission. Walker states that out of 676 who appeared at the first summons only 128, including college servants, did not deny the Visitors' authority[1], while in nine colleges only fourteen fellows submitted. He admits that some who had stood out at first afterwards submitted, but of these, he says, there were "comparatively few." If taken by itself, this last statement might be misleading, but elsewhere in the course of his attempt to arrive at a fair estimate of the number of ejections, Walker allows that 125, not including commoners, may have ultimately withdrawn their opposition and retained their places[2], and

---

[1] Walker: *Sufferings of the Clergy*, Pt. i, 135, note.
[2] *Ibid.* Pt. ii, 138.

this figure again is not very far from that to be obtained from Burrows' list.

According to the latter authority about 150 of those who, from first to last, tendered their submissions had been on the foundations of their respective colleges before the appointment of the Visitors, while the total number of those who undoubtedly submitted, exclusive of servants, amounted to 301, besides 103 from the various halls[1].

It will have been seen from the foregoing remarks that Walker's estimates do not always tally with one another. The 400 ejections reckoned up in the note appended to the Oxford list does not bear any very close relation to the figures revealed by the list itself; the "comparatively few" submissions mentioned on page 135 of Part I does not coincide with the 125 submissions which he concedes elsewhere. In view of the fact that he very properly does not pretend to give more than approximate figures, these discrepancies are matters of very slight importance, and merely have the effect of obscuring his real opinion. When, however, his various statements are brought into relation with one another, they do not appear to be very excessive. The general effect of the examination of Walker's figures and a comparison with Professor Burrows' lists is to show that there were fewer expulsions and more submissions than has been represented.

The sequestrations were, of course, spread over a considerable period, but nearly all of them took place under the first board of Visitors and before the year 1652. The next matter that must claim attention is the general character of the men who filled the vacant places.

The first care of the Visitors, Walker tells us, was to

---

[1] The halls were essentially Puritan in tone, see Burrows, *Register of the Visitors*, p. xxv.

provide for themselves and for those who had been associated with them in the work of purging the University. Then, quoting *Dr Allestry's Life*, he states that the places of the ejected Royalists were filled by "an illiterate rabble, swept up from the plough tail, from shops, and grammar schools, and the dreggs of the Neighbour University[1]," while the "sacred rewards and titles of learning," that is to say the honours and degrees, were "prostituted" to the "lust and ambition of everyone who was distinguish'd by ignorance, enthusiasm, treason and rebellion[2]." He admits, indeed, that the Visitors appointed a standing committee to examine the candidates from Cambridge and elsewhere, but this examination he clearly regards as a mere formality, since later on he suggests, on Wood's authority, that the Visitors were open to corruption[3].

It was almost inevitable that, in order to fill the vacant places in the colleges and in the University, recourse should sometimes be had to methods of which the honesty, as well as the expediency, was at least doubtful. That certain of the Visitors and of those who had assisted them in their work should, in some cases, have taken the places of those whom they had expelled, was clearly in defiance of a natural conception of justice, and laid them open to the application of the maxim that "it is only the hangman's fee to have the dead-man's clothes." It is unlikely that the action of the Visitors was influenced to any appreciable extent by this fact, since the wholesale expulsions which took place were to a great extent due to outside causes, but such a tribunal should have been composed of those to whom no charge of selfish motive could apply.

[1] Walker: *Sufferings of the Clergy*, Pt. i, 140.
[2] *Ibid.* Pt. i, 141.   [3] *Ibid.* Pt. i, 139.

There is also some truth in the assertion that preferment was given as a reward for past service in the Parliamentary cause. Successful soldiers, such as Jerome Zanchy, who received a fellowship at All Souls, formed a somewhat incongruous element in the reformed University, while an unnecessary amount of offence was given by the lavish grants of honorary degrees to those who had been closely connected with the King's overthrow and death. There is evidence, too, that interest could sometimes be made in the case of sons of distressed Parliamentarians. Thus, on October 23, 1648, we find the London Committee making a recommendation to the Visitors on behalf of Sir Robert King, in consideration of his "sufferings and services," with a view to obtaining the next vacant fellowship at All Souls for his son. And again, on the same date, a recommendation for a student's place in Christ Church is made in the case of a son of "Mr Vincent Cupper, whoe hath eight children, and suffered much for the Parliament[1]."

The character of the delegates or "informers" as possible candidates for preferment has already been discussed. Another class who, according to Walker, took an important part in the scramble for the vacant places was "a tribe of ignorant enthusiasts and schismatics" from Cambridge, not regular members of that University, but a "colony of Presbyterian or Independent novices," who had betaken themselves thither "after it had been reformed into confusion[2]."

How many there were of these Cambridge immigrants it is impossible to say with any degree of certainty. In a list of "Persons appointed by the Visitors or elected under their sanction" which Professor Burrows appends to his edition of the Register, the names of sixty-four

---

[1] Burrows' *Register of the Visitors*, p. 206.
[2] Walker: *Sufferings of the Clergy*, Pt. i, 139–40.

Cambridge men appear, but there may have been others whom it has not been possible to identify. The greater number of these are unknown to fame, but the list includes such men as John Wallis, a celebrated mathematician who became Savilian Professor of Geometry, Nathaniel Sterry who was made Dean of Bocking after the Restoration, Stephen Charnocke, a well-known author, and Seth Ward, afterwards successively Bishop of Exeter and of Salisbury.

Something may be learnt concerning the general character of the "intruders" from the regulations which controlled the admissions. On July 5, 1648, a committee was appointed for the express purpose of examining candidates for fellowships, scholarships, or other places in the University. The names of its members are given in the order of the above date, and it was, says Professor Burrows, "a very competent Committee[1]." Probably a great part of this "examination" was concerned with the religious views of the candidates, for this was a point on which the Visitors always showed themselves to be exacting. A more explicit order was made in 1653. On November 1 in that year the Visitors decreed that no scholar should be eligible for the place of probationer, fellow, or chaplain unless he submitted to the Visitors a testimonial "subscribed by the hands of foure persons at the least, knowne to the Visitors to be of approved godliness and integrity[2]." The impolicy of such regulations was severely censured by those who valued learning above the type of piety which was likely to find favour with the Visitors. Gerald Langbaine, the Provost of Queen's, spoke in no uncertain terms on the subject in a letter to John Selden, written a week after the issue of the order.

"I was not so much troubled," he wrote, "to hear of

[1] Burrows' *Register of the Visitors*, p. 141.   [2] *Ibid.* p. 368.

that fellow who lately in London maintayned in publick that learning is a sin, as to see some men (who would be accounted none of the meanest among ourselves here at home) under pretence of piety, go about to banish it in the University. I cannot make any better construction of a late order made by those we call visitors, upon occasion of an election last week at All Souls Coll., to this effect, that for the future no schollar be chosen into any place in any college, unless he bring a testimony under the hands of 4 persons at the least (not electors) known to these Visitors to be truly Godly men, that he who stands for such place is himself truly Godly, and by arrogating to themselves this power, they sit judges of all men's consciences, and have rejected some against whom they had no other exceptions (being certified by such to whom their conversations were best known to be unblamable, and statutably elected after due examination and approbation of their sufficiency by the Society) merely upon this account that the persons who testified in their behalf are not known to the Visitors to be regenerate. I intend e're long," he concludes, "to have an election in our College, and have professed that I will not submit to this order[1]."

But though the effect of the Visitors' policy would lead, as Langbaine foresaw, to a considerable amount of injustice and to the reduction of scholarship to a position of secondary importance, it is improbable that persons of gross ignorance, and still less of bad character, would have gained admission. In Exeter, Mr Boase states that the Rector's "care in the election of fellows was very singular[2]," and even Anthony Wood allows that there were some "good scholars and well-bred persons[3]."

---

[1] Tanner MSS. (Bodl.) 52, fol. 60.
[2] C. W. Boase: *Registrum Collegii Exoniensis*, p. cxxiii.
[3] *Hist. of Oxford*, iii, 634.

So much for the rank and file of the "intruders."
Of those who succeeded to official positions it is possible
to speak rather more explicitly. Walker, after a sweeping
condemnation of the manner in which the fellowships
had been filled, proceeds to state that "the first and
highest places of the University" were no better provided
for. In support of this, he instances Dr Hoyle and
Du Moulin, the two new Professors of Divinity and
Ancient History respectively. The former's lectures, he
says, had "neither method nor argument in them, and
seem'd to shew him ignorant, even of the most common
and ordinary rules of logick." The latter he only accuses
of tiring himself " as well as the auditory with the praises
of the Parliament[1]."

Neither of these men, certainly, were men of any
great eminence, although Hoyle was a man of whom the
University need not have been ashamed. He had been
educated at Magdalen Hall, and had afterwards held the
divinity professorship at Trinity College, Dublin. Of
Du Moulin little is known except that he has been
condemned by Anthony Wood. But neither of these
two are really fair examples of the new occupants of the
various University chairs. Although possibly the most
distinguished men of the time, Sheldon, Sanderson,
Hammond and Morley, were among those who refused to
submit, some men of distinction were left, and the
"intruders" were not all as intellectually contemptible as
royalist historians represented[2].

But it was not the condition only of the Puritan
nominees which their adversaries questioned. Two or
three instances are given by Wood to show that the honesty
of the new officials was not above reproach. Robert Harris,
the President of Trinity, is charged with appropriating

---

[1] Walker : *Sufferings of the Clergy*, Pt. i, 141.
[2] Burrows' *Register of the Visitors*, p. lxxxiii.

two bags of money found in the President's lodgings, and the President and fellows of Magdalen are said to have broken open a chest left to the college by Dr Humphrey, and to have converted the contents to their own use, although the fund had been bequeathed for the public good of the society[1]. Heylin and Fuller both corroborate this story, the latter adding that "though one must charitably believe the matter not so bad as it is reported, yet the most favourable relation thereof gave a general distast[2]." Mr Macray also narrates the incident with some additional facts. Apparently the newly-appointed officials of the college came across the chest by chance while searching in the Muniment Room for the original statute book. They divided the 1411 gold pieces among the members of the college and persuaded John Wilkinson to take his share as President. After his death, the matter came to the knowledge of the Committee of Parliament and they instituted an inquiry, with the result that the money began to be repaid. In 1679 all had been restored except Wilkinson's 100 pieces and 300 more which were due from ten fellows[3]. The incident does not appear capable of any but an unfavourable construction though an attempt was made to justify it on the grounds that the college was in debt and that the fellows misunderstood the character of the fund[4]. Dr Reynolds, the Vice-Chancellor, and Ralph Button, one of the new Canons of Christ Church, are likewise accused of an intention to rifle the contents of Bodley's and Saville's chests, but in this case it is not definitely asserted that their purpose was dishonest, and as officers of the University they may be allowed to have had the

[1] A. Wood: *Athenae Oxon.* (1692), ii, 748.
[2] Heylin: *Exam. Hist.* (1659), i, 268 ; Fuller: *Church Hist.* (1655), bk. ix, 234.
[3] Macray: *Register of Magdalen College*, New Series, iii, 121.
[4] *Oxford College Hist. Series*, Magdalen, pp. 169-70.

right to inspect the University chests[1]. The Royalists' practice of concealing public property possibly gave the Visitors an additional excuse for search.

Another instance of spoliation was the seizure of Bishop Waynflete's mitre and other " Popish Reliques" at Magdalen which took place in January 1646/7. After the Restoration, the college endeavoured to regain the lost treasures or their money value, and, in the course of the legal investigations, it transpired that the goods had been seized by one Michael Baker, described as a "messenger of the Exchequer," acting "by colour of an Order" of the House of Lords. According to Baker's own statement, the mitre and a considerable quantity of copes and other valuable ecclesiastical vestments, "estimated by severall persons which viewed them at Oxford to be worth two thousand pounds," were taken to London by the carrier and were there delivered " to Mr Alexander Thaine then deputy to James Maxwell als. Lord Deirlton, and, sold by him, part to one Mr Wheeler a Goldsmith, other part kept and disposed of by the said Mr Thaine to his owne use." Thaine pleaded the Act of Oblivion, and the Magdalen men, who seem to have met with a considerable amount of discouragement in the pursuit of their case, were unable to obtain compensation[2].

The work of the Visitors had, naturally enough, caused satisfaction to those who had succeeded to places under their auspices. On November 1, 1648, Convocation addressed a letter of thanks to the Speaker, in which they expressed their gratitude for the great favours bestowed on "this Seminary of Piety and Acts, by

[1] Wood: *Athenae Oxon.* (1692), ii, 748–9.
[2] An account of the proceedings is printed, from the MS. in the Tanner Collection, in J. R. Bloxam's *Register of Magdalen College*, ii, 341. A copy of Baker's statement before the Lords Commissioners of the Treasury is in the British Museum, Add. MSS. 32,094, fol. 3.

whose goodnesse and bounty they begin now to live and move againe."

"Wee must ever mention with all thankefulnes," the letter proceeds, "the care you have had for purginge these Fountaines and that notwithstanding all your burdens that lay upon you and publique pressures, you have devised liberall thinges for the incouragement of learning : so that were there no other argument, this place alone were enough to confute that unjust calumny of perverse men that you intend to bring˓ in darkenesse and Barbarisme on this knowing Nation[1]."

The "Fountaines," however, were destined to be purged still further. A certain amount of interference with University and college statutes was not only necessary to the work of "regulation," but was, as we have seen, practically justified by the wording of the Treaty of Surrender. It may, indeed, be doubted whether, in the disordered state in which the University was left by the war, any reorganisation would have been possible without occasional alterations in college constitutions.

Though the action of the Visitors in this respect may have been unduly prolonged, it was not dictated by any other motive than that of precaution, and in some cases their interference was justified. As late as November 1657, they conducted an inquiry into the case of All Souls College, where fellowships had been frequently bought and sold[2]. A letter of this period which seems, from internal evidence, to be written from and about All Souls, suggests that the early work of the Visitors had not been effectual in restoring order.

"Here is much talk," the letter runs, "of a new Visitation in September next to enquire how exercise is perform'd, and colledg statuts observ'd. Our colledg

---

[1] Tanner MSS. (Bodl.) 57, fol. 397.
[2] See *Cal. of S. P. Dom.* 1657–8, pp. 181, 236, 260, 272.

can give but a poor accompt, wherever ye fault will light, for wee have had no exercise, discipline, nor respect to statut since the Reformation[1]."

As soon as a college was judged to be sufficiently "reformed" to administer its own affairs without detriment to the well-being of the University, full power to do so was granted and further interference on the part of the Visitors ceased.

But the public mind did not cease to interest itself in the Universities. The period of the Commonwealth and Protectorate was essentially a period of experiment and of radical ideas in matters constitutional and institutional, and it was not unnatural that the tendency of the time should have led men's thoughts in the direction of University reform. Some reference has already been made to the attitude of the "Barebones" Parliament and the writings of William Dell and John Webster[2]. Another interesting scheme of reform was published in June 1659 in a pamphlet entitled "Sundry Things from several hands concerning the University of Oxford[3]."

The pamphlet, which is republican in tone, begins with a petition in which Parliament is asked to "enact freedom of opinions" at the University and to carry out various reforms in its government. Since degrees had been improperly conferred, the petition asked that all which had been bestowed since the surrender should be "cassated and nulled by some solemn act, as being no longer characters of merit, but cheats wherewith to amuse the ignorant." None were to be Heads of Houses but such as were "entirely affected for a Republique," and if

---

[1] MS. J. Walker (Bodl.) c. 9, fol. 195, printed in G. B. Tatham : *Dr John Walker*, p. 332. The letter is addressed to Jeremy Stephens and is signed "M.A."—probably Martin Aylworth, an elderly fellow of All Souls who had submitted to the Parliamentary authority. The letter is dated July 26, but the year is not given.

[2] See *ante*, pp. 137 *et seq.*   [3] Brit. Mus. *King's Pamphlets* E. 988 (25).

it should be found impossible to provide a sufficiency of suitable governors, the number of colleges should be reduced rather than that they should become "nurseries for such as may hereafter be as thorns in your sides." There was to be no Chancellor and power was not to be given to any of the clergy, "who have been so notoriously corrupt, negligent, and malicious" as Visitors, but there should be "a kind of Censor" with power to punish offences and "influence all elections for the advantage of such as are actively obedient and deserving."

The petition is followed by what is described as "a slight model of a Colledge to be erected and supplied from Westminster School." The Dean and Canons of Christ Church were to be abolished and their incomes devoted to the new college, the supreme control of which was to be in the hands of the governors of Westminster. As for the studies, the "model" had several novel suggestions. The "novices of the foundation" were to be provided with books, clothes, diet, chambers, furniture, and "physick in case of indisposition" at the college charge. The discipline was to be strict, and the course of study designed to fit men for the several professions. There were to be two professors in Divinity, one in Civil Law and Politics whose duty it should be to dispose the students "to prefer a Commonwealth before Monarchy," a professor in the philosophy of Descartes and one in the philosophy of Gassendi. There was to be a "School of Experiments in Optiques and Mechaniques for the instruction of the Gentry," professors of Physick and Anatomy, a Chemist and a professor of "useful Logick and civil Rhetorick."

The body of public opinion, however, at that time, was sufficiently conservative to preserve the Universities from the ill-digested schemes of theoretical reformers who, to use Wood's expression, "made it their business to scribble books to incite the rabble to lay these antient fabricks equal with the ground[1]."

Another scheme of a different kind, of which nothing came, was that of the conversion of S. Mary's Hall into a college which should support ten "godly, able men," to be engaged in drawing up "a generall synopsis of the true reformed Protestant Christian Religion professed in this Commonwealth." It was also to receive "poore Protestant Ministers and Schollars, being forraigners and strangers borne[2]."

In his general summary of the effect of the Visitation upon Oxford, Clarendon, after accusing the Puritan rulers of filling the fellowships with incapable Presbyterians and with endeavouring to extinguish all good literature, explains how the natural disastrous results of so much "stupidity and negligence" were almost miraculously averted, and gave place to "a harvest of extraordinary good and sound knowledge in all parts of learning." This happy consummation is mainly attributed to "the goodness and richness of the soil[3]," which triumphed over the evil effects of the seed sown upon it, but such an unconvincing explanation would not have been needed if the historian had not set himself to reconcile two contradictory facts. On the one hand there is the assertion that the natural effect, if not the design, of the Visitation was to ruin the University, and on the other, there is the fact that at the Restoration, Oxford was "abounding in excellent learning and devoted to duty and obedience." The true solution, it need hardly be said, is to be sought elsewhere. The Visitation in fact, whatever its defects, as regards its influence upon the University was not such as Clarendon and others have described it.

[1] Wood : *Hist. of Oxford*, iii, 696.
[2] See a draft of the scheme in Brit. Mus. Add. MSS. 32,093, f. 399.
[3] *Hist. of the Rebellion* (ed. Macray), iv, 259.

The Government, especially during the later years of
the Protectorate, did not show themselves careless of the
interests of the University. The grant of £2000 per
annum towards the increase of the stipends of Heads
of Houses has been noticed already[1]. In the case of
Oxford, some similar grants were made to certain pro-
fessorships. £80 per annum was granted, by way of
augmentation, to Seth Ward as Professor of Mathematics,
by an order of June 29, 1658[2], and on January 22, 1658/9
Dr Thomas Clayton, Professor of Physic, received an
augmentation of the same amount, to be paid "out of
the revenues of the new Windsor almshouses[3]." Wood
further records that the Protector ordered £100 per
annum to be paid out of the Exchequer for the encouragement of a Reader in Divinity, and that he
bestowed "25 antient MSS." on the Library at his own
expense[4].

Some attempt has already been made at a comparison
between those who were expelled from the chief offices in
the University and those who took their places, and it
has been seen that, on the question of mere ability, the
change was not always for the worse. Several of the
new Heads, like Conant and Staunton, evinced an amount
of interest in the moral and intellectual well-being of the
undergraduates which had not been common in earlier
times and was certainly not often found in the Oxford of
the Restoration. As to the new fellows, the experience of
the various colleges differed enormously. Lincoln seems
to have been the most unfortunate, but in most cases the
"intruders" adapted themselves to the traditions of the

[1] See *ante*, pp. 131–2.
[2] *Cal. of S. P. Dom.* 1658–9, p. 66. On Jan. 6, 1658/9 Ward petitioned for
a continuance of his augmentation, which had been paid for three quarters
and then suspended. *Ibid.* p. 243.
[3] *Ibid.* p. 263.
[4] A. Wood : *Hist. of Oxford*, iii, 667.

place, and administered the affairs of their colleges sufficiently well[1].

The generality of those who entered the University during the period of the Commonwealth and Protectorate were probably drawn from a rather different class from that which had supplied the colleges at an earlier date, though a change from an aristocratic to a more plebeian membership seems to have begun some years before the outbreak of the war[2]. It was ceasing to be the fashion for men of position to send their sons to the University, and therefore the falling-off in the numbers of the nobility and gentry, which Wood laments[3], was not wholly due to the Puritan ascendency. At the same time, it is probable, as Wood leads us to believe, that a class of *novi homines*, whose fortunes were founded on the triumph of the Parliamentary party, men, possibly, who had speculated successfully in confiscated lands, began to send their sons to the University. In point of numbers the colleges did well[4], and there is evidence that, far from wishing to ruin the Universities, the Puritans fully appreciated their value as a training ground for the ministry. Under the relaxed discipline of the Restoration, the numbers decreased.

The picture which Wood gives of the manners and morals of Puritan Oxford is not wholly unfavourable to those who exercised authority there. It shows, of course, the strict enforcement of the Puritanical system, a rigid discipline as regards the conduct, and a severe supervision as regards the spiritual welfare of the undergraduates. Expulsion, says Wood, was the ordinary result of

[1] See *Oxford College Hist. Series*, University, p. 120 ; Balliol, p. 141 ; All Souls, p. 135 ; Magdalen, p. 168 ; Lincoln, p. 116, etc.
[2] D. Macleane : *History of Pembroke College, Oxford*, p. 241.
[3] A. Clark : *Life and Times of Anthony Wood*, i, 301.
[4] See *Oxford College Hist. Series*, Christ Church, p. 71 ; Merton, p. 92; Wadham, p. 67.

swearing or cursing[1]; "public drunkenness" was punished very severely; May-games, "morrices," and "Whitsun ales" were discountenanced, and it was only at "Act times" that the authorities would permit "dancing the rope, drolles, or monstrous sights to be seen[2]."

Catechising was frequent and prayers took place "in most tutors' chambers every night[3]," but Walker states that the celebration of the Holy Communion was entirely neglected by the University and college authorities[4]. On this last point the evidence is conflicting. "To prepare the citizens and scholars for the Holy Communion" was one of the professed objects of the Seven Preachers[5], and a notice in Wood's *Athenae* speaks of Samuel Parker as constantly partaking of the Sacrament in a Presbyterian meeting-house[6]. On the other hand, other authors besides Walker have testified to its neglect. It may be that it was regularly celebrated in the Presbyterian churches in the city, and for that reason was deemed unnecessary in the colleges.

The liturgy of the Church of England was, of course, rigorously suppressed, but services were held in secret "in the house of Mr Th. Willis, a Physician, against Merton College Church" and "Prayers and Surplices" were "used on all Lord's Days, Holy Days and their Vigils, as also the Sacrament according to the Church of England administered[7]."

Whether the ideals of the governors were reflected in the conduct of the governed is perhaps doubtful.

---

[1] In Christ Church, members were fined a shilling for every oath, and on the third offence were to be proceeded against as scandalous persons. *Oxford College Hist. Series*, Christ Church, p. 76.

[2] A. Clark: *Life and Times of Anthony Wood*, i, 299.   [3] *Ibid.* i, 300.

[4] Walker: *Sufferings of the Clergy*, Pt. i, 143.

[5] Burrows: *Register of the Visitors*, p. llx.

[6] A. Wood: *Athenae Oxon.* (1692), ii, 615.

[7] A. Wood: *Hist. of Oxford*, iii, 613.

Dr Fowler, indeed, expresses his suspicion that "this constant succession of sermons...must have produced such utter weariness in the minds of many of the students as to prove a hindrance rather than an incitement to religious thoughts and a godly life[1]," and Wood's evidence points to a similar conclusion. If the undergraduates might not frequent taverns, they could yet "send for their commodities to their respective chambers and tiple and smoake till they were overtaken with the creature": if "common players" were not admitted into the University and the undergraduates were themselves prohibited from acting, they still could, and probably did, indulge therein "by stelth[2]."

The ordinary studies of the University were not neglected. At Christ Church the tutors were directed "to reade constantly to their scholars in approved classicall authors[3]," and on July 20, 1649, the Committee for the Reformation of the University ordered that "either the Latin or Greeke be stricktly and constantly exercised and spoken, in their familier discourse within the said severall Colledges and Halls respectively, and that noe other language be spoken by any Fellow, Scholar, or Student whatsoever[4]." According to Wood, disputations and lectures were well and frequently performed, besides the public discussions in the Schools known as "coursing," which were carried on with so much spirit that they ended "alwaies in blowes, and that in the publick streets, to the great scandall of the gown[5]."

But speaking generally, the general tone of life, if

[1] T. Fowler: *Hist. of Corpus College, Oxon.* p. 222.
[2] A. Clark: *Life and Times of Anthony Wood,* i, 298–9.
[3] *Oxford College Hist. Series,* Christ Church, p. 74. On the other hand the system at Balliol was lax. *Ibid.* Balliol, p. 142.
[4] Burrows: *Register of the Visitors,* p. 249.
[5] A. Clark: *Life and Times of Anthony Wood,* i, 300. Boase: *Registrum Collegii Exoniensis,* p. cx.

not the standard of scholarship, seems to have improved, and this is no slight justification of the Visitors' work. The eradication of abuses had been the object of Laud and his antagonists alike, and the proper method of attaining that object had been one of the questions involved in their larger differences. Laud's reforms had never had a fair trial, and the system which obtained at Oxford after the Restoration, in its relation to life and conduct, was far removed from his. The Puritans, on the other hand, had the opportunity of putting their system to the test. It is not necessary to speculate as to whether, quite apart from the doctrinal views involved, the new order would have been to the ultimate interest of the University and the nation. Judged by its immediate results, the work of the Visitors marks an improvement in many aspects of the University life, and to that extent, at all events, must be considered a success.

CHAPTER VI

THE FATE OF THE EJECTED CLERGY

In the foregoing chapters an account has been given of the manner in which the Episcopal Church was overthrown and the Puritan ascendency established. It still remains to be seen how the clergy of the Church of England fared during the later years of the Civil War and under the Commonwealth and Protectorate, when the government of the country was under the influence of the new power.

The ruin of the King's cause left the mass of the loyal clergy in a condition of extreme destitution. The greater part of the cathedral and parochial sequestrations had taken place before the close of the war, and a very large number of ejected clergymen had been cast adrift upon the country with practically no prospect of employment or means of subsistence. Of these the more fortunate were able to find a home with relations or friends, but a considerable proportion had been driven to take refuge with one or other of the King's garrisons. The gradual surrender of these fortresses, and the emigration of the more powerful Royalists to the Continent, still further reduced the resources of the unfortunate clergy, and rendered them almost entirely dependent on charity. The majority preferred to stay in England rather than to take refuge abroad, even at the risk of being committed to prison, as many of the more influential actually were. In a letter to Gilbert Sheldon, dated October 29, 1650, Henry Hammond refers to their melancholy prospect in a tone of resignation.

"What you foresee, as possible, concerning our common condition," he writes, "may not be far off, yet truly I have not yet considered of it, being much inclined to wait God's providence, and to stay here in or out of prison as long as we may, and when nothing but going beyond the sea will free us from spiritual imprisonment, then to prefer banishment as the less evil[1]."

A certain number, however, who had been closely associated with the King, repaired to the exiled Court in France. The Bishop of Galloway, Dr George Morley, afterwards Bishop of Winchester, Dr John Cosin, Dean of Peterborough, and Dr Stewart, Dean of St Paul's, are amongst those whom Evelyn mentions as attending there during his visit to Paris in 1651[2]. With a few exceptions almost all the members of the little Court were exceedingly short of funds, and often in most necessitous conditions. The Earl of Norwich writes pathetically to Secretary Nicholas that "since I see noe hope of mony from your Court, I must retire where I may mend my ould breeches and put a crust of new bread in my belly without farther disgrace in soe visible a place[3]," and a similar picture is given in a letter from Lord Hatton during Cosin's illness. "Mr Deane Cosins," he writes, "is exceeding ill and I cannot thinke he will last long....He is exeeding poore and necessitous, even to the want of necessityes for his health, and hath not anything heere coming in[4]."

In England the royalist clergy were often no better off. The wife of the Dean of Bristol, a correspondent

---

[1] Quoted in *Illustrations of the State of the Church during the Great Rebellion*, published in the *Theologian and Ecclesiastic*, vii, 119.

[2] *Memoirs of J. Evelyn* (1819), i, 257.

[3] *Nicholas Papers* (Camden Soc.), iii, 15.   [4] *Ibid.* ii, 102.

informed Nicholas in January 1645/6, was "in a very sad and miserable condicion," so much so that his maid had been seen "in the market sellinge of rosemary and bayes to buy bread[1]." In view of this general indigence, a fund was started, largely through the agency of Henry Hammond and Jeremy Taylor, for the dispensation of charity to the needy clergy[2]. Lord Scudamore was one of the leading contributors[3], and good work was no doubt achieved by this organisation, but its effects could only have been felt by a comparatively small number. The great majority of the clergy were to a large extent dependent upon the treatment accorded to them by the Government.

When the county sequestration committees had been formed, directions had been given that if the ejected minister were married and had a family, a sum of money was to be allowed for their support. In the Earl of Manchester's commission of January 22, 1643/4, it was ordained that "the said Earl of Manchester shall have power to dispose of a fifth part of all such estates as they shall sequester, for the benefit of the wives and children of any of the aforesaid persons[4]." Although the wording of the ordinance seems to suggest that these grants were merely at the discretion of the Earl of Manchester, there is little doubt that either then, or soon afterwards, it was intended both in the Eastern Association and elsewhere, that they should be made in every case where they could fairly be claimed. If, however, it could be proved that the ejected clergyman had other sources of income, or was not solely dependent upon his cure, the money was not granted, and this explains why

[1] *Nicholas Papers* (Camden Soc.), i, 68.
[2] J. E. Bailey: *Life of Fuller*, p. 406.
[3] *Illustrations of the State of the Church during the Great Rebellion* (*Theologian and Ecclesiastic*, xii, 173).
[4] *Acts and Ordinances of the Interregnum* (Ed. C. H. Firth and R. S. Rait), i, 372.

the articles of accusation almost invariably conclude with a deposition by witnesses as to the value of the living and the private or other means of the accused clergyman. In the case of Dr Nicholas Grey, who was ejected from the living of Castle Camps in Cambridgeshire, the Committee for Plundered Ministers ordered that no "fifths" should be paid, since Grey was "also schoolmaster of Eaton Colledge whereby he hath a subsistance," but on being informed that this was not the case, they ultimately reversed the order[1].

The good behaviour of the ejected clergyman and of his wife were also taken into consideration and no allowance was made to those who persisted in an open defiance of the Parliamentary power. The authorities, however, showed considerable discrimination, and, in one case, where the petition of a clergyman's wife was refused, "in regard of the malignancy proved against her," the Committee for Plundered Ministers saw no ground for withholding relief from her children[2]. When the ejected clergyman had neither wife nor child, no help was given[3].

Within these limits, the Parliamentary authorities were peremptory in enforcing payment, though they appear to have experienced considerable difficulty in

[1] Brit. Mus. Add. MSS. 15,669, fol. 140, 187.

[2] "This Committee have taken into consideration the cause returned ag^t Mrs Jacob of Dalingoe in the County of Suff, why hee (sic) should not have a fift parte of the profittes of the sd rectory sequestred from her husband and in regard of the malignancy proved against her doe conceive her wholly unworthy of any allowance notwithstanding which this Committee see noe cause why the children of the sd Mr Jacob should not have reliefe out of the sd rectory and doe therefore order that the sd children shall have the fift parte of the profittes of the sd rectory," etc. The grant was subsequently questioned on the ground that the children were grown up. Add. MSS. 15,669, fol. 53 b, 64.

[3] John Tolly, applying for maintenance out of the rectory of Little Gransden, was informed that as he had neither wife nor child it was "against the general course of this Committee to grant any maintenance." Add. MSS. 15,669, fol. 117 b.

doing so. In August 1645, the Committee for Plundered Ministers, who were frequently invoked as a court of appeal, ordered that "whosoever shall neglect to pay the fifth part of the profits of such living as he enjoyeth by sequestration, contrary to any order in that behalfe, and shall not upon summons show good cause for his non-payment thereof shall be sequestered[1]," and there are several instances, recorded in their minutes, in which they insisted upon payment being made[2]. In the case of the living of Weldrake in Yorkshire, for example, acting in the spirit of the foregoing decree they threatened to eject the "intruding" minister, one Henry Bayard, unless he paid the "fifth" to his predecessor's wife within a fortnight[3]. The same policy prevailed even after the Committee for Plundered Ministers had been dissolved, for in the instructions issued to the Major-Generals in 1656, it was laid down "that where a fifth has been allowed to wives and children of sequestered ministers, and is detained, they shall cause it to be paid, unless they find just cause to the contrary[4].

But although the intention of the Government in this matter was clear, the question was a constant source of friction between the ejected clergy and their unlawful successors. At first the intruders endeavoured to evade the law on the ground that the original order of 1644 had not specifically included clergymen among other delinquents, and Fuller, in his *Church History*, mentions many other subterfuges to which they had recourse[5]. The new incumbents complained that the parishioners

---

[1] Add. MSS. 15,669, fol. 239.

[2] For example, in a dispute between French, the "intruding" minister at Cottenham, Cambridgeshire, and Mrs Manby, the wife of the ejected rector, they decided in favour of the latter, though in this case they allowed her only £60, the living being valued at £500. Add. MSS. 15,670, fol. 170 b.

[3] Add. MSS. 15,670, fol. 220.

[4] *Cal. of S. P. Dom.* 1656–7, pp. 45, 144.

[5] J. E. Bailey: *Life of Fuller*, p. 378.

were incited to withhold the payment of their tithes, and consequently refused to pay a fifth part of their income to their predecessors. Very likely in some cases, they had reason on their side, and the behaviour attributed to some of the Episcopalian clergy was hardly creditable. Cases of incitement to withhold tithes are common among the entries of the Committee for Plundered Ministers, and in some cases open violence broke out[1].

The difficulties experienced by the ejected clergymen, however, did not always arise from the intruders only, for not infrequently it was the local committee which stood in their way. This was the case with Walter Bushnell, the ejected minister of Box in Wiltshire who applied for his fifths in 1658. Bushnell maintained that his living was worth £100 per annum, and produced tenants who were prepared to lease it at that rent. This the commissioners refused to accept, alleging in the first place that the living was not worth more than £90, and, in the second, that Bushnell himself had removed more fixtures from his vicarage than he was entitled to, and that his personal estate amounted to more than £500. The result of a long and tedious suit was that the commissioners granted him £12 per annum until further notice, and omitted to pay the arrears which were due to him[2]. In some districts it seems to have been the practice of the local committee to dole out allowances in small sums rather than to pay a fixed proportion of the value of the living. Thus the standing committee for Cornwall, in the years 1646 to 1649, paid out £326. 3s. 8d. to the wives of sequestered clergymen. The sum was distributed among nineteen persons in small payments varying from £3 to £24[3].

---

[1] See *ante*, p. 72.

[2] *A Narrative of the Proceedings of the Commissioners*, etc., by Walter Bushnell (1660), pp. 236–248.   [3] MS. J. Walker, c. 10, fol. 126 b.

This illustrates the obstacles which the ejected clergy-man frequently had to overcome, and even when the fifth was obtained it was hopelessly insufficient for the support of a family. For the injustice of the intruders and the local authorities however, the Government was only indirectly responsible. That they occasionally acted with consideration towards those whom they had deprived of the means of livelihood is evidenced by occasional payments to individual sufferers. For example, on January 2, 1655/6, the Committee for Plundered Ministers ordered the payment of £5 towards the relief of Peter Warner, "one of the late singing-men" in Chester cathedral[1], and on July 15 of the same year they directed the treasurer to pay £20 to several "members and officers of the late hierarchy," attached to the cathedral[2]. Similar payments of £10 and £5 were made in subsequent years[3].

In the earlier stages of the Puritan ascendency, a very large number of Episcopalian clergy, a considerable proportion of whom were drawn from the Universities, were not only deprived of their benefices but committed to prison for their enmity to the cause of the Parliament. The *Commons' Journals* contain many orders consigning offenders of this sort to imprisonment.

At first the prisoners were confined in the ordinary London gaols, but as the number increased, other accommodation had to be provided, and the Parliament took the course of converting the London palaces and houses of the bishops into prisons. This not unnaturally outraged the Royalists' sense of justice and decency, and was regarded as an act almost of sacrilege, but from the point of view of the prisoners there is no doubt that it

---

[1] *Plundered Ministers Accounts, Lancs. and Cheshire*, ed. W. A. Shaw, ii, 108.

[2] *Ibid.* ii, 145.   [3] *Ibid.* ii, 203, 209, 298.

was a decided change for the better. The conditions of imprisonment at Lambeth or Ely house, even when the quarters were full and overcrowded, would be infinitely more healthy than those to be obtained in a common gaol of the period, and it is therefore not surprising to find that Sir Roger Twysden, to whose experiences of prison life it will be necessary to refer more than once, used all his interest to get himself transferred from the "Counter" in Southwark to Lambeth Palace, and that he was sincerely grateful to the friend through whom his object was accomplished[1].

The formal order by the provisions of which Lambeth Palace was converted into a place of detention for political prisoners was not made until January 1642/3[2], but it had already been used for that purpose for some months before, and as early as the previous September Col. Henry Brooke, a captured Royalist, had been conveyed thither[3]. The ordinance of January 1642/3, however, laid down the regulations under which the new prisons were to be managed, and these are instructive as showing on what sort of footing the inmates were to be treated. On the whole, and having regard to the times, the regulations do not appear at first sight to be harsh or unreasonable. The prisoners, indeed, were compelled to pay for the privilege of being lodged at Lambeth. It was decided that "the Keeper, for the time being, may receive of ordinary persons, at entrance, twenty shillings and not above; of Esquires and Knights, forty shillings and not above; and for any of higher degree, five marks, and not above." It was further laid down that "the Keeper for the time being may take of every prisoner, for his chamber, weekly, a reasonable allowance, according to

---

[1] Twysden's *Journal* (*Archaeologia Cantiana*, iv, 178).

[2] *Commons' Journals*, ii, 894, 914.

[3] J. Cave-Brown, *Lambeth Palace*, p. 235.

the room or rooms he shall desire to make use of : and
for such as shall provide their own furniture, to have so
much abated of their rent, as the same is worth." With
regard to the property of the Archbishop, it was allowed
that furniture might be removed by his servants to any
repository sanctioned by the Parliament, while the gardens,
fishponds, etc., were to be safeguarded from spoliation[1].

The next step taken by the Parliament was to
appoint a Keeper, and the person they selected for the
post was the notorious Alexander Leighton. This man
had been a bitter enemy to Episcopacy, and had been
sentenced with cruel severity by the Star Chamber for
the publication of his book, *Sion's Plea against the
Prelacie*. He had lately been liberated by Parliament
and indemnified for his sufferings. He has generally
been looked upon as one of those hot-headed fanatics
who did so much harm to the cause which they espoused,
and, although it is stated that he always spoke of his
enemies with forgiveness, one would naturally suppose
that at this date, he could hardly have regarded the
Episcopalian clergy with anything short of extreme
bitterness. To place such a man in the position of
gaoler over his enemies was an act of such apparent
injustice that the violent condemnation with which it has
sometimes been assailed is at least excusable[2]. We shall
have occasion below to observe Twysden's description of
him, but in the meantime it may be noted that the only
charge which Nalson brings against him is that of extor-
tion and of having made "that persecution which was so
great a crime in others a lawful and gainful calling in
himself[3]."

[1] *Commons' Journals*, ii, 913.
[2] Thus Mr Cave-Brown (*Lambeth Palace*, p. 235) asserts that in this
appointment, "the intense malevolence of the triumphant faction proclaimed
itself."
[3] J. Nalson: *Impartial Collection*, i, 512.

Mr Cave-Brown, in his history of Lambeth Palace, states that as a result of the ruthless overcrowding of the prisoners, a fever broke out amongst them in the summer of 1645 and caused "an appalling mortality," and to the same effect Bishop Kennett's *Register* narrates that of nearly a hundred ministers who were brought out of the west and imprisoned at Lambeth "almost all" were destroyed. Whether, as Mr Cave-Brown suggests, many of those who died were removed elsewhere for burial it is not possible to say, but the burial register of the Lambeth parish church includes the names of seventeen prisoners who died between July and December in that year[1]. This certainly was a high proportion for such a short period, but if the fever was as universal in its effects as Kennett's *Register* represents, it is at least curious that Twysden, who was there at the time, makes no mention of it.

No doubt the treatment which the prisoners received depended very much on their ability to pay, and it is probable that amongst the less fortunate in this respect, both clergy and laity, there was much real hardship and suffering. Twysden, although his whole estate had been sequestered, must have belonged to the former class, and his position cannot have been exceptional, for the majority of the better sort would have been able to pay for privileges and such comforts as were obtainable. Twysden, then, on his arrival at Lambeth, was assigned as a lodging a set of rooms which had been occupied formerly by one of the Archbishop's chaplains[2]. It comprised three rooms and a study, according, as he says, "to most of the buildings of that house," and for this he paid at first a rent of twelve shillings a week. But finding that his stay at Lambeth was likely to be

[1] J. Cave-Brown : *Lambeth Palace*, pp. 239–40.
[2] *Archaeologia Cantiana*, iv, 176.

protracted, he demurred at paying this high rate in future, and, in company with some other prisoners, he went to Leighton and told him so. Leighton, however, or possibly his deputy—for Twysden says that the Keeper himself "meddled not much with the prisoners[1]" —refused to make any reduction, and even threatened him with "harder usage," but upon Twysden making an appeal to some influential friends, his case was brought before the Committee for Prisoners[2]. Here it was decided that he should pay forty shillings entrance fee, and eight shillings a week for his rooms in the future. His relations with Leighton do not appear to have been altogether unfriendly, in spite of the latter's grasping demands. He "parted with very great kindnesse from Doctor Leighton"; he says, "the man beeing no ill dispositiond person, but one who loved the Presbytery, and loved money." The general impression, in fact, gained from his account, is that, except for the avarice of the gaolers, the treatment at Lambeth was not severe and that Dr Gardiner is justified in saying that their "confinement was made as easy as was compatible with privation of liberty[3]."

The next expedient to which the Parliament had recourse for the disposal of their prisoners is not open to a similar defence. At the beginning of August in the year 1643, the order was suddenly given that a certain number of prisoners should be transferred to two ships then lying in the Thames. Walker assumes that this was merely a new method of dealing with the ever-increasing numbers for whom it was necessary to find accommodation, but Twysden suggests, far more plausibly, that it was due to motives of public policy[4]. At that date, a series of reverses inflicted upon the Parliamentary

---

[1] *Archaeologia Cantiana*, iv, 177.   [2] *Ibid.* IV, 178.
[3] S. R. Gardiner: *Commonwealth and Protectorate*, iii, 312.
[4] *Archaeologia Cantiana*, iii, 149.

armies in almost every direction had left the King free, if he would, to strike at the capital, and it was generally believed in London that this was the move which he would adopt. In this expectation, therefore, Parliament was anxious to place as many of their prisoners as possible beyond the reach either of recapture or of inflicting injury upon the Parliamentary cause. But whatever the motive, it was ordered on August 7 that "the Committee for Prisoners shall consider what prisoners are fit to be put on shipboard ; and shall send them to the Committee for the Militia, to give order for putting them on ship-board accordingly : and the masters and captains of the Ships contracted with by the militia, to this purpose, are hereby authorised and required to receive them, and to keep them in safety till further order[1]." This was accordingly done, but the scheme raised great complaints from those who were subjected to this new form of imprisonment. On August 15, barely a week after the original order had been made, a "humble petition of divers Knights, Doctors in Divinity, and Clergymen, Esquires, Gentlemen, Commanders, and Officers, prisoners in the ship called the Prosperous Sarah, now riding in the river of Thames" was read, and referred to the Committee for the Militia. In view of the complaints contained in this petition, the same Committee was recommended "to take care, that the prisoners aboard the two ships be accommodated according to their several quality and conditions ; and that the commoner sort be separated from the better ; and that they do particularly take care of the sick, the wounded, and such as are upon exchange[2]." About three weeks later, that is to say, on September 6, the Commons

---

[1] *Commons' Journals*, iii, 197. Four days previously to this, *i.e.* on August 3, a committee of four had been appointed to treat with the Committee for the Militia on this subject.   [2] *Ibid.* iii, 205.

decided to abandon the scheme finally, and accordingly
ordered that the prisoners should be removed and returned to their former prisons, and that "the ships be
forthwith discharged from any further entertainment of
the State in this kind[1]."

The short space of time during which the prisoners
were left on board the ships is in favour of Twysden's
theory of the reason for which they were sent thither, for
by the time that the last mentioned order was made, it
had become apparent that the expected advance on
London was not to take place. The fact that only
two ships seem to have been engaged, to some extent
makes against the theory, because a very small proportion of the prisoners could have been bestowed on
board them, but the terrible overcrowding of the vessels
gives additional weight to the assumption that their
employment was in the nature of a temporary expedient
to be abandoned when the need for it was past.

The evidence of the order of August 15 seems to
show that the Parliament had not intended that the
confinement on board ship should involve any unnecessary hardships, but there can be no doubt that the
sufferings of the unfortunate prisoners, during the short
time that they passed there, were very intense. Twysden,
who spent three days on the "Prosperous Sarah,"
graphically describes the "small Collyer's barke where
wee lay, styfled with heat and lack of ayr, pent in an
unhealthy, uneasy, obscure roome[2]," and his account is
substantiated in an extremely interesting letter written
by Richard Sterne, formerly Master of Jesus College,
Cambridge, describing his prison experiences to a
Mr Sayer, who appears to have been a friend to him
in his affliction and to have advanced him money for
his support.

[1] *Commons' Journals*, iii, 229.   [2] *Archaeologia Cantiana*, iii, 153.

The letter[1], which is dated from Ely House, October 9, 1643, is largely taken up with expressions of gratitude for this timely assistance, rendered necessary by the sequestration of all the writer's property. Speaking of his imprisonment he says he had already been fourteen months in confinement, "nineteen weeks in the Tower, 30 weeks in Lord Peter's House, 10 days in the Ship, and 7 weeks here in Ely House. The very fees and rent of these several prisons," he goes on, "have amounted to above £100 besides diet and all other charges, which have been various and excessive, as in Prisons is usual.... If my friends had not made my credit better than it deserves to be, and supplyd my occasions, I should have kept but an hungry and cold house both here and at home. And all this while," he complains, "I have never been so much as spoken withal, or called either to give or receive an accompt why I am here." Describing the imprisonment on the ships, he says that they "lay (the first night) without anything under or over us but the bare decks, and the cloaths on our backs; and after we had some of us got beds, were not able (when it rain'd) to ly dry in them, and when it was fair weather, were sweltered with heat and stifled with our own breaths; there being of us in that one small Ipswich coal-ship (so low built too, that we coud not walk, nor stand upright in it) within one or two of threescore; whereof six Knights, and 8 Doctors in Divinity, and divers Gentlemen of very good worth."

The whole letter is couched in moderate language, and contains hardly an allusion to or a reflection upon the Parliamentary authorities. The writer was merely describing his circumstances to an intimate friend, and had no particular reason to magnify his sufferings. There

---

[1] The letter is printed in Walker's *Sufferings of the Clergy*, Pt. ii, 370. The original is in the Walker Collection. MS. J. Walker, c. 4, fol. 116.

is little reason to doubt the substantial accuracy of the account.

But although the hardships of imprisonment, especially to the poor, are by no means to be minimised, the chief objections to it were the illegality of detaining men who very often had never been even heard in their own defence, the length of time during which they were so detained, paying heavy fees all the while for their maintenance, and the impossibility in the majority of cases of getting their petitions answered or their complaints redressed. For all or most of this, the Parliament was primarily responsible, but nevertheless it is not easy to assign the blame to them in every case. Their general attitude towards prisoners, but particularly towards prisoners of war, seems to modern eyes to be entirely cruel and unjustifiable, for, although the barbarous proposal, attributed to them by Walker[1], of selling prisoners as slaves to the Turks, is not authenticated, the practice of sending prisoners of war to serve in the plantations of Virginia is an established fact[2]. Some of the Scots, captured at the battle of Dunbar, were so disposed of. They were not slaves in the technical sense, but rather bound servants, and in Massachusetts, John Cotton informed Cromwell, the principal buyer allowed the prisoners to cultivate land for their own advantage and so to redeem their freedom. At the same time, although Cotton states that the owners desired "to make their yoke easy," it cannot be supposed that the fate of the unfortunate prisoners was desirable nor can their treatment be regarded as humane[3]. But charges of cruelty towards

---

[1] Walker, Pt. i, 58.

[2] See S. R. Gardiner : *Civil War*, iv, 193, 207 ; *Commonwealth and Protectorate*, ii, 63, iii, 309, 338–9.

[3] A Collection of original papers relative to the History of the Colony of Massachusetts Bay (Boston, 1769), p. 235, quoted by Carlyle. *Cromwell's Letters and Speeches*, iii, 9.

prisoners of war were made from both sides alike, and the Parliamentarians complained bitterly of the horrible places in which their own captured soldiers were confined at Oxford and of the barbarous conduct of William Smith, the Provost Marshal[1].

With regard to the political prisoners, the attitude of the Parliament was, of course, entirely different, yet even here in a less degree they are blamable, not on account of the harshness of their orders—for in this respect they often acted with consideration—but in putting unfit persons in a position of authority. It was in this direction that oppression was chiefly experienced. It was likely enough that in the case of the imprisonments, as in that of the sequestrations, the subordinate agents of the Parliament meted out harsh treatment to their victims, and extracted as much profit from them as they were able. The masters of the prison ships, for example, seem to have been reluctant to surrender such profitable freight, and had to be summoned to show cause why they did not give up the prisoners in accordance with the Commons' order[2]. Such men probably had little consideration for the persons or the pockets of their victims[3]. On the other hand, arbitrary exaction was not universal amongst those with whom the prisoners came into contact, and it was not uncommon for the members of some of the Parliamentary committees to behave with courtesy and consideration towards the prisoners who came before them[4].

---

[1] See *The Prisoners Report or a true Relation of the cruell usage of the Prisoners in Oxford. King's Pamphlets*, E. 93 (23). Ludlow's *Memoirs* (ed. Firth), i, 87.　　　　[2] *Commons' Journals*, iii, 239.

[3] See Twysden's *Journal*: "Beefore wee had anything out of the shippe which for necessyty wee carryed in, 20 shillings was to bee payd for our lodging." *Archae. Cant.* iii, 153. On the other hand, Henry Wollaston, the keeper of Newgate, asserted in a petition of Nov. 4, 1656, that he had paid over £700 towards the maintenance of prisoners who otherwise "must have perished." *Cal. of S. P. Dom.* 1656–7, p. 152.　　　　[4] *Archae. Cant.* iv, 147.

CHAPTER VII

RELIGIOUS FREEDOM UNDER THE PURITANS

THE question of the Puritans' consideration for the consciences of their opponents is of peculiar interest because the conditions were to a great extent new. As long as the Presbyterians were in power there could be no question of toleration, for it had no place in their conception of the church polity, and they occasionally used means to suppress other forms of "heresy" beside the practices of the Episcopal Church[1]. The principles of the Independents, on the other hand, if pursued to their logical conclusion, would have allowed liberty to individual congregations to use whatever form of service they pleased within certain broad limits. Speaking generally, therefore, the issue between tolerance and intolerance depended upon the ultimate supremacy of the Independent or Presbyterian party[2].

The Independents had hoped, by overthrowing the episcopal rule, to find freedom : the Presbyterians, on the other hand, evinced an inclination to use the opportunity, which their early ascendency gave them, in enforcing a system more rigid than that which had gone

---

[1] On May 1, 1645, the Committee for Plundered Ministers committed two men to the City Marshal "for anabaptisme." They were subsequently discharged on bail. Brit. Mus. Add. MSS. 15,669, fol. 63, 73.

[2] W. A. Shaw: *Hist. of the Eng. Ch.* 1640–60, ii, 33–54.

before, and it is probable that their policy in this matter did more than anything else to discover the fundamental division between the two great forces in the Puritan movement. The Independents complained that the Presbyterians gave them worse terms than those which they could have obtained from the Episcopalians, that they had endeavoured "to twist their interest with the Parliament, as the Bishops did with the King[1]."

The controversy between them, in the imperfect form in which it appears in the pamphlet literature of the time, followed familiar lines and concerned itself mainly with the proper function of the civil power in affairs of religion. "Either the Civill, or the spirituall State must be supream : which of these must judge the other in spirituall matters ?" So the root of the question is stated by one who took the side of toleration[2].

On the one side the Independents contended that if the right to enforce doctrines were allowed to rest with the civil power, then the canons of orthodoxy would change with the Government, and Queen Mary must be justified for having persecuted those who dissented from the established religion[3]. They held that the fallacy of the Presbyterian position, as of that of all persecutors, lay in the fact that they claimed to be "competent examiners and judges of other men differing in judgement from them," whereas, according to the opposite theory, every man had an equal right to toleration provided that his principles were not dangerous to the State[4]. Opinions differed as to the limits to liberty which political expediency should define, but while some

---

[1] *Truth, still Truth*, etc., by Henry Burton, p. 31 ; *Tolleration Justified and Persecution Condemned*, p. 2.

[2] *The Necessity of Toleration in Matters of Religion*, by Samuel Richardson, 1647. *King's Pamphlets*, E. 407 (18), p. 11.

[3] *Ibid.*

[4] *Tolleration Justified and Persecution Condemned*, pp. 3, 8.

were disposed to make exceptions in the case of Papists and Episcopalians, others were prepared to include even Arminians and Adamites[1]. "Of all sects of men," it was said, "those deserve least countenance of a State that would be Persecutors, not because of their consciences in the practice and exercise of their Religion, wherein the ground of freedome consists; but because a persecuting spirit is the greatest enemy to humane society[2]." The more blasphemous the opinion, the same writer insists, the more easily should it be suppressed by reason and argument[3].

The case against toleration, on the other hand, was well put in "A Letter of the Ministers of the City of London presented the first of January 1645 to the Reverend Assembly of Divines." As some of the dangers to the Church which a toleration would involve, the authors allege that the people's minds would be subverted, that the life and power of godliness would "be eaten out by frivolous disputes and janglings," and that other sects and heresies would be encouraged to strive for the same liberty. Further, it would be difficult to discriminate in granting toleration, but to grant it to all could "scarce be cleared from great impiety[4]." A letter purporting to come from the "Ministers about Colchester," written about the same date, also pleads against a toleration of Independency on the ground that experience and reason alike proved that it was "The Mother of Contention, the Root of Schism, the Back-door of Heresie, the Nullity of Church Government, the plain Breach of Covenant with God and Man[5]." The

---

[1] See *The Humble petitions of the Brownists*, printed in the year 1641. *King's Pamphlets*, E. 178 (10).

[2] *Tolleration Justified*, etc. p. 7.   [3] *Ibid.* p. 8.

[4] *A Letter of the Ministers of the city of London*, pp. 3, 4.

[5] *A True Copy of a Letter from divers Ministers about Colchester in the County of Essex, to the Assembly of Divines, against a Toleration.*

Presbyterians in fact started from the position that it was impossible that all doctrines should be true and therefore that a general toleration meant a toleration of error[1]. One writer, who showed a certain breadth of view in his treatment of the subject, while admitting that everyone ought to examine and judge for himself, urged that everyone was not intellectually capable of doing so, and that therefore it was necessary that there should be the guidance of a clear understanding "expounding according to the general rules of interpretation laid down in the Scripture[2]." It was the duty of Parliament at that juncture, he proceeded, to bring in a form of Church government. When that had been done, it would be time to consider whether other sects should be given toleration. In the meantime, he pointed out, false opinions could not be disposed of by argument, because the subjects under dispute were often matters of faith rather than of reason, and he was accordingly prepared to defend persecution, the end of which he saw to be "neither onely, nor alwayes the good of the party punished, but of others, that they may either be warned by his example, or preserved by his restraint[3]." He attributed the prevalence of heretical opinion very largely to "wordly lust, whether it be a content or discontent," and thought that many adhered to the Independents "rather out of policy than conscience[4]." It is interesting to compare these views with those which inspired Laud's policy towards dissenters and to observe that men who had so little else in common were at least agreed in their distrust of unrestrained religious enthusiam.

Dated February 11, 1645/6. *King's Pamphlets*, 669, f. 10 (42). See also *The Humble Petition of the Ministers of the Counties of Suffolke and Essex concerning Church Government. King's Pamphlets*, E. 339 (11).

[1] *Anti-Toleration, or a Modest Defence of the Letter of the London Ministers*, etc. p. 28.

[2] *Ibid.* p. 9. [3] *Ibid.* p. 24. [4] *Ibid.* pp. 22-23.

During the period of the Presbyterian ascendency
the attitude of the Government towards adherents of the
Episcopal Church found expression in the work of
the committees rather than in the formulation of
Parliamentary ordinances. It was, of course, wholly
unfavourable to their religious liberty, but it was so
largely determined by the political situation that it is
difficult to form an opinion of the probable effect of the
Presbyterian rule under less complex conditions.

The triumph of the Army meant the triumph of
Independent principles, and there is some evidence that
where the problem was not complicated by secular
politics, the time was not unpropitious for a broad-
minded venture in the direction of religious freedom.
An instance is provided in the history of the Roman
Catholic colony of Maryland.

After the success of the Puritan cause in England,
Lord Baltimore displaced Greene, the Roman Catholic
governor, in favour of William Stone, a Protestant and
a Parliamentarian, but in the year 1649 he submitted to
the colony a draft of a Toleration Act which was passed
in an assembly largely composed of Romanists. The
preamble of the act is especially interesting. It began
with the admission that "the inforceing of the conscience
in matters of Religion hath frequently fallen out to be of
dangerous Consequence in those commonwealthes where
it hath been practiced," and the act went on to decree
that no person "professing to beleive in Jesus Christ"
should be in any way "troubled, molested or discountenanced for or in respect of his or her religion nor in
the free exercise thereof...nor any way compelled to the
beleife or exercise of any other Religion against his or
her consent, soe as they be not unfaithfull to the Lord
Proprietary." This protection to the Roman Catholics
in the enjoyment of religious freedom was withdrawn in

1654, but the act was revived in 1658 and constitutes a noticeable landmark in the development of the theory of toleration[1].

But in England religious differences were to such a large extent the badges of political parties that no Government was prepared to disregard them, and it is therefore hardly surprising if the liberty in matters of religion which followed the rise of the Independents was understood only in a very limited sense, and went very little way towards a complete scheme of toleration. The numerous proposals in this direction which were formulated or discussed invariably stopped short at "Popery and Prelacy" and the use of the book of Common Prayer. The nearest approach to a complete toleration was probably contained in the series of proposals drawn up by the Independent party and submitted to the King in August 1647. They contemplated a wide liberty of worship and the abrogation of all acts and clauses which enjoined the use of the Prayer Book. Several even of the bishops, to whom, at the King's direction, Sheldon submitted the proposals, were in favour of compliance. The Bishop of Oxford (Robert Skinner) wrote that "in such a strait, such a toleration is...not only lawful but expedient[2]": and Ussher agreed that "in such exigents" a Christian prince has "a latitude allowed him[3]." The Bishop of Rochester (John Warner) was more guarded, but thought that such a toleration would be admissible if the tolerated religions "be not destructive to the catholic faith, or the real settled peace of the kingdom; or so that he [the King] oblige not

---

[1] *Select Charters illustrative of American history*, ed. W. Macdonald, p. 105.

[2] Letter from the Bishop of Oxford to Sheldon, printed in H. Cary's *Memorials*, i, 329.

[3] *Ibid.* i, 335.

himself to such a toleration for ever, but until he may regain the power given him by God, whereby to reduce them, by a Christian and meek way, to one right and well-grounded religion[1]."

As the negotiations proceeded, however, the limits of the proposed liberty became more strictly defined. Following on the formulation of the " Heads of the Proposals " by the Army in August 1647, the House of Commons also took up the subject of toleration, and on October 13, 1647, passed a series of resolutions. While allowing for liberty of worship, they distinctly stated that "their indulgence shall not extend to tolerate the use of the book of common prayer in any place whatsoever[2]." The same reservation was made in their proposals submitted to Charles at Carisbrooke in the following December[3]. The subsequent enactments of the Independents adopted a similar attitude towards Episcopacy in general. Both the " Agreement of the People," and the " Instrument of Government," while allowing for a toleration of " such as profess faith in God by Jesus Christ," provided that it should not necessarily extend to " Popery and Prelacy[4]."

But although the Prayer Book had been placed under the ban, its abolition had been a work of time. The Presbyterians, especially in Scotland, were particularly bitter against it, but natural opposition of principles prevented them at first from carrying the Independents with them. A first step was made in January or February 1643/4 when both Houses of Parliament petitioned the Assembly of Divines to provide them with a minister " to pray to God with them." " By these

---

[1] H. Cary: *Memorials*, i, 346.
[2] *Commons' Journals*, v, 333.
[3] W. A. Shaw : *Hist. of the Eng. Ch.* 1640–60, ii, 70.
[4] S. R. Gardiner : *Constitutional Documents*, pp. 370, 416.

means," wrote Baillie, "the relicks of the Service-Book, which till then were every day used in both Houses, are at last banished[1]." On November 21, 1644, the "Directory for Worship," which was to take the place of the detested Prayer Book, was finished ; on January 3 following, it was passed by the Lords, and on February 27, the Scots Commissioners were able to report that it had been approved by the Assembly and Parliament of Scotland. Subsequently some small alterations were made at the desire of the Scots, but on March 5 the Directory was adopted, together with an ordinance "for the taking away of the Book of Common Prayer, and for establishing and observing of this present Directory throughout the kingdom of England and Dominion of Wales[2]."

In the Preface to the Directory, it was stated that "long and sad experience hath made it manifest; that the Leiturgie used in the Church of England (notwithstanding all the pains and religious intentions of the compilers of it) hath proved an offence, not onely to many of the Godly at home, but also to the Reformed Churches abroad." Many had been kept from the Lord's Table and "divers able and faithfull ministers debarred from the exercise of their ministry," while Papists had been able to boast that "the Book was a compliance with them in a great part of their service[3]. It was therefore ordered that the Book of Common Prayer "shall not remain, or be from henceforth used in any Church, Chappel, or place of public worship."

On August 26, 1645, this was supplemented by the issue of a further ordinance, providing for the effective

[1] *Baillie's Letters* (1841), ii, 130.
[2] W. A. Shaw : *Hist. of the Eng. Ch.* 1640–60, i, 350, 353, 354.
[3] *Acts and Ordinances of the Interregnum* (Ed. C. H. Firth and R. S. Rait), i, 582 *et seq.*

distribution and enforcement of the Directory, and naming the penalties to be incurred by those who continued to use the Prayer Book. It was ordained that " if any person or persons whatsoever, shall at any time or times hereafter, use, or cause the aforesaid book of Common-Prayer to be used in any Church, Chappel, or publique place of worship, or in any private place or family...every such person so offending therein, shall for the first offence forfeit and pay the sum of five pounds of lawfull English money, for the second offence the sum of ten pounds, and for the third offence shall suffer one whole year's imprisonment without bail or mainprize[1]."

Two years afterwards, a further blow at the Church service was dealt by an ordinance making it illegal to observe the feasts of Christmas, Easter and Whitsuntide[2].

According to the letter of the law, then, the Episcopalians and their Prayer Book were to be suppressed with a heavy hand. How far was this suppression made a reality by the ruling power ?

On the whole, it would be correct to say that the Common Prayer was absolutely banished, and that the Church service could only be performed privately and by stealth.

In December 1647 complaints were made to the House of Commons to the effect that malignant ministers were countenanced in some parts of London "where they preach and use the Common Prayer Book contrary to the ordinance of Parliament," upon which the House ordered that the Committee for Plundered Ministers should be directed to examine and punish any who had been accessories to such proceedings[3]. Possibly as a

[1] *Acts and Ordinances of the Interregnum* (Ed. C. H. Firth and R. S. Rait), i, 755 *et seq.*

[2] *Ibid.* i, 954, June 8, 1647.

[3] Rushworth : *Historical Collections*, vii, 944, quoted in J. E. Bailey's *Life of Fuller*, p. 416.

result of this order, Fuller, who shortly before had been acting as lecturer at S. Clement's, Eastcheap, ceased to officiate in that capacity[1] The Church of England was, in short, to use Evelyn's words, "reduced to a chamber and conventicle, so sharp was the persecution[2]." Writing on March 18, 1648/9, Evelyn again records that " Mr Owen, a sequester'd and learned minister, preached in my parlour and gave us the blessed Sacrament, now wholly out of use in the Parish Churchs," and again he speaks of the Sacrament being "administered to me and all my family in Sayes Court," his London house[3]. When his second son was born, the christening was privately performed by the same Mr Owen "in my library at Sayes Court,... because the Parish Minister durst not have officiated according to the forme and usage of the Church of England[4]." On Christmas Day in 1657, a celebration of the Holy Communion in Exeter chapel was interrupted by a party of soldiers, who took the names of the offenders and detained some as prisoners. "When I came before them," writes Evelyn, "they tooke my name and abode, examin'd me why, contrarie to an ordinance made that none should any longer observe ye superstitious time of the Nativity (so esteem'd by them), I durst offend, and particularly be at Common Prayers[5]."

But though this was the case generally, there was a certain number of churches where the clergyman continued to use the liturgy of the Church of England, either with or without the connivance of the ruling power. Mr Bailey, indeed, states that under the Protectorate "the country clergy in possession of the parochial livings were permitted to use the Common Prayer if the local ecclesiastical boards did not object, or to use it with modifications," a practice to which we

---

[1] J. E. Bailey: *Life of Fuller*, 415.   [2] *Memoirs of J. Evelyn* (1819), i, 302
[3] *Ibid.* i, 236, 269.   [4] *Ibid.* i, 272.   [5] *Ibid.* i, 308.

shall refer again later, but, in opposition to this, he quotes the opinion of Mr Lathbury who believed that "in the country the letter of the declaration against the Common Prayer was strictly observed[1]." The available evidence supports the latter view, but a few cases on the other side are well authenticated. Robert Skinner, Bishop of Oxford, held the rectory of Launton during the whole period of the Commonwealth and read prayers and conferred orders there[2]: Heylyn built an oratory in his house at Abingdon and "had constant prayers and sacraments for his own family, and some particular neighbors who had a desire to hear the service and receive the Sacrament according to the Church of England[3]," and other instances are recorded[4]. In London, it was reported in May 1658, that at S. Peter's, Paul's Wharf, "the Common Prayer Book has been many years used by disaffected persons[5]," and at S. Bennet's hard by, the liturgy was constantly used, and the Sacraments administered during the Commonwealth[6].

Under Cromwell, as we shall see presently, there was a greater measure of connivance, but during the earlier years of the Puritan ascendency, the Episcopalian, even when he dared to use the Prayer Book at all, was obliged to do so with extreme caution. Hacket, while officiating at S. Andrew's, Holborn, had his life threatened by a soldier, because he used the Church liturgy, and Dr Sanderson, while reading prayers at Boothby Pagnell,

[1] J. E. Bailey: *Life of Fuller*, pp. 597–8.
[2] Stoughton: *Church of the Commonwealth*, p. 308.
[3] *Historical and Miscellaneous Tracts of...Peter Heylyn* (1681), p. xxvi.
[4] One of John Walker's correspondents told him that John Waltham, the incumbent of Dodbrooke, "notwithstanding frequent complaints made against him...still read a considerable part of ye comon prayer as the Rubrick directed." G. B. Tatham: *Dr John Walker and the Sufferings of the Clergy*, p. 194. See also *ibid.* p. 294.
[5] *Cal. of S. P. Dom.* 1658–9, pp. 13–14.
[6] J. E. Bailey: *Life of Fuller*, p. 507.

had his book torn from him by a party of soldiers[1]. Under these circumstances, it was found necessary to disguise the fact that they used the obnoxious book. Sanderson, for example, after the incident just mentioned, "did vary somewhat from the strict rules of the rubric[2]," and Edward Rainbow and Bull compiled prayers of their own based on those in the Prayer Book[3]. This method was adopted by a considerable number of the Episcopalian clergy who retained their livings and outwardly conformed to the new *régime*, and many of the prayers so compiled have been preserved[4].

The experience of Hacket and Sanderson seems to prove that the Prayer Book was as unpopular as ever, but the attitude of a certain section of the clergy in this matter suggests the question how far this was really the case in the country at large. On the one hand, it appears from an allusion contained in a letter from Henry Hammond to Sheldon, written on May 23, 1654, that there was a movement on foot, even amongst the clergy themselves, in favour of the disuse of the Prayer Book. Those who took part in the movement very likely felt that the probability of the restoration of Episcopacy in its old form was too remote to warrant them in holding out indefinitely, and therefore began to contemplate the advisability of some form of compromise. At the same time they were unwilling to do so without authority and some of the deprived bishops seem to have been consulted on the matter[5].

But though few of the bishops would have viewed

[1] J. E. Bailey: *Life of Fuller*, p. 433.

[2] Stoughton: *Church of the Commonwealth*, p. 325.

[3] Walton's *Lives* (ed. T. Zouch, 1796), p. 461.

[4] Stoughton: *Church of the Commonwealth*, p. 340. J. E. Bailey: *Life of Fuller*, p. 610. J. F. Chanter: *Life and Times of Martin Blake*, p. 134.

[5] See the letter in the *Illustrations of the State of the Church* (*Theologian and Ecclesiastic*, xv, 184).

such a proceeding with favour, there was about this time a movement from two opposite quarters in the direction of compromise. Baxter's "Voluntary Associations[1]" represent the beginnings of a more liberal spirit on the part of the Presbyterians and Independents, while a corresponding tendency amongst a section of the Episcopalian party can be traced in some letters written by Dr John Gauden to Dr Bernard in 1656. The letters contain the outlines of a scheme of limited Episcopacy, to which the Doctor had been drawn by the observation of a movement amongst ministers of very different opinions towards "a fraternall accord as to the maine[2]." He found, he says, that "all sides are content to remitt of former rigors and distances[3]," but he was underestimating the difficulties of the business. The fact was that he spoke for the moderate Episcopalians only, men who had always taken a broader view of the position of the Church of England. Divines of the Laudian school were still as much opposed as ever to a relaxation of principles in deference to Puritan demands, and the course which political affairs had taken had tended only to strengthen their uncompromising hostility.

Amongst the people generally, Dr Gardiner states, there was no trace of any demand for the restoration of the Prayer Book[4], but this is somewhat of an overstatement. Besides the evidence contained in Evelyn's *Memoirs*, there are several indications of a tendency in its favour. For example, on a Sunday in September 1649, the Common Prayer was read in many churches in London, and a band of soldiers was called out to interrupt the services[5]. And again, in 1653, there was a marked increase of the illicit use of the Church liturgy,

[1] W. A. Shaw : *Hist. of the Eng. Ch.* 1640–60, ii, 152 *et seq.*
[2] Thurloe : *State Papers*, v, 598.   [3] *Ibid.* v, 600.
[4] *Commonwealth and Protectorate*, ii, 84–5.   [5] *Ibid.* i, 173.

synchronising in this case with a wave of royalist sympathy[1]. In a petition to the Protector, dated December 18, 1654, divers Puritan ministers, in praying for continuance in their cures after the legal incumbent's death, complain that they were displeasing to their congregations because they were divided from them and their party and did not use the service book[2]. In November 1657, Sir Thomas Evelyn received a complaint from the Council in reference to the behaviour of Leonard Hudson, whom he had entertained as his household chaplain. The Council had been informed that Mr Byfield of Long Ditton "has daily received great interruption from Leonard Hudson...who, being prelatical, gathers a concourse of people of like views, and uses the words of the Book of Common Prayer[3]." In May 1658, Thomas Jessop, minister of Luton in Bedfordshire, complained that he had served the cure for eight years, "struggling against a malignant and prelatical party, because I was not episcopally ordained, and they now withdraw the people from my communion and worship in prelatical form[4]." As a last piece of evidence, may be taken a minute of the proceedings in Council, under date December 22, 1657 : "To advise his Highness to send for Mr Guning and Dr Taylor, and require an account of the frequent meetings of multitudes of people held with them, and cause the ordinance for taking away the Book of Common Prayer to be enforced[5]."

The question of the administration of the Holy Communion "occasion'd great and long debates in the House of Commons" and "took up at times the debates

[1] *Commonwealth and Protectorate*, ii, 300.
[2] *Illustrations of the State of the Church* (*Theologian and Ecclesiastic*, xvi, 187). The author gives no reference for this.
[3] *Cal. of S. P. Dom.* 1657-8, p. 159.   [4] *Ibid.* 1658-9, p. 37.
[5] *Ibid.* 1657-8, p. 226.

of the House for several months[1]." The principal change proposed was in the matter of suspension in cases of "ignorance and scandal," and the scheme which eventually took shape in an ordinance of Parliament aimed at investing the "Elders" of the congregation with a power to decide who were fit persons to be admitted to the Sacrament. This restriction upon the right of the individual to take part in the most solemn service of the Church was severely criticised by Selden and Whitelock who argued that there was no justification for the new power of rejection and that the elders were, in any case, an unsuitable tribunal to exercise it[2], but the contrary opinion prevailed and an ordinance was issued on October 20, 1645[3].

General rules were laid down for the guidance of the elders of the congregation. In the first place certain fundamental doctrines are stated as necessary to those who were to be admitted to the Sacrament, and the ordinance then proceeds to enumerate the various forms of "scandal" which would justify suspension, idolatry and sabbath-breaking taking place beside breaches of the moral and civil law. Appeal was to be allowed, in the case of any person who felt himself to be aggrieved, to a series of superior tribunals culminating in Parliament itself.

It was obviously the intention of the Government to impress upon the minds of ministers and of their congregations that the Holy Communion was a solemn and awful thing and it seems clear that it was so regarded. The diary of Ralph Josselin, the incumbent of Earl's Colne, describes fully the careful searchings of heart

[1] Rushworth: *Historical Collections*, vol. vi, pp. 203, 205.
[2] *Ibid.* pp. 203–5.
[3] *Acts and Ordinances of the Interregnum* (Ed. C. H. Firth and R. S. Rait), i, 789.

which preluded the "first celebration of the ordinance,"
after an intermission of many years, in February 1649/50.
"Jan: 30, wee mett at priory," he writes, "divers presd
y^t persons must make out a worke of true grace on y^r
hearts in order to fellowship and this ordinance." Two
meetings were held at his house "to take names and
admitt by joynt consent." He "admonisht divers," and
admitted others but "divers christians hung backe,"
and then finally the service wás performed.

"Wee all sat round and neare ye table; ye bread
was broken not cutt in blessing it ; ye Lord pourd out a
spirit of mourning over Christ crucified on me and most
of ye company, and my soule eyed him more y^n ever, and
God was sweete to mee in ye worke[1]."

The liberty to preach stood on a different basis to
the liberty to use the liturgical forms of the Episcopal
Church. The use of the Prayer Book had been condemned by ordinance, but as long as the Episcopalian
clergy gave an outward conformity to the Puritan discipline, their public preaching could be tolerated without a
breach of the law. It is not to be supposed, however, that
the Puritan Government, as a general rule, was disposed
to grant such toleration, especially if the clergyman in
question had been connected with the royalist cause, and
the cases in which liberty to preach was allowed or
connived at were in the nature of exceptions.

The account of the means by which the Episcopalian
clergy first regained entry to the pulpits of parish churches
reveals the Puritans in a position of being hoist with
their own petard. In 1641, as a blow against the rigour
of the Laudian system, the Parliament had passed an
ordinance allowing parishioners liberty "to set up a
lecture, and to maintain an orthodox minister at their

[1] *Ralph Josselin's Diary*, edited by E. Hockliffe (Camden Series iii,
vol. xv), pp. 82–4.

own charge, to preach every Lord's day where there is no preaching, and to preach one day in every week where there is no weekly lecture." It was under the protection of this ordinance, that Fuller and other Episcopalian divines began to preach in London in 1647 and 1648[1]. The Parliament endeavoured to put an end to this state of things, and Fuller himself, as has been seen, was obliged temporarily to desist, but the practice continued to some extent throughout the length of the Commonwealth period. In view of the antagonism with which the Episcopalian incumbents had viewed the Puritan lecturers in earlier times, it is particularly interesting to notice that the Puritans themselves, when established as parish ministers, frequently were no less sensitive on the subject of these supplementary sermons, from whichever party they proceeded[2].

A dispute which occurred at S. Botolph's, Aldgate, provides an interesting example of this, and is worth describing at length. The parties to the quarrel were Zachary Crofton, the incumbent, and John Simpson, who had been authorised by an order in Council, dated February 10, 1656/7, to lecture in the church on Sunday afternoons and on one week-day. On July 31, 1657, Crofton wrote to Simpson to inform him that if the order by which he invaded his church gave him any power, the late revolution had made it void, since the Protector had sworn to govern according to law. He announced his intention of preaching on the afternoon of Sunday, August 2, between one and two o'clock, and therefore desired him to cease his "future pains there" and to signify the same to his friends, in order that there

---

[1] J. E. Bailey: *Life of Fuller*, p. 412.

[2] This, however, was not always the case. For example, Fuller seems to have been on friendly terms with Simon Ash the incumbent of S. Bride's where he was lecturer in 1655. See Bailey's *Life of Fuller*, p. 589.

might be no disturbance. On August 4, a large number of "Common Councilmen, Churchwardens and other well-affected inhabitants" petitioned the Protector on Simpson's behalf, and Crofton was summoned to answer for his contempt of the order in Council. On August 14, the same petitioners complained that on August 9, Crofton had refused Simpson the pulpit and "kept it, being guarded by constables of Middlesex, who have no authority within the liberties of the City of London, and caused much disturbance, hazarding bloodshed." The quarrel continued during the succeeding months, and finally, on information that he preached against the Government, Crofton was referred to the Committee for Ejecting Scandalous Ministers[1]. After the Restoration, Crofton again got into trouble, though he petitioned for pardon on the ground that he had been "loyal in the worst of times and suffered sequestration and imprisonment." In a contemporary letter, however, he was described as a "Presbyterian, a subtle, witty man,...bitter against the Bishops and...a great vexation to them[2]."

A somewhat similar case occurred at Tewkesbury in August 1658. On the 19th of that month, John Wells, the minister in possession, wrote to the Council on the subject of "a malignant lecturer put in upon me....I appointed Thomas Holtham," he informed them, "to stop Mr Hopkins at the Church door, whilst he was coming to preach his lecture on a Tuesday." A disturbance followed, and ended in the lecturer's favour. Hopkins succeeded in preaching, and Holtham was imprisoned on the Act "for disturbing of ministers on the Lord's day[3]."

[1] *Cal. of S. P. Dom.* 1657-8, pp. 48, 50, 62, 64, 65, 133.
[2] *Ibid.* 1660-1, pp. 536, 546. A full account of Crofton and of the incident referred to in the text will be found in *Eng. Hist. Review*, vol. x, p. 41.
[3] *Cal. of S. P. Dom.* 1658-9, p. 117.

But though, in the case of royalist clergy, un-authorised "lecturing" was checked, at the same time, even during the early years of the Puritan ascendency, a small number of well-known divines were allowed to preach unmolested. On December 20, 1647, it was brought to the notice of the Commons that Archbishop Ussher was in the habit of preaching in Lincoln's Inn Chapel, and the House, after a debate, decided that he might continue to do so, although he had formerly adhered to the enemy, on condition that he took the Negative Oath[1]. Fuller, though silenced about the end of 1647, was preaching again in 1649[2], and in 1650 not a few had begun to re-engage in their calling[3].

How far Cromwell's views of toleration extended, it is difficult to decide. If one may judge from his recorded utterances, it would seem that he was far in advance of the great majority of his contemporaries on this important subject, and that he possessed in a remarkable degree the true spirit of toleration. During the course of the Civil War when acting as a General in the employ of a Presbyterian Parliament, he frequently impressed upon the ruling powers that the triumph of their cause was being won by men who would not be contained within the Presbyterian fold, and on one occasion at least he gave unmistakable expression to his view of the narrow policy that would force the people into a rigid conformity.

"We look at ministers," he wrote to the Governor of Edinburgh Castle in September 1650, "as helpers of, not lords over, God's people. I appeal to their consciences, whether any person trying their doctrines, and dissenting, shall not incur the censure of Sectary?

---

[1] Rushworth: *Historical Collections*, vii, 937–8. The House, however, proceeded to say that "delinquent ministers should not take encouragement at this" and gave directions that they should be silenced.
[2] J. E. Bailey: *Life of Fuller*, p. 433.   [3] *Ibid.* pp. 508–9.

And what is this but to deny Christians their liberty, and assume the Infallible Chair[1]?"

Later, when invested with power to formulate his views with greater authority, he insisted again and again upon the truth, once forcibly put into words by himself, that liberty of conscience is a "fundamental," "a natural right," and that "he that would have it, ought to give it[2]."

It is more difficult to say what was the motive force which induced his attitude of mind. At times, as Lord Morley has said, his tolerance seems to proceed "from a rich fountain in his heart of sympathy with men[3]," but at times again it is checked, if not definitely coloured, by the statesman's view of what is expedient. "The State, in choosing men to serve it," he had once written, "takes no notice of their opinions; if they be willing faithfully to serve it, that satisfies[4]." Nor is it possible to say whether his refusal to extend toleration to Papists, sprung from motives of public policy or from the common intellectual inability to pursue conclusions to their logical outcome. "I meddle not with any man's conscience," he wrote to the Governor of Ross in October 1649, "but if by liberty of conscience, you mean a liberty to exercise the Mass, I judge it best to use plain dealing, and to let you know, where the Parliament of England have power, that will not be allowed of[5]."

Even here, however, he claimed that his rule was marked by more lenient treatment, and in his letter to Cardinal Mazarin on the subject of indulgence for the Roman Catholics, while refusing to make a public declaration for that purpose, he reminded his correspondent

---

[1] Carlyle's *Cromwell's Letters and Speeches* (Centenary edition, 1902), ii, 232.   [2] *Ibid.* iii, 147.
[3] Morley : *Oliver Cromwell* (Macmillan, 1904), p. 379.
[4] Carlyle's *Cromwell's Letters and Speeches*, i, 182.   [5] *Ibid.* ii, 83.

that, under his government, there was "less reason for complaint as to rigour upon mens' consciences than under the Parliament[1]." Even if he himself had wished for a wide toleration, he must have realised that men's minds were not prepared for it and that the time was not ripe. On the other hand, he was willing to act with some leniency, where political considerations did not forbid. Certainly, under his rule, a considerable amount of freedom was allowed, and the condition of the Episcopalians improved. Ussher was on terms of friendship with him, and remained unmolested at Lincoln's Inn Chapel. On his death the Protector contributed £200 towards the expenses of a public funeral and permitted the Church burial service to be used[2]. Peter Gunning, to mention another instance, officiated constantly, and in spite of occasional interruptions, at Exeter Chapel, and George Wilde preached twice at least in London[3]. Neal, indeed, states that several of the clergy at this time "indulged the public exercise of their ministry without the fetters of oaths, subscriptions or engagements," and besides Wilde, he instances Hall, afterwards Bishop of Chester, Pearson, Ball, Hardy, Griffith and Farringdon[4]. This represents the moderate school of Episcopalian divines. Stricter churchmen, like Henry Hammond and Herbert Thorndike, deprecated any form of compliance, and would not have availed themselves of the liberty even had it been offered[5].

On February 15, 1654/5, a proclamation on religious liberty was issued, which, without specifying the tolerated sects, promised freedom "to all persons in this

[1] Carlyle's *Cromwell's Letters and Speeches*, iv, 5.
[2] Stoughton: *Church of the Commonwealth*, pp. 304-5.
[3] Once on April 15, 1655, at S. Gregory's, and once on Dec. 25 in the same year. See *Memoirs of J. Evelyn* (1819), i, 293, 297.
[4] *Hist. of Puritans* (1822), iv, 72.
[5] Stoughton: *Church of the Commonwealth*, pp. 332, 335.

Commonwealth fearing God, though of differing judgments, by protecting them in the sober and quiet exercise and profession of religion and the sincere worship of God[1]." In some respects, these provisions represent the high-water mark of religious toleration during the Interregnum, but they were destined soon to be curtailed. In the following month, a royalist insurrection under Col. Penruddock broke out in Wiltshire, and, though it was all over within a month, it served, in conjunction with the real or supposed assassination plots of the following summer, to give a new turn to the Protector's ecclesiastical policy. He now began to treat the Royalists as a class apart, and this necessarily involved restrictive measures towards the royalist clergy. On August 24, the Major-Generals were instructed to inquire into the execution of the law for the ejection of scandalous ministers[2], but a much more serious blow was dealt on September 21, by the issue of a series of orders for "securing the peace of the Commonwealth." Two clauses related to the royalist clergy. The fifth directed that "From November 1st, 1655, none of the party [i.e. the Royalists] are to keep in their houses chaplains, schoolmasters, ejected ministers, or fellows of colleges, nor have their children taught by such": the sixth ordered that "none who have been, or shall be, ejected from any benefice, college, or school, for delinquency or scandal, are after 1. Nov. 1655, to keep any school, preach, or administer the sacraments, marry persons or use the Book of Common Prayer, on pain of 3 months imprisonment; on a second offence, 6 months; and on a third, banishment." A saving clause was added: "unless

[1] Gardiner: *Commonwealth and Protectorate*, iii, 260. The proclamation excluded the more violent sectaries "under the names of Quakers, Ranters, and others."
[2] *Ibid.* iii, 321.

their hearts are changed, and they obtain the approval of the Commissioners for Public Preachers[1]." It was found impossible to put the whole of these orders in force within the time mentioned, and by a subsequent declaration of November 24, the day by which the royalist clergy were to lose their chaplaincies was altered to January 1. In this case also, a saving clause was appended to the effect that to those who had given "a real testimony of their godliness and good affection to the present government, so much tenderness shall be used as may consist with the safety and good of this nation[2]."

Yet, even with this proviso, the declaration fell like a thunderbolt amongst the royalist clergy. Under the milder administration of the laws against delinquents many had returned to the exercise of their duties[3], either in parishes or, more commonly, in private families, but according to the strict interpretation of the new edict, they saw themselves not only deprived of their homes at the present, but also cut off from all hope of maintenance for the future. Some letters written about this time to Sancroft by Thomas Holbeach, the rector of Chastleton, illustrates the consternation that the declaration had caused.

"My state is this," he writes on January 5 ; "I have hitherto, since I heard the news, continued my course without the least fayling either of service, sermons, or communions in their solemnity, and upon the first of this present [month] I preached for ought I know my last." In a week or two he hopes to know "what will be done,

---

[1] *Cal. of S. P. Dom.* 1655, p. 347.

[2] Gardiner : *Commonwealth and Protectorate*, iii, pp. 334–5.

[3] Walker states (*Sufferings of the Clergy*, Pt. i, p. 171) that this was due to the Act of Oblivion passed on February 24, 1651/2, but this excepted all guilty of "high treason (other than for words only)" and would not have covered the case of the great majority of royalist clergy.

and learne what will be the penalty of offenders, or upon
what terms favour may be hoped. For my part," he
continues, " I expect none, but yet have no mind to cast
off my calling and subsistence till I must needs, and
yet shall never regard either so much as to deale un-
worthily for the enjoyment of them." He asks, therefore,
for information and advice. " How many are by this
cashiered that you know of? Doe any of perfect
integrity continue on still? May the administration of
the Sacrament be continued in ritus et leges ecclesiae
Anglicanae¹?"

On January 27, he stands "still at gaze expecting
the issue²," but on February 10, he writes that he is "still
suspended as before, and the rather because as yet no
Commissions are come into our county by whom that
I should have any restitution." A lady neighbour was
endeavouring to make interest on his behalf with Sir
William Fleetwood, "but against this I have this to
object, that upon what tearmes his allowance would be
granted I am utterly ignorant: the least, I believe, will
be approbation and affection to the present government,
and whether I have such or noe, I would not willingly
be asked." He asks Sancroft to let him know how
matters were tending. "Some say that [it] is the
generall ayme to bring all to such addresse and acknow-
ledgment³."

In his next letter, dated March 16, he shows that he
has given up hope of a favourable issue of his case. The
contents of Sancroft's last letter "confirme me in myne
opinion at first and make good your judgment that all
this is but dallyance and dissimulation, but ruine, as farre
as can be, is the designe. Accordingly, therefore, I am
disposing of myne affaires, having begun to sell both

¹ Tanner MSS. (Bodl.), 52, fol. 100.
² *Ibid.* fol. 104.   ³ *Ibid.* fol. 109.

books and goods, and intending to goe on, that the proceeds of them may be a subsistence to us. Only I procure my place till May daie, because by that meanes I hope the better to induce my Parishioners to pay what we agreed for for the whole year. You say very right if my sequestration had not been taken notice of, I might have adventured to have gone on, but the malice of some made that knowne soone enough to cut the throat of any such purpose, and now my forbearance hath published it farre and wide[1]."

Holbeach's case was not singular. After January 1, clergymen, who had in the past suffered sequestration, were frequently deprived of the cures which they held, or hindered from obtaining livings to which they sought admission. In practice, however, if a candidate received the approval of the Commissioners for Approbation, a license to preach could generally be obtained from the Protector. For example, on November 11, 1656, permission to exercise his ministry was granted on the petition of William Belke. He had been sequestered from Wotton in August 1644, but the Committee for Plundered Ministers had informed him, on December 5, 1645, that "their censure was to be no obstacle" to his obtaining other employment, as they were satisfied of his conformity to Parliament, orthodoxy and good life. On this, he had been presented to the living of Chilham, and had preached until he was silenced by the Protector's declaration[2].

There are also numerous cases, preserved among the State Papers, where clergymen received licenses to enable them to enter upon a cure. On March 30, 1658, John Halke, who had been sequestered in 1646, petitioned for restoration to the liberty of preaching, and, on a

---

[1] Tanner MSS. (Bodl.), 52, fol. 113.
[2] *Cal. of S. P. Dom.* 1656–7, p. 154.

favourable report from three Puritan divines, he received an order permitting him to "exercise his gifts" if approved by the Commissioners for Approbation[1].

In January 1656/7 Robert Jennings, who had been ejected from his living at the visitation of the county of Oxford, was "freed from ejectment" and enabled to preach, after being approved[2]. On June 10, 1658, a license to preach was granted to Michael Jermin, D.D., who had been deprived of two benefices, one in London, and another in Sussex[3], and other instances of similar petitions might be given.

The verdict was not always favourable. In October 1658, Henry Beesley, who had been ejected from his parsonage, petitioned for a reference to Council, that, by their approbation he might be restored to the ministry. He submitted a certificate of his fitness, but his petition was dismissed. It had probably been brought to the notice of the Council that, in the previous April, he had been convicted of "public and profane scoffing and swearing[4]."

On the whole, it does not seem that the severe declarations of September and November 1655 affected the general position of the royalist clergy very seriously. In an interview with some of the leaders of the moderate Episcopalians in 1656, Cromwell practically undertook that they should not be molested as long as they caused no disturbance[5]. Dr Gardiner states that as far as private chaplains were concerned, there is no evidence that any ejections took place in consequence of this order, and that even Walker "did not succeed in producing a single instance of a chaplain or a schoolmaster reduced to poverty by this action of the Protector[6]."

[1] *Cal. of S. P. Dom.* 1657-8, pp. 351, 375.   [2] *Ibid.* 1656-7, p. 231.
[3] *Ibid.* 1658-9, p. 57.   [4] *Ibid.* pp. 28, 54, 157.
[5] Gardiner: *Commonwealth and Protectorate*, iii, 323, 336.   [6] *Ibid.* p. 336.

As a matter of fact, this is not quite correct, for Walker, although he admitted that the ordinance was allowed to drop, nevertheless states that, through fear of the consequences, "a great deal of disturbance" was occasioned amongst the clergy, and he instances Hales, a former Canon of Windsor, who was actually led to relinquish his chaplaincy on that account[1]. In the main contention, however, Dr Gardiner is no doubt correct, and here again instances of dispensation are not wanting. By an order of July 1, 1656, Dr Allestree was allowed to officiate as chaplain to Sir Anthony Cope[2], and Arthur Leonard, chaplain to the Earl of Banbury, petitioned for a similar license in September following, though in this case the result is not stated[3].

Outwardly, however, there was no relaxation of the law. The ordinances against "scandalous" ministers, under which head royalist clergymen would not infrequently be included, were still enforced, and from time to time the authorities were even urged to "renewed diligence" in the work[4]. In April 1657 a debate took place on the subject, and was the occasion of some complaints being made against the injustice of the commissioners. On the other hand, it was considered that the good work done had justified their existence, and it was decided that the ordinances should remain in force for three years, unless Parliament should take further notice of the subject in the meantime[5]. It was not until the last months of the Interregnum that the principle, tacitly recognised by Cromwell, took shape in a formal statement. On March 16, 1659/60, an Act, dealing with the question of complaints against undue

[1] Walker: *Sufferings of the Clergy*, Pt. i, 195.
[2] *Cal. of S. P. Dom.* 1656-7, p. 3.   [3] *Ibid.* p. 107.
[4] *Ibid.* 1657-8, pp. 50, 63, 112.
[5] Stoughton: *Church of the Commonwealth*, p. 146.

sequestration, ordered that ejected ministers were to be capable of holding livings if blameless and of sound doctrine[1].

In the appointment of ministers to livings, under the Puritan *régime*, the rights of patrons were recognised, except in the case of "delinquents." The Long Parliament had not interfered with the existing system and though patronage was condemned in a resolution of the Nominated Parliament, it was accepted by the Protector in 1654[2]. Where the patron was a delinquent, considerable concessions were made to the principle of popular election, subject to the control of the officially appointed authorities. Under the Long Parliament, the county committees appointed to livings in the gift of delinquents, but the wishes of the parishioners were generally consulted, and nominations to Crown livings were made by the parishioners directly[3]. The work of examining and approving candidates for preferment was, from November 1647 to its dissolution in March 1652, performed by the Westminster Assembly of Divines[4]. On March 20, 1653/4, Cromwell replaced this system by the institution of a body of Commissioners for the Approbation of Public Preachers, better known under their shorter title of "Triers."

This body was composed of ministers and laymen and met in London. The right of presentation was left with the legal patron, provided that the vacant living was filled up within six months. The candidate was obliged to procure a certificate testifying to his "holy and good conversation," signed by at least three persons, of whom one was to be a minister. So provided, he presented himself before the commissioners in London, to

[1] *Acts and Ordinances of the Interregnum* (Ed. C. H. Firth and R. S. Rait), ii, 1469.
[2] Gardiner, *Commonwealth and Protectorate*, ii, 84, 321 ; iii, 22.
[3] *Ibid.* ii, 84. [4] *Camb. Mod. Hist.* iv, 362.

"be judged and approved...to be a person for the Grace of God in him, his holy and unblameable conversation, as also for his knowledge and utterance, able and fit to preach the Gospel[1]." The power of the commissioners was retrospective, and they were empowered to examine all who had been presented to livings since April 1, 1653.

The proceedings of this tribunal were bitterly assailed in the pages of contemporary royalist tracts, one of the best known of which, Anthony Sadler's *Inquisitio Anglicana*, was written by a clergyman who had himself failed to obtain approval. Walker condemns the commissioners in the strongest terms, and regards their institution as a blow aimed chiefly at the royalist clergy. It "was done," he says, "with a particular regard to the exclusion of the old loyalists, and no doubt, of those young ones likewise who might have arisen, and been then ready to offer themselves." And again : "it is undeniable both from the subsidiary ordinance before mentioned[2], and from the whole course of the proceedings of these Commissioners, that the old Loyalists were excluded from the benefit of approbation[3]." He further accuses them of corruption. They "might not only...be well suspected," he says, "of practising, but are also well known in fact, to have practised such partialities and corruptions, under the great temptations of so high a trust, as, I think, I hardly ever met with, so much as charged on any bishop, by the worst of his enemies[4]."

This view is manifestly one-sided. Walker states that he had seen some of the records of the commissioners when he was searching in the Lambeth Palace Library[5],

[1] *Acts and Ordinances of the Interregnum* (Ed. C. H. Firth and R. S. Rait), ii, 855.
[2] Probably Cromwell's "Silencing Edict" of Sept. 21, 1655.
[3] John Walker : *Sufferings of the Clergy*, Pt. i, pp. 171, 173.
[4] *Ibid.* Pt. i, p. 172.
[5] *Ibid.* Pt. i, p. 173. Probably the two volumes containing certificates of approbation. Lambeth Palace Library MSS. 996–7.

and he mentions that an answer to the *Inquisitio Anglicana* was published under the title of *Mr Sadler Examined*[1], but he does not seem to have referred to the *Inquisitio*, and he had never seen the answer.

The answer to which he refers was published in the same year as the *Inquisitio*, and was probably written by Philip Nye, one of the commissioners[2]. Naturally, it gives a very different version of their proceedings. The author explains that the delay in hearing cases, one of the complaints brought by Sadler and others, was occasioned by the press of applications from those whose tenure of preferment required confirmation. He declares that the details of Mr Taylor's case, quoted by Sadler, are falsely reported, and that approval was withheld because the commissioners discovered that Taylor's certificate was forged. This, Nye says, was so plainly proved that Taylor himself "could not at last but acknowledge it[3]." Similarly he accuses Sadler of misrepresentation in his own case. Sadler had stated that the commissioners' minute-book merely recorded that "such an one was examined, and no more." Nye refutes this. The entry distinctly stated he was "not approved[4]."

According to Nye, the ordinary method of procedure was as follows: "1. Although the certificate do not satisfie so fully, yet they call in the person. 2. If they finde him so qualified, as if he had a good certificate, they might approve, he is no longer necessitated to any personall attendance, but may by any friend or sollicitor exhibite his better certificate, and by the same hand receive the instrument of his admittance. 3. If a man be in any respect doubtfull, they take the trouble of

---

[1] John Walker: *Sufferings of the Clergy*, Pt. i, p. 177.
[2] *Mr Sadler Re-examined.* Brit. Mus. E. 818 (10).
[3] *Ibid.* p. 6.   [4] *Ibid.* p. 9.

enquiry upon themselves (as in this instance[1]) for having the advantage of frequent posts in the compasse of a week or ten daies they can understand from any part of England, and know of what repute the man is whencesoever he comes. This Mr Sadler laieth to their charge, pag. 2., as a crime. 'They have by their informers (saith he) intelligence from all parts[2].'"

The charge of corruption Nye indignantly repudiates. "I do not beleeve it can be said of any of them, that ever they have attempted directly or indirectly to pleasure themselves or any relation or friend of theirs, with any living that for want of their approbation hath hitherto become vacant; much less to disapprove anyone upon such a vile consideration....Many good livings," he goes on, "that were in his Highnesses gift had been void...which (for fit men) they might as likely have procured if their design had been for livings[3]." He admits that money was offered: "Twenty, forty pounds at a time hath been offered me to get a person approved, but I never heard of a farthing offered to put any man by....Ten persons (if of worth) have been put into places with less trouble, then ordinarily one man is disapproved. The indulgence of the Commissioners is such, and their unwillingness to misunderstand of any person's worth, that liberty is given to those that for present are disapproved, to return and be examined again even toties quoties[4]."

At the same time, Nye passes over almost without comment the verbatim account which Sadler had given of his own examination. He merely says that he had heard some of the commissioners "wonder with what

---

[1] *i.e.* Taylor's case.

[2] *Mr Sadler Re-examined*, p. 5; cf. *Sufferings of the Clergy*, Pt. i, pp. 173-4.

[3] *Mr Sadler Re-examined*, pp. 7-8; cf. *Sufferings of the Clergy*, Pt. i, pp. 172, 174.   [4] *Mr Sadler Re-examined*, p. 10.

conscience he could offer...to be deposed for the truth of them[1]."

The minutes of the commissioners' proceedings are lost, and the only extant records of their work are contained in one or two volumes of certificates of approbation[2]. Under these circumstances it is difficult to form an estimate of their character. On the whole it is reasonable to suppose that the accounts given by aggrieved persons, and reproduced in Walker's pages, are considerably overdrawn. Others besides Royalists were rejected, and, though the natural tendency of the commissioners would be to exclude any whose opinions were widely at variance with their own, we have already seen that not a few royalist clergy did obtain their approval[3]. On the other hand, the accounts, given by Sadler and others, though possibly inaccurate as to the details, show that the actual examination turned largely upon the question of whether or no the candidate were possessed of the Grace of God, and at what exact date the work of regeneration in him began. The result was often a confused and unedifying discussion on points which neither the candidate nor the commissioners understood. The lines upon which the "Triers" proceeded, in fact, made it inevitable that many worthy men would be rejected and not a few hypocrites received, but the highly-coloured accounts by royalist pamphleteers must be accepted with reserve.

The exclusion of able clergymen was the more to be regretted, because, in the early years of the Puritan *régime* at all events, there seems to have been a great dearth of

---

[1] *Mr Sadler Re-examined*, p. 8.

[2] Lambeth Palace Library MSS. 996-7. See W. A. Shaw: *Hist. of the Eng. Ch.* 1640-60, ii, 472.

[3] Stoughton : *Church of the Commonwealth*, pp. 105-7. In a few cases, examination by the "Triers" may have been evaded. It was so in the case of Edward Rainbow. See *Dict. Nat. Biog.*

ministers to serve the cures throughout the country, caused by the wholesale ejection during the Civil War. In many cases pulpits were filled by unordained and uneducated men. Evelyn speaks of the pulpits of the London churches being "full of novices and novelties," and "Independents and Phanatics[1]." On one occasion, at Rye, he heard "one of their canters, who dismiss'd the assembly rudely and without any blessing," and on another he was surprised to see "a tradesman, a mechanic" step into the pulpit[2]. In many cases too the churches were without regular incumbents. At the Savoy Conference, Bishop Morley asserted that this had been so, and instanced the parish of Aylesbury. Baxter denied this, but the Church Survey of 1650 shows Morley to have been correct[3]. The same survey shows that in 1650, out of the fourteen churches in the town of Cambridge, only three, S. Peter's, S. Bene't's and S. Andrew's had settled ministers[4].

In the meantime, the exiled church was taking steps to preserve its continuity. The Bishop of Oxford, Robert Skinner, and the Bishop of Chichester, Henry King, both contrived to confer orders in England[5], and Evelyn mentions an ordination being held in Sir Richard Browne's chapel in Paris in June 1650, when "the Bishop of Galloway officiated with greate gravity[6]."

A more important question was that of the consecration of bishops. When, after the execution of the King, and the failure of Charles II's campaign at Worcester, the prospect of the ultimate triumph of the royalist cause

---

[1] *Memoirs of J. Evelyn* (1819), i, 247, 262.   [2] *Ibid.* i, 265, 272.
[3] Stoughton : *Church of the Commonwealth*, p. 434 ; Brit. Mus. Lansdowne MSS. 459.
[4] Brit. Mus. Lansdowne MSS. 459, fol. 152.
[5] Stoughton : *Church of the Commonwealth*, p. 308. *Clarendon State Papers* (1786), iii, App. p. c.
[6] *Memoirs of J. Evelyn* (1819), i, 244.

seemed to depend upon the dim and uncertain chances of the future, the danger that the regular Episcopal succession might be interrupted became apparent, and the importance of providing in time against such an event began to agitate the minds of churchmen and to find expression in the secret correspondence which was maintained between the adherents of the Episcopal Church at home and abroad. In a letter from Henry Hammond, probably to Bishop Wren, dated October 14, 1651, the writer says that he has been "put in mind by G[ilbert] S[heldon] to be a remembrancer to some of those who are concerned, to think of doing somewhat to preserve a church among us, lest it perish with their order[1]," and to the same effect, a correspondent, signing himself "Belleau," tells Sheldon, in a letter from Paris on October 4 of the same year, that he hopes shortly "there will be a course taken to perpetuate that church, which methinks can never fail[2]." The main difficulty at that time was to collect a sufficient number of bishops to perform the ceremony in proper form, without exciting the suspicion of the Puritan government[3], but the project was not allowed to drop, and we find Dr Duncan writing to Clarendon in June 1655 in a strain that suggests that this difficulty was likely to be overcome[4]. The fateful year 1659, however, found the Episcopalians still considering ways and means.

The situation had by this time become serious, for the surviving bishops were in advanced years, and it would be "almost a Miracle," Clarendon wrote, " if the Winter

---

[1] Quoted in *Illustrations of the State of the Church* (*Theologian and Ecclesiastic*, ix, 294).   [2] *Ibid.* x, 328.   [3] *Ibid.* vi, 298.

[4] "I consulted often with those five Bishops, to whom I was directed, viz., Ely, Sarum, Rochester, Lichfield, and Chichester; and they were all very glad to hear that care was taken for the preservation of their Order: and ready to advise, and do anything in their power that might further it." *Clarendon State Papers*, iii, App. p. c.

doth not take away half the Bishops that are left alive[1]."
In the event of this gloomy foreboding being fulfilled, those
who were moving in the business foresaw that the continuity of their church was in imminent danger, for the
assistance of a continental church could not be invoked
except at the price of sacrificing the distinctive purity of
their own[2]. Nor did it seem that the brightening
horizon of the royalist cause, even if it heralded the
restoration of the King, was bringing any certain promise
for the Episcopal Church.

"I will tell you a Phancy of my own," wrote
Clarendon on July 8, 1659. "...The late Revolutions in
England, and the several Humours, and Distempers, and
Jealousies in several factions amongst themselves, make
it a very natural Supposition, that there may fall out
some avowed Treaty with the King; and then the
Presbyterians will not be over modest, in valuing and
computing their own Power....If I were a Presbyterian
(and they have many wiser Men, and who know better
how to compass what themselves desire) I would not
propose to the King to do any formed Act to the
Prejudice of the Church; because I should despair of
prevailing with him; but I would beseech him to suspend the doing any Thing, that should contribute to the
former Establishment, till there might be such a mature
Deliberation, that the best Provision might be made to
compose all Differences: and if I could prevail thus far;
I should hope by some continued Suggestions (which
would be speciously enough administered by Persons
of very distinct Interests) to spin out the Time, till all
the Bishops were dead[3]." "Both the Papist and Presbyterian," he wrote again on September 29, "value

[1] *Life of John Barwick* (1724), p. 462.
[2] *ibid.* p. 200.
[3] *Ibid.* pp. 425-6.

themselves very much, upon computing in how few years the Church of England must expire[1]."

Such considerations spurred the royalist churchmen on in the prosecution of their design. In England, one of the prime movers was John Barwick, sometime Fellow of S. John's College, Cambridge, and a firm adherent of the royalist cause, who was in consultation with the bishops and kept up a correspondence upon that and other subjects affecting the King's interest with Clarendon in France. Some time in the earlier half of the year 1659 a list had been drawn up with the King's sanction containing the names of those whom it was proposed to present to bishoprics, and this was forwarded to England and "much facilitated," Barwick wrote, "the work in several instances."

"The grand Affair of the Church," he says in the same letter, "is still in motion towards that Happy Conclusion, which his sacred Majesty is so piously zealous for, with what speed may reasonably be used in a Matter of so great Importance and Difficulty[2]." The question for the moment was that of procedure. The dispersal of the members of the cathedral chapters had, of course, rendered impracticable the regular practice of electing by means of a *congé d'élire*, and at an earlier stage of the deliberations, in 1655, it had been proposed that the King should send a mandate to three or four of the bishops to proceed by way of collation. Dr Cosin had gone so far as to draw out a proper form for this purpose[3], and Clarendon seems again to have suggested this method in 1659. Barwick, however, writing after a consultation with the Bishop of Ely, urged several

---

[1] *Life of John Barwick*, p. 450.

[2] Barwick to Lord Chancellor Hyde, June 21, 1659. *Life of John Barwick*, p. 411.

[3] *Clarendon State Papers*, iii, App. p. cii.

objections against this course and advised that the King should rather grant a commission to the bishops to consecrate fit persons to definite sees, and this view seems to have been accepted by the King[1]. A third expedient, proposed both in 1655 and 1659, was to appoint the selected persons to sees in Ireland, where the method of election was different, with the intention that they should exercise their functions in England. "The Bishop of Derry," Clarendon wrote, "is so positive for the Irish Way...which he thought would clearly elude all those formalities, which seem to perplex us[2]." Dr Cosin, however, had already pointed out that this would be in effect to adopt the practice of the Roman Church, which had been so justly condemned by Bishop Jewel, and that no one would be found willing to accept consecration to a bishopric in a place "where he never intends to come[3]."

Nothing, however, was destined to come of these anxious consultations, and the fears which had inspired them were, in the event, proved to be groundless, but it is a little difficult to discover, from the letters that have survived, why the project was not put into execution. The difficulty did not come from the Court in France. "The King hath done all that is in his Power to do," wrote Clarendon on September 29, "and if my Lords the Bishops will not do the rest; what can become of the Church[4]?" The obstacle, if obstacle there was, must therefore have come from the churchmen in England, and yet, with the exception of Skinner of Oxford and

[1] "We adhered to that Method and Order; much preferring the Bishop of Ely's Judgment and Advice, in that point, before any Man's: And upon the same Ground His Majesty is very willing to change, and acquiesce in the Opinion and Resolution now propos'd." Hyde to Barwick, July 8, 1659. *Life of John Barwick*, pp. 424-5,
[2] *Ibid.* p. 424.   [3] *Clarendon State Papers*, iii, App. p. cii.
[4] *Life of Barwick*, p. 449.

Brownrig of Exeter, who were said to be opposed to the consecration of new bishops[1], the rest seem to have been agreed not only on the principle but also on the method. Fortunately for the Church, the omission to provide for the future caused no serious results, and the hierarchy was peaceably re-established in the midst of the royalist reaction which accompanied the Restoration.

[1] *Life of Barwick*, p. 218.

CHAPTER VIII

CHURCH PROPERTY

HITHERTO we have been discussing the Puritan rule in its effect upon persons and in its attitude towards the members of the Episcopal Church of England. It may not be considered irrelevant to speak in conclusion of the treatment accorded to the cathedrals and places of worship in which the services of that Church had been carried on.

The general confusion into which the country was plunged by the Civil War naturally rendered a considerable amount of destruction to the fabric of churches inevitable, but the damage done may be divided into two classes; that which was caused by military operations, and that which was the result of the unrestrained violence of soldiers and mobs. The former class of destruction is evidenced by the appeals for rebuilding funds which found their way to the Government during the later years of the Protectorate. For example, there is a petition presented in July 1657, by the inhabitants of Oswestry, whose church "was pulled down in the late war, for the safety of the garrison[1]." Again, there is a petition from the inhabitants of Rushall, Staffordshire, presented in May 1658, to the effect that "during the late war, Rushall Hall was a garrison for the Parliament, and Capt. Tothill, the governor, was obliged to demolish the parish church"; and a somewhat similar petition came from the inhabitants of Edgbaston[2].

[1] *Cal. of S. P. Dom.* 1657–8, p. 32.   [2] *Ibid.* 1658–9, p. 1.

Of the damage done by the Parliament's soldiers, several accounts remain. The letters of one Nehemiah Wharton, written from the Roundhead army, and preserved among the State Papers, give a good idea of the behaviour of the soldiers during the early years of the war[1]. When Waller captured Winchester in March 1644, the town was given over to plunder, "some of the tombs, images, escutchons, etc., in the cathedral being barbarously thrown down by the soldiers[2]." In 1654 Evelyn found Worcester cathedral "much ruin'd by the late warrs[3]," and at Lincoln the soldiers had taken all the brasses from the gravestones.

In some cases no doubt the Parliamentary leaders endeavoured to check the violence of their troops, but the party as a whole was anxious to see the work of destruction carried on. The *Commons' Journals* of the first few years of the Long Parliament show how determined the Puritans were on a thorough reformation in respect to ceremonies and innovations, and how far they were prepared to go in the direction of destroying the sculptured figures and other marks of "superstition" which the churches throughout the country contained. Altars were to be pulled down, superstitious pictures and stained-glass windows defaced, and vestments destroyed[4]: the directions were wide, and subject to few reservations.

A special commission under Sir Robert Harley was appointed in April 1643 with the object of furthering the campaign of destruction, but the work had begun with the meeting of the Long Parliament, before any ordinance

[1] Quoted in Stoughton : *Church of the Civil Wars*, p. 248 *et seq.*
[2] J. E. Bailey: *Life of Fuller*, p. 317.
[3] *Memoirs of J. Evelyn* (1819), i, 282.
[4] A cryptic order of May 31, 1643, directs that the copes at Westminster Abbey, St Paul's, and Lambeth, are to be "burnt and converted to the relief of the poor in Ireland!" *Commons' Journals*, iii, 110.

to that purpose had been issued[1], and a considerable reformation must have taken place in those churches either where the congregation was opposed to the ritualistic "innovations" or where the authorities thought it best to anticipate the attentions of the official iconoclasts[2]. The Subdean and Prebendaries of Westminster, for example, presented a certificate to the Committee for Demolishing Monuments of Superstition in 1643, to the effect that they had removed the Communion-table to the body of the Church, taken away all candlesticks and pictures, defaced crosses and crucifixes and "left off an ancient custom of that Church to minister the Communion in wafers[3]." Those who took this course acted wisely, for though the task of destruction in churches was usually entrusted to the churchwardens, in the Eastern Association the execution of the Parliament's instructions acquired an additional terror by the appointment of the notorious William Dowsing.

Dowsing's commission began with a reference to an ordinance of August 26, 1643, whereby it had been decreed that "all Crucifixes, Crosses, and all Images and pictures of any one or more persons of the Trinity, or of the Virgin Mary, and all other Images and pictures of Saints, or superstitious inscriptions in or upon all and every the said churches," etc. shall be taken away or defaced. Inasmuch, however, as many such superstitious images and inscriptions still remained in the Associated Counties "in manifest contempt of the said ordinance," the holder of

---

[1] *Diary of John Rous* (Camden. Soc. 1856), p. 99. Under the date November 17, 1640, Rous notes that "Many railes [*i.e.* altar-rails] were pulled downe before the parliament: at Ippiswich, Sudbury, etc. Marlowe, Bucks, the organs too."

[2] *Ralph Josselin's Diary* (Camden Series iii, vol. xv), p. 12. "This Michaelmas (1641), upon an Order of the House of Commons to that purpose wee tooke downe all images and pictures and such like glasses."

[3] *Hist. MSS. Com. Rep. on the MSS. of the Duke of Portland*, vol. viii, p. 4.

the commission was required to repair to that district and put the ordinance in execution. It was dated December 19, 1643, and was addressed "to Willm Dowsing Gen. and to such as he shall appoint[1]."

The journal in which Dowsing chronicled his proceedings provides us with a very fair idea of the thoroughness with which he fulfilled his mission. There is no attempt to gloss over the facts. The details of the ruthless destruction seem to be set down in a spirit of conscious pride at work well done. The following are a few characteristic extracts taken from the proceedings in Cambridgeshire.

"Bourne. We did downe 2: Angells, tooke a superstitious inscription in brasse and one of the Virgin Mary, and divers other Popish pictures, and gave order to take downe 2 Crosses in the Steple, and on the Chancell.

"Teversham. Mar: 26: We brake 2 Crucifixes in the Chancell, and there was Jesus writen in great Capitall Letters on six Arches in the Church, and in 12: places in the Chancell, and Steps there ye pavement diged up: the 6 Jesus in the Church, I did out, and 6 in ye Chancell, other six I could not reach, but gave order, to doe them out."

A good example of what came under the head of "superstitious inscriptions" is found at Hatley S. George, where Dowsing notes that "there was written over a coat of armes, Will: St George gave a Hide of Land in Haslingfield with his Daughter, to be nun in Clerkenwell, in the tyme of King Henry 2nd wch we burnt[2]."

Altogether Dowsing appears to have visited nearly sixty churches in Cambridgeshire, and wherever he went he left a track of ruin behind him. There seems to be almost a note of disappointment in the report for Ashley,

[1] Evelyn-White : *The Journal of William Dowsing*, pp. 6–7.
[2] *Baker Collection*, xxxviii, fol. 458, 471, 473.

"Only a Crosse, on the top of the Church," but this is a solitary instance, most churches offering an ample field for his destructive genius. Pre-Reformation brasses, which contained "popish" invocations, stained-glass windows, sculpture of all kinds, organs, almost everything of a decorative character, no matter what its antiquity, were cleared away or defaced: the churches which he or his deputies visited were literally stript of their contents.

As this was the course of action authorised by Parliament in the case of the ordinary parish churches, one would have been led to expect that the cathedrals, as offering a fairer field for their iconoclastic zeal, would have fared even worse, and at one time this promised to be the case. In February 1650/1, a proposal was brought before the Commons that "all Cathedral churches, where there are other churches or chapels sufficient for the people to meet in for the worship of God, be...pulled down and sold, and be employed for a stock for the use of the poor." Fortunately, this never became much more than a proposal, and though a beginning was made with Lichfield cathedral, the agents of the Parliament got no further than taking the lead from the roof and destroying the great bell[1]. On July 9, 1652, the project was again broached, but on this occasion it was proposed that a selected number of cathedrals should be demolished or sold, and that the proceeds should be devoted towards making up the deficit in the state finances. As in the former case, one cathedral, Canterbury, was actually threatened, but the proposal again fell to the ground[2]. A certain section of the Parliament, however, evidently were loath to relinquish the idea, and it was brought up again in January 1652/3,

[1] Gardiner: *Commonwealth and Protectorate*, ii, 23.
[2] *Ibid.* p. 187.

only to be laid aside again[1]. A rather different proposal, affecting Rochester, was made in October 1657, when it was suggested that the cathedral should be sold, to enable the Government to pay the arrears due to wounded seamen, but the scheme was frustrated by the dissolution of Parliament[2]. In spite, therefore, of these attempts, the majority of the cathedrals, with the exceptions already mentioned, remained without serious damage. The cathedral which suffered most from the ill-usage of the time was undoubtedly S. Paul's.

"One of the first acts...of the Parliament," writes Dean Milman[3], "was to seize and appropriate to other uses the sum remaining out of the subscription for the repairs of the Church in the chamber of the city of London. This sum amounted to above £17,000. The scaffolding erected around the tower was assigned to Col. Jephson's regiment for £1,746. 15. 8d, due as arrears of pay. On striking the scaffolding, part of the south transept, with its roof, came down." In 1631 when the repairs, now so rudely interrupted, were started, complaints had been brought to the notice of the Government to the effect that the cathedral premises had been subjected to abuses and had been "used like a street for carriage through of all burthens, provisions and necessaries men have to use, or pass from place to place, whereat good men are much scandalized." A series of orders had accordingly been issued to check this profanation[4], but now the abuses returned in an aggravated form. The portico itself was let out for shops, and the body of the building became a cavalry stable[5]. Sir Philip

---

[1] Gardiner: *Commonwealth and Protectorate*, ii, 211.

[2] *Cal. of S. P. Dom.* 1657-8, pp. xiv, 121-2. A similar proposal, affecting Ely cathedral, was made in 1648. See A. Kingston: *East Anglia and the Great Civil War*, p. 332. [3] *Annals of St Paul's*, p. 347.

[4] Rushworth: *Historical Collections*, ii, 91.

[5] *Annals of St Paul's*, p. 353.

Warwick, who had paid a visit to the cathedral "purposely to observe," records that the carved work on the portico was "broken down with axes and hammers, and the whole sacred edifice made not only a den of thieves, but a stable of unclean beasts[1]." In February 1658, it was reported that the Convocation House, attached to S. Paul's, "lies on a heap, roof and floor fallen down, windows broken, iron and lead embezzled, the whole building ruinous and very dangerous, and the waste ground spread with soft-stone and rubbish[2]."

It is clear, then, that the treatment of the cathedral by the Puritans was not dictated by any artistic appreciation or sentimental respect for the past. In this, as in other matters, a practical sense of what was expedient was the main-spring of their action, and it may be that motives of this kind indicated another use for the cathedral buildings. On August 15, 1651, about a year before the scheme for sale or demolition was broached for the second time, Parliament resolved that "the minster of Peterborough should be employed for the public worship of God, if the inhabitants would pay for the maintenance of the services[3]," and, a few years later, similar orders were made in connection with other cathedrals. On July 1, 1656, it was ordered, on the petition of the Mayor and citizens of Gloucester, "that the late cathedral, with its utensils, cloisters, churchyards, library and schoolmasters' and other houses, be henceforth enjoyed by them, for the preaching of the word, education of children, and other public uses[4]." In Wells, a similar petition from the inhabitants in the same month, led to a quarrel with the celebrated Dr Cornelius Burgess, who in

---

[1] *Sir P. Warwick's Memoirs*, p. 80.
[2] *Cal. of S. P. Dom.* 1657–8, pp. 280–1.
[3] Gardiner: *Commonwealth and Protectorate*, ii, 23.
[4] *Cal. of S. P. Dom.* 1656–7, p. 3.

March 1649 had purchased the manor of Wells from the Trustees for the sale of Bishops' lands, and had settled there. The petition had intimated that, as the single parish church in the town provided insufficient accommodation, the cathedral had been made use of, but it was "much in decay." "Many pious people," however, were disposed to contribute towards its repair, and the petitioners therefore asked that the lease of the cathedral might be continued to them. This was done, but in the following March, the inhabitants complained that they were obstructed by Burgess, who had "got possession of the church without order, threatens those whom we put in to take care of it, keeps it locked, and admits none save at his pleasure." On being required by the Government to deliver up the keys, Burgess justified his opposition by saying that the petition was the work of a few men only who sought "to bring back an old malignant, who took arms against Parliament[1]."

In Exeter the Puritans were credited, not only with having built a brick wall in the middle of the cathedral to divide the building into two, but also with having put up for sale thirteen out of the seventeen churches in the city. After the Restoration a number of the freemen of Exeter presented a petition to Parliament praying that the offenders might be compelled to make good the damage which they had done, and our information as to the circumstances is largely derived from papers drawn up in connection with their suit.

[1] *Cal. of S. P. Dom.* 1656-7, p. 23 ; 1657-8, pp. 336, 379. On January 11, 1652/3 Burgess had presented a petition to Quarter Sessions stating that he had been authorised by Parliament to preach in the Cathedral, and complaining that the religious exercises were much disturbed "by certen people who usually come into the Cloisters and there continue walkinge up and downe & talkinge all sermon tyme." *Somerset Quarter Sessions Records*, vol. iii, ed. E. H. Bates Harbin (Somerset Record Soc. 1912), pp. 198-9.

According to the version of the petitioners, the fifth article of the treaty, by which Exeter was surrendered to Sir Thomas Fairfax in 1646, had secured the churches from being defaced, but the Mayor and others of the Presbyterian party embarked upon an elaborate conspiracy to root out Episcopacy from the city. Having " purged " the city Chamber of fifteen out of its twenty-four members, and obtained, by means of disfranchising "most of the cittizens," the election of two men after their own heart to represent the city in the Parliament of 1656, they seized and shut up the cathedral and thirteen parish churches and procured an act entitled " An Act for promoting and more frequent preaching of the Gospell and maintenance of Ministers in the City of Exeter and the uniting of parrishes and parrish churches in the City."

" By vertue whereof," continue the petitioners, "they divided that famous cathedral church, they pull downe the walls, seats, stalls of the Bishop, Deane, Canons, prebends, viccars and Choiristers, destroy and melt the organs of that Church (worth 1500l[1]) ruined the holy Ghost Chapell, Library, Chapter house, vestery, and drawne downe the Cloisters and digged up the burying place within it," and committed other acts of vandalism and sacrilege.

In August 1657, according to the same account, the Common Council of the city required an inventory of church property from the churchwardens of thirteen churches and sent the city bellman to proclaim that the materials, sites and grounds were for sale. The churchwardens, supported by a number of the inhabitants, presented a petition against this proceeding, partly on the grounds that, if it were carried out, there would be an insufficient supply of churches. The reply of the Mayor and his supporters was to indict " for a supposed ryott,' those of the churchwardens who had refused to give up their keys, and though the jury returned an ignoramus, they were bound over.

The churches so seized were disposed of in various ways. One was "pulled downe and left open to all uncleanes" and six others were stripped of all their contents so that "only the bare walls and ruinous carcases" remained. Two of the churches, S. Mary Steps and S. Paul's, were sold, apparently to the parishioners, for £130 and £110 respectively, and others were disposed of in a similar way and for similar sums. It was alleged that Trinity church was leased with the express proviso that it should not be "employed to God's service."

As a final charge against the Mayor and Chamber the petitioners stated that they had "destroyed the Byshops, the Deanes and many of the Canons howses within the Citty of Exeter, making a Sugar howse of Byshops Pallace the Deanes dining-roome a meeting-place for Anabaptist, and his howse into 60 seuerall dwellings of the baser sort of people. Archdeacon Cotter's howse puld down and the materialls taken away. Canon Berry's howse converted to an Inne howse, and the Treasurers howse made a Bridewell." The petition contained other complaints not directly concerned with the cathedral and church buildings[1].

The petition was referred by the Lords to a Committee for Petitions[2], and on September 1, 1660, the House issued an order, on the report of the Committee, to the effect that the churches and all belonging to them should be restored to the churchwardens and repaired at the expense of the parishioners, and that the Chamber

---

[1] The foregoing details are taken from some papers in the Walker Collection (Bodleian Library, MS. J. Walker, c. 4, fol. 253–300).

[2] *Lords' Journals*, xi, 91.

of Exeter were to remove the wall in the cathedral at their own charge[1].

The above version of the story comes, of course, from the side of the petitioners, and the only surviving indication of the line of defence put forward on behalf of the Mayor and Chamber is contained in a counter petition addressed by them to the House of Lords on November 30, 1660, in which they sought to excuse their failure to obey the order of the House. They stated that they had already given notice to the church-wardens to fetch away the bells and other materials, but "as for plate none was taken, and few of the churches were touched by the petitioners, and those the smallest and least useful, thirteen out of the eighteen churches of Exeter being incapable of receiving such a congregation as could maintain a preaching minister." They contended that the construction of the offending wall and seats was made before June 24, 1660, and their action was covered by the Act of Indemnity. They pointed out that the cathedral now provided for the accommodation of two congregations and that if the existing arrangement were abolished before the other churches were restored "thousands of people" would have no place to resort to for the worship of God. They further pleaded that the removal of the wall by them would constitute a trespass and could not be carried out without danger to the fabric, in preserving which "they and others" had "in these miserable times spent 2,400ll[2]."

[1] *Ibid.* 152 and *Hist. MSS. Com. 7th Rep.* App ndix, p. 129. According to a copy of the decision of the Lords Referees i the Walker Collection (MS. J. Walker, c. 4, fol. 288), Allhallows was excepted from the list of churches to be restored. The papers in this collection contain various statements of lawyers' fees in connection with the freemen's case. One item in Alan Pennye's accounts, £460 "dew unto me p. bond from the Lord Berkeley and diverse other sums from other Lords to wyn them to act for us," has a sinister appearance. MS. J. Walker, c. 4, fol. 295, 299.

[2] *Hist. MSS. Com. 7th Rep.* Appendix, p. 136.

This last argument had been anticipated by their opponents. "They will object for the Maior," ran the statement of the freemen's case, "that they have bestowed 1700l[1] in erectinge a brickwall and repairinge that Cathedrall Church without which it would have beene like St Paule's in London." Their answer was "that then that Church was in good repaire and that this wall weakned the Church by the erectinge whereof they did take away the bazis of the pillers and the tops of the pillars and vaults over it are broken, that they haue since weakned the marble pillars in the Quire of the Cathedrall by hewinge away the bazis thereof makinge many great holes therein to fasten the beames for their galleries[1]."

The further history of the case need not detain us. It will be observed that the defendants did not deny the main facts alleged against them and only urged a justification which, from the Puritan point of view, would no doubt have appeared sufficient. The facts, when presented with due allowance for exaggeration on the part of the loyal citizens, accord sufficiently well with the other evidences of the attitude of the Puritan party towards the cathedral and church buildings of the country.

---

[1] MS. J. Walker, c. 4, fol. 273.

APPENDIX I

(Bodleian Lib. MS. J. W. c. 5. fol. 288.)

(See p. 46.)

"An Inventorie of the goods and chattells of Isaack Allen Rector of Prestwich taken [before] us whose names are here subscribed Jan: 28, 1644. An [ ] hed the 30th of Octob: 1645 by

> John Wrigley
> Peter Walker.

> > James Wroe
> > John Scoales
> > Roger Walwarke.

As followeth.   Imprimis in the great Parlour.

	£	s.	d.
Three tabells	1	10	00
one Court Cupboard	0	10	00
three field Chayres	1	10	00
two formes, five buffett stooles	0	18	00
seaven cushinns	0	7	00
fire shovell and tongues	0	2	00

Item in the Hanging Chamber

one standing bedd with the furniture thereunto			
belonging	5	0	00
one table, one Court Cupboard	0	13	4
two field Chayres, two buffett stooles ...	1	6	8

Item in the Apple Chamber

One Canopie bedd, with two Curtaines ...	1	0	00
one Chayre	0	6	8

Item in the Studdio

one hundred and fiftye bookes			
one chayre			

Item in the yellow Chamber

    one standing bedd with Curtaines, Vallence, a
feather bedd, one blankett, Caddow, and
boulster. Questioned as belonging to Anne
Allen   3   6   8

    one Chayre and two buffett stooles   0   8 00

    one Court Cupboard and a little table   ...   0   6   6

Item in the Chappell Chamber

    two standing bedds, one feather bedd and a
wool bedd, two coverings, and blanketts, two
bolsters and two pillows   8   0 00

    one Court Cupboard, one round table   ...   0 10 00

    one Chayre, three buffett stooles   0   8 00

    one Cupboard-Cushin, one trunke   0   4 00

Item in the brushing Chamber

    one Cupboard and two Coffers   1   0 00

    foure paire of sheetes   1   0 00

    six table Cloathes   0   5 00

    one pillow beare, and five napkins   0   2 00

Item in the maides Chamber

    three little bedds with furniture for two   ...   3   0 00

Item in the Maisters Chamber

    one standing bedd, with Curtaines, Valence,
Caddow, one fether bedd, two blanketts, two
bolsters and sheetes   3   6   8

    one presse, one twigg Chayre   1   6   8

    one little table   0   4   0

Item in the Clossett

    two Coffers, seaven Cupboard Cloathes   ...   0 13   4

    two dosen and tenne table napkinns   ...   1 12 00

    six paire of sheets, foure table cloathes   ...   3   0 00

                           Summa totalis   £41 16   6

                [fol. 288 *b*.]

In the little parlor

    one table three chayres [one] stoole 0 10 00

    one forme, foure Cushens   0   1   6

In the servants Chamber

    one bedd with its furniture 0 13   4

In the lowe Celler

    foure beefe tubbes 0 16 00

	£	s.	d.
one turnell, one hogshead	o	6	oo
two barrells, and two firkins	o	3	oo

In the lowe parloure

| one standing bedd, one canopie bedd, with one fether bedd, two blanketts, one Caddow one Coverlett and Curtaines ... ... | 2 | 3 | 4 |
| two tables, one Chayre ... ... | o | 3 | oo |

In the Hall

three tables	1	10	oo
three formes	o	7	oo
five Cheeres	o	10	oo
five Cushinns	o	1	oo

In the Buttery

| two cupboards the greater 15s the lesse 5s eight pewter dishes 16s, two flaggons 1s 6d one quart one pint 2s 6d foure pottingers, two salts, five Saucers 5s two dosen and a halfe of trenchers 1s 6d a napkin presse 2s | 1[1] | 8 | 6 |

In the Cellor

| three hogsheads ... ... | o | 2 | oo |

In the Brewhouse

| one meltarke, and two malt-arkes ... ... | 2 | 10 | oo |
| five brewing vessells ... ... | 1 | 10 | oo |

In the Kitchen

| eight pewter dishes two chamber potts 13s 4d, three brasse potts, one brasse morter, one posnett £1 6s 8d, two brasse pannes two skelletts, a frying pan 4s, two dripping pannes, eight spitts, two chayres £1 1s. ... ... | 3 | 5 | oo |

In the Larder

| three Ranges, two Cheeseboards, one coffer, one tresse ... ... | o | 5 | oo |

In the day-house

| six Ranges for milke 6s, seaven milk basons 4s 8d, seaven Cheesefatts 2s two milke boards five cheeseboards 7s, one Cheesepresse 4s, five milke pannes and a butter tub 2s 4d and a Churne 2s 6d ... ... | 1 | 8 | 6 |

---

[1] A mistake for £2.

	£	s.	d.
In the Cheese Chamber			
One Arke, foure Cheesboards	o	8	oo
In the servants Chamber			
two bedsteds with Cloathes	1	o	oo
In the outhouses			
one baye of heye in the kilne two bayes of heye for the horses	10	o	oo
four Cart Chestes	o	14	oo

Summa totalis　£29 15 2

[fol. 289.]

	£	s.	d.
Item two forkes and two [ ]	o	2	6
two Cole Carts, two [ ] shod wheeles a drug [ ] Clog wheeles	4	o	o
A Cole waine	o	6	o
A harvest Cart and a turf Cart and a paire of Clogwheeles	1	13	4
Two ston trowes	o	4	o
Three kine	9	o	o
Foure sterkes	6	13	4
One horse and a mare	2	10	o
One paire of iron trese a Cart saddle, three olde Collers and two halters	o	11	o
Two plowes, a paire of plow-irons	o	5	o
a spade, a forke, a hatchett, and a muck-forke	o	3	o

Summa totalis　£25 8 2

The totall summe of the whole inventorie (the books being not prized) is　£96 19 10

The glebe togeather with Mr Ashtons land prizes as followeth viz:

	£	s.	d.
Imprimis. In meddowing, six Ackers at 13s 4d an Acker per ann.	4	o	o
Item. Plowing ground foureteene Ackers at 10s an Aker p. annum	7	o	o
Item. Pastureing grounde, twenty Ackers at 6s 8d an Acker p. annum	6	13	4

Sum: total　£17 13 4

APPENDIX II

THE CASE OF SYLVESTER ADAMS

(See p. 102.)

The voting of the Heads of Colleges on Dec. 18, is recorded as follows:

"1. Dr Ward gave his opinion pro affirmatione.

2. Dr Collins saith, Mr Adams is coming one, and so stay a while to draw him further on.

3. Dr Smith the like, and desireth to deferre the sentence a while.

4. Dr Comber desireth that Mr Adams may haue time to advise and consider how farre he voluntarily will make satisfaction before any be enioyned.

5. Dr Bambrigge pro affirmatione, but for the time when it shal be done is content when you Mr Vice-Chancellor and (sic) next will.

6. Dr Cosen disliketh the recantation propounded in some particulars.

7. Dr Bachcroft thinketh fitt he shall renounce what is contrary to the Doctrine of the Church of England according to the recantation now read.

8. Dr Laney disliketh the recantation propounded in some particulars.

9. Dr Love approveth the recantation read.

10. Dr Martin doth not yet thinke it fitt the recantation should be enioyned to Mr Adams nor anie other upon any ground yet made knowne to him.

11. Dr Sterne doth not assent to the recantation read.

12. Dr Holdsworth approveth the recantation, but liketh that a longer time be giuen to the deliberate upon it.

13. Dr Eden doth not agree to the recantation read."

Upon this, the Vice-Chancellor warned Adams not to leave the town without his leave.

At the meeting on March 2, 1638, it is stated that "Mr Vice-Chancellour did read unto him the foresaid forme of acknowledgement conceaved in writing, and asked him two severall times whether hee would voluntarily submitt thereunto; but hee bothe times expressely refused to subscribe the same. Whereupon Mr Vice-Chancellour upon the said recantation deliuered in writinge his sentence and censure of Mr Adams his said sermons and subscribed the same with his owne hand."

It is not stated that any alteration had been made in the recantation. The Vice-Chancellor's sentence ran as follows: "I having diligently perused the Sermon of Mr Adams, fellow of Peterhouse in this University, concerning the necessity of confessing of our sinnes to a Preist, and having sundry times convented him thereupon, and finding him still obstinate in his false doctrine, I doe sentence him so farre forth as is in me to recall his error and giue satisfaction to the Church by the publiq and audible pronouncing of this forme here underwritten.

"Whereas upon Sunday the 25 of June last, in my publiq Sermon upon these words S. John 20, 23 'whose sinnes ye remitt they are remitted, and whose sinnes ye retaine they are retained,' I delivered this Doctrine, That a speciall confession unto a Preist (actually where time or opportunity presents it selfe, or otherwise in explicit intention and resolution) of all our sinnes committed after Baptisme, so farre forth as we doe remember, is necessary unto salvation, not only necessitate praecepti butt also necessitate medii, so that according to the ordinary or revealed meanes appointed by Christ there can be no salvation without the aforesaid confession; upon more mature thoughts and better information, I doe finde that this Doctrine then delivered was both erroneous and dangerous, having no warrant from the word of God, and crossing the Doctrine of our Church, as may appeare by her Liturgie in the second exhortation at the Communion, and in the visitation of the sick, and in the second part of the Homilie of Repentance; As therefore in generall I doe acknowledge in the words of the aforesaid homilie that it is most evident and plaine that this auricular confession hath not his warrant of God's word, and that therefore being not ledde with the conscience thereof, if wee with feare and trembling and with a true contrite heart use that kind of confession which God doth comãnd in his word [namely an unfeigned confession unto Almighty God himselfe] then doubtlesse (as he is faithfull and true) he will forgiue us our sinnes and make us cleane from all our wickednes; so in the case of a troubled or doubtfull conscience, I doe conforme my opinion unto the direction of our Church, which in her Liturgie doth exhort and require those whose consciences are troubled with any weighty matter to a speciall confession, so that they who cannot quiet their owne consciences are to repaire to their owne or some other discreet and Learned Minister of God's word, to open to him their greife, that so they may receiue such ghostly counsell, advise and comfort, as their consciences may be relieued, and by the ministry of God's word they may receiue comfort and the benefitt of absolution, to the quieting of their consciences, and the avoyding of all scruple and doubtfullnes: butt it is against true Christian liberty that any man should be bound to the numbring of his sinnes as it hath been used heretofore in the times of Ignorance and blindness. This I do acknowledge to be the Doctrine of the Church of England concerning confession and to it I doe ex animo subscribe and am heartily sorry for what ever I haue delivered to the contrary.

"And if Mr Adams refuses to make this publiq acknowledgement of his error, then my sentence is that he shall undergoe the punishment which the University Statutes cap: 45 de concionibus doe appoint to be inflicted. And I require the Register to make an act as well of this my sentence as of the forme of recantation inioyned by me, wherein he is charged with no other butt his owne words in his sermon, and appointed to recall his false Doctrine in no other butt the words of the Liturgie and Homilie of our Church. This I require to be Registred that so it may appeare, that I haue done my part to assert and maintaine the Doctrine of our Church.

R. Brownrigg, procan: "

Eleven other Heads then signed the document, though rather as expressing their individual opinions than as giving their consent to the proceedings.

"I do give my consent unto the vice-chancellor's sentence before specifyed. Samuel Ward.

And so doe I. Tho. Bainbrigg.

I am of opinion that the doctrine dd. [delivered?] by Mr Addams in the sermon mentioned was both erroneous and scandalous, and that it is most fitt hee should make the recantation proposed, unlesse hee will wilfully crosse his owne doctrine, and refuse to Confesse his faulte for the obtaining of his absolution. Tho. Paske.

And soe doe I. Tho. Bachcroft.

I doe assent unto the sentence of the Vice-Chancellor. Rich. Love.

I doe conceive the recantation sett by Mr Vice-Chancellor to Mr Adams to be both aequall and moderate, and the least satisfaction which Mr Adams can make for the scandalous doctrine he delivered.

Ri. Holdsworth.

The foresaid Recantation is not allowed for that it charges particular confession to be contrary to the Liturgy and any other part of the established doctrine of the Church of England by me B. Lany.

I having declared my mind both privately and publiquely sundry times to Mr Adams concerning his sermon and refus'd of late his Questions tending the same way, yet forbeare to enioyne Recantation becaus it is not to be layd by our Statutes, but upon that which cleerly crosses the doctrine of the Church of England whereas our Articles condemn not Confession at all. S. Collins.

I desire that this Recantation may be qualified in some particular expressions thereof before I giue my assent thereunto, which particulars I haue declared by my suffrage in Court. Jo. Cosin.

Bycause the Church of England in so many places adviseth us to speciall confession I conceive the recantation praedict., in that it charges particular confession as contrary to the doctrine of our Church, is not to be approved. Wm. Beale.

I doe not find that the Church of England hath anywhere determined Confession to a priest to be a thing unnecessary, but that in divers places it urges the practice of it. And therefore I conceive that the sermon in question hath not incurred the punishment mentioned Cap. 45 of the University Statutes. Rich. Sterne."

"Which done," the record informs us, "Mr Vice-Chancellour did dismisse the meeting, but not the cause," and we are left to assume that the verdict of the majority was put into execution.

The above account is taken from the entries in the *Acta Curiae* preserved in the University Registry. There is another short account given in Bennet's *Register* (*Emmanuel College Records*), p. 182, which differs in some particulars. According to this account "the following Heads voted that he should be enjoyned to recant...viz: the Vice-Chancellor himself, with Dr Love, Master of Benet, Dr Bambridge, Master of Christ's, Dr Bancroft (*sic*) of Caius and Dr Holdsworth of Emmanuel. The Master of Sidney, Dr Ward, had joined in the complaint, but was not present at the hearing. On the other side he [Adams] was supported by the High Church Party or Friends of Archbishop Laud, of whom Dr Cumber, Master of Trinity, Dr Cousins of Peterhouse, Dr Smith of Magdalene, Dr Martin of Queens' and Dr Eden of Trinity Hall all voted in his favour, and being thus acquitted by 8 to 5 he received no censure for his behaviour." From the names mentioned, this seems to refer to the meeting on December 18.

The version given in Cooper's *Annals* (iii. 287) is taken from the Baker MSS., and the account of the voting on December 18 again does not tally with the record in the *Acta Curiae*.

APPENDIX III

THE SEIZURE OF COLLEGE PLATE AT CAMBRIDGE
(See p. 105.)

College accounts are a rather uncertain guide to the chronology of the events which they illustrate, as the record of expenditure on various occasions is not uncommonly contained in a general statement at the end of the year, but two or three stray entries in the accounts of Trinity College for 1642 suggest a connection with Cromwell's attempt to intercept the plate which was being sent to the King.

In the Senior Bursar's accounts we find the following entries :

"Given to those that carried the University plate into our
    Tower . . . .   ii. s.

Spent at the entertainment of Captain Cromwell and his
    gentleman soldiers . . . .   ix s. v^d

To Chambers and Wright for laying up ye College Plate
    when wee were in danger of the Soldiers . . .   v. s."

And in the Steward's Book :

"Bestowed on the Soldiers and those that watcht the Plate
    in the new Court . . . . £1. 11. 4."

The allusion to the soldiers seems at first to imply that these payments belong to February or March 1642/3, *i.e.* after the occupation of the town by the Parliamentary troops, and if so, it is clear that some at least of the University and College plate was not sent to the King, but was retained and afterwards bestowed in a place of safety when the danger of plunder seemed imminent. In support of this theory it may be noticed that it appears from the Bursar's books that in 1648 the authorities at Trinity look up some treasure which had been concealed during the troubles[1].

But it is also possible that they refer to the previous July, when Cromwell made a sudden descent upon the town and seized the plate belonging to some of the colleges as it lay ready for a convenient opportunity to be despatched to the royalist headquarters. On this hypothesis, the payments may be connected with a probably unsuccessful attempt on the part of the College to save the plate from seizure at the last moment.

In the Bursar's accounts for the following year appear the following cryptic entries :

"Spent by William Linkey in his journey to seeke for the
    plate . . . . iii ll.

Spent by Cooke in a journey to look for the plate .   . xlv. s. vi. d.

To John Rooke for a journey about the plate   .   . ii. s. vi. d."

In the absence of further evidence, it is only possible to hazard the conjecture that a consignment of the College plate had been despatched, and had failed to reach its destination, but that the College authorities were not satisfied of its irrevocable loss.

[1] Quoted in A. Kingston's *East Anglia in the Great Civil War*, p. 286.

INDEX

Abbot, George, Archbishop of Canterbury, 10, 21, 152
Abdy, John, 121 n., 122
Abingdon, 156, 224
Adamites, 216
Adams, Sylvester, 99–102, 268–71
Advertisements of 1566, The, 12, 15
Agreement of the People, The, 220
Akehurst, Alexander, 143
Alchorne, Edward, 60
Allen, Anne, 265
Allen, Isaac, 46, 79, 80, 264–7
Allestree, Richard, 240
Andover, 62
Appleby, Thomas, 123 n.
Approbation of Public Preachers, Committee for, 5, 236, 238–9, 241–5
Arkesden, 87
Armagh, Archbishop of, see Ussher
Arminians, 216
Arminius, spread of the doctrine of, 8
Arrowsmith, John, Master of S. John's College, Cambridge, 125 n., 126 n., 132 n., 144
Arundell, Francis, 121 n.
Ash, Simon, 116 n., 230 n.
Asheton, Col. Ralph, 79
Ashley, 255–6
Ashton, ——, 267
Aylesbury, 157, 246
Aylworth, Martin, 190 n.

Babington, Churchill, estimate of the clergy, 42
Babington, Humphrey, 122
Baillie, Robert, 29, 221
Bainbrigg, Thomas, Master of Christ's College, Cambridge, 100, 119, 268, 270–1
Baker, John, 85
Baker, Michael, 188
Baker, Thomas, 116 n., 120, 144
Baldero, ——, 123 n.
Ball, Samuel, 87
Ball, ——, 234
Baltimore, Lord, see Calvert
Banbury, Earl of, see Knollys
Barnard, Nathaniel, 97–8

Barnstaple, 71 n., 87
Barrey, George, 121 n.
Bartlow, 85–6
Barton, Francis, 122
Barwick, John, 249–50
Bastwick, John, 25
Batchcroft, Thomas, Master of Gonville and Caius College, Cambridge, 100, 119, 120, 268, 270–1
Baxter, Richard, 24, 226, 246
Bayard, Henry, 202
Bayley, ——, 50–1
Bayly, William, 122
Beale, William, Master of S. John's College, Cambridge, 96 n., 101–3, 105, 119, 271
Beales, 63
Beardhall, George, 87
Beaumont, Roger, 50
Beesley, Henry, 239
Belke, William, 238
Belleau, 247
Benefices, number of, 52; plurality of attacked, 33, 75; patronage, 241; service of during Interregnum, 246
Berkeley, Lord, 262 n.
Bernard, Nicholas, 226
Bernard, Richard, author of The Faithfull Shepheard, 42
Berry, Canon, 261
Beverley, 155
Birche, Thomas, 79
Bishops, exclusion of from House of Lords, 33–6; proposal to replace authority of by a commission, 35; consecration of, 246–51
Bishops' lands, sale of, 36–8
Blake, Martin, 71 n.; 87
Bocking, 184
Bolton, Samuel, Master of Christ's College, Cambridge, 125, 132 n.
Bond, John, Master of Trinity Hall, Cambridge, 125 n., 132 n.
Boothby Pagnell, 224
Boreman, Robert, 122
Bottisham, 82
Bourne, 255
Box, 203

Williams, ——, 70
Willis, Nathaniel, 121 n.
Willis, Thomas, 195
Wiltshire, 203, 235
Winchester, 253
Winchester, Bishops of, see Morley and Neile
Winchester College, 130, 131, 140
Winchester, diocese of, 12
Windsor, 193, 240
Wisbech, 49, 50
Wollaston, Henry, 213 n.
Wood, Anthony, 139, 153, 155, 159, 163-4, 182, 185, 191, 194-6
Woodruffe, George, 112
Wootton, 81
Worcester Cathedral, 253

Worthington, John, Master of Jesus College, Cambridge, 132 n., 141, 145
Wotton, 238
Wotton, William, 122, 123 n.
Wren, Matthew, Bishop of Ely, 247
Wright, Ezechiel, 146
Wright, ——, 272

Yarmouth, 71
Yelden, 61
York, Archbishop of, see Williams, John
Yorkshire, 48, 202
Young, Thomas, Master of Jesus College, Cambridge, 125 n., 126, 134, 136

Zanchy, Jerome, 183
Zouch, Dr, 172